Climate Justice and the Economy

As climate change has increasingly become the main focus of environmentalist activism since the late 1990s, the global economic drivers of CO_2 emissions are now a major concern for radical greens. In turn, the emphasis on connected crises in both natural and social systems has attracted more activists to the Climate Justice movement and created a common cause between activists from the Global South and North. In the absence of a pervasive narrative of transnational or socialist economic planning to prevent catastrophic climate change, these activists have been eager to engage with advanced knowledge and ideas on political and economic structures that diminish risks and allow for new climate agency.

This book breaks new ground by investigating what kind of economy the Climate Justice movement is calling for us to build and how the struggle for economic change has unfolded so far. Examining ecological debt, just transition, indigenous ecologies, social ecology, community economies and divestment among other topics, the authors provide a critical assessment and a common ground for future debate on economic innovation via social mobilization.

Taking a transdisciplinary approach that synthesizes political economy, history, theory and ethnography, this volume will be of great interest to students and scholars of climate justice, environmental politics and policy, environmental economics and sustainable development.

Stefan Gaarsmand Jacobsen is an Assistant Professor at Roskilde University, Denmark.

Routledge Advances in Climate Change Research

Globalizing the Climate
COP21 and the Climatisation of Global Debates
Edited by Stefan C. Aykut, Jean Foyer and Edouard Morena

Adapting Infrastructure to Climate Change
Advancing Decision-Making Under Conditions of Uncertainty
Todd Schenk

Local Action on Climate Change
Opportunities and Constraints
Edited by Susie Moloney, Hartmut Fuenfgeld and Mikael Granberg

Pricing Carbon in Australia
Contestation, The State and Market Failure
Rebecca Pearse

The Paris Framework for Climate Change Capacity Building
Mizan R. Khan, J. Timmons Roberts, Saleemul Huq and Victoria Hoffmeister

The Anthropology of Climate Change
An Integrated Critical Perspective
Hans A. Baer and Merrill Singer

EU Climate Diplomacy
Politics, Law and Negotiations
Edited by Stephen Minas and Vassilis Ntousas

The Global Climate Regime and Transitional Justice
Sonja Klinsky and Jasmina Brankovic

Climate Justice and the Economy
Social Mobilization, Knowledge and the Political
Edited by Stefan Gaarsmand Jacobsen

(Series page: https://www.routledge.com/Routledge-Advances-in-Climate-Change-Research/book-series/RACCR)

Climate Justice and the Economy

Social Mobilization, Knowledge and the Political

Edited by Stefan Gaarsmand Jacobsen

LONDON AND NEW YORK

from Routledge

First published 2018 by Routledge

2 Park Square, Milton Park, Abingdon, Oxfordshire OX14 4RN
52 Vanderbilt Avenue, New York, NY 10017

Routledge is an imprint of the Taylor & Francis Group, an informa business

First issued in paperback 2020

British Library Cataloguing-in-Publication Data
A catalogue record for this book is available from the British Library

Library of Congress Cataloging-in-Publication Data
Names: Jacobsen, Stefan Gaarsmand, editor.
Title: Climate justice and the economy: social mobilization, knowledge and the political / edited by Stefan Gaarsmand Jacobsen.
Description: Abingdon, Oxon; New York, NY: Routledge, 2018. | Series: Routledge advances in climate change research |
Includes bibliographical references and index.
Identifiers: LCCN 2017060248 | ISBN 9781138234741 (hbk) |
ISBN 9781315306193 (ebk)
Subjects: LCSH: Environmental policy–Economic aspects. | Climatic changes–Economic aspects. | Environmentalism. | Environmental justice.
Classification: LCC HC79.E5 C5946 2018 | DDC 363.738/74–dc23
LC record available at https://lccn.loc.gov/2017060248

ISBN: 978-1-138-23474-1 (hbk)
ISBN: 978-0-367-45901-7 (pbk)

Typeset in Times New Roman
by Deanta Global Publishing Services, Chennai, India

Contents

Contributors

Sam Bliss is a PhD student at the University of Vermont, USA, studying the ecological economics of food systems, with and without markets. He previously studied at the Autonomous University of Barcelona, Spain, as a Fulbright student researcher. Together with Professor Giorgos Kallis, Sam is currently finishing up a book on the claims and the ideology of post-environmentalism, provisionally titled *Kiss Nature Goodbye*.

Patrick Bond is a Professor of Political Economy at the Wits School of Governance, South Africa, and from 2004–2016 directed the University of KwaZulu-Natal Centre for Civil Society, South Africa. He has lived in Southern Africa since 1989 and was editor or author of more than a dozen policy papers in the Mandela government. His books include *BRICS* (edited with Ana Garcia, 2015), *Elite Transition* (2014), *South Africa – The Present as History* (with John Saul, 2014), *Politics of Climate Justice* (2012), *Durban's Climate Gamble* (2011) and a dozen others.

Ulrich Brand is a Professor of International Politics at the University of Vienna, Austria, since 2007. Before he worked as an Assistant Professor at Kassel University, Germany, and taught and did research at several universities in Europe, North and Latin America. He works on theories of international and state politics, environmental policies, biodiversity, NGOs and social movements and was a member of the Expert Commission "Growth, well-being and quality of life" of the German Parliament.

Stefan Gaarsmand Jacobsen is an Assistant Professor at Roskilde University, Denmark, currently working on the project 'Sustainable Rationalities'. Funded by the Danish Research Foundation, the project investigates the economic imaginaries of contemporary critical environmental organizations. Prior to this, Jacobsen was part of the research project *Economic Rationalities in History* (ECORA) at Aarhus University, Denmark, where he published critical perspectives on the development of liberalist economic thought and attempts to democratize the economy from below.

Georges Alexandre Lenferna is a Fulbright Scholar and PhD Candidate at the University of Washington, USA, focusing on climate ethics and justice. In Climate Justice advocacy, he has recently served in roles such as Climate

Justice Steward with the Alliance for Jobs and Clean Energy, a fellow with Carbon Washington, a research consultant with 350.org, and as a leader and member of numerous divestment movements.

Emanuele Leonardi is a Post-Doctoral Researcher at the Centre for Social Studies of the University of Coimbra, Portugal. His research interests include André Gorz's political ecology, logics of exploitation in contemporary capitalism, Climate Justice movements and their critique of carbon trading. He is the author of *Lavoro Natura Valore: André Gorz tra marxismo e decrescita* (2017) and has published articles in journals such as *Capitalism Nature Socialism*, *Ephemera* and *Soft Power*.

Gerda Roelvink is a Senior Lecturer in Geography and Urban Studies in the School of Social Sciences and Psychology at Western Sydney University, Australia. Her research expertise is in the field of diverse economies, focusing in particular on collective action and economic transformation. Gerda's work on diverse economies includes the book *Building Dignified Worlds: Geographies of Collective Action* and the co-edited volume *Making Other Worlds Possible: Performing Diverse Economies*.

Leah Temper is a Researcher in Environmental History and Ecological Economics at the Autonomous University of Barcelona, Spain, and a freelance environmental journalist and video artist. Her area of study is Ecological Conflicts and Social Metabolism and she has done fieldwork in Israel, Kenya, Ecuador and India, studying conflicts related to land use, mining and energy. She is the coordinator and co-editor of the *Global Atlas of Environmental Justice* (EJatlas) and director of the Seeds of Survival Program.

Brian Tokar is a Lecturer in Environmental Studies at the University of Vermont, USA, and serves on the boards of the Institute for Social Ecology and 350Vermont. His most recent book is *Toward Climate Justice: Perspectives on the Climate Crisis and Social Change* (Revised edition, 2014).

Rikard Warlenius has a PhD in Human Ecology and currently teaches economic history at Stockholm University, Sweden. His research interests include climate justice, ecological economics and uneven development.

Abbreviations

CAN	Climate Action Network
CCS	carbon capture and storage
CSE	Center for Society and Environment
CDM	Clean Development Mechanism
CJ	Climate Justice
CJA	Climate Justice Action
CJM	Climate Justice Movement
CJN!	Climate Justice Now!
CO_2	carbon dioxide
COP	Conference of Parties
CSO	civil society organizations
CTW	Carbon Trade Watch
EAC	Energy Action Coalition
EPA	Environmental Protection Agency
FOE	Friends of the Earth
FSC	Forest Stewardship Council
GDP	gross domestic product
GGCJ	Greenhouse Gangster vs. Climate Justice
GGGJ	Grassroots Global Justice Alliance
GHG	greenhouse gas
GMO	genetically modified organism
IEN	Indigenous Environmental Network
ILO	International Labour Organization
IMF	International Monetary Fund
IPCC	Intergovernmental Panel on Climate Change
NASA	National Aeronautics and Space Administration
NGO	nongovernmental organization
PCCCRM	People's Conference on Climate Change and the Rights of Mother Earth
PPM	parts per million
REDD	Reducing Emission from Deforestation and Forest Degradation
RT	Rising Tide
UN	United Nations
UNFCCC	United Nations Framework Convention on Climate Change
WTO	World Trade Organization
WWF	World Wildlife Fund for Nature

Editor's preface

Stefan Gaarsmand Jacobsen

If Climate Justice were a struggle of words, then the 2015 Paris Agreement would have been the final victory. In his opening speech for the Conference of the Parties (COP) 21st meeting in Paris, French President Francois Hollande seemed completely convinced and even morally committed to the cause. Recounting the fact that recent victims of record summer temperatures in 2015 had to be counted in the "millions" and the economic losses in the "billions", he continued,

> How could we accept that the poorest countries, those that emit the fewest greenhouse gases, those that are the most vulnerable, should once again be worst affected? It is in the name of climate justice that I speak to you today. It is in the name of climate justice that we must take action.
>
> (Hollande 2015)

Further testifying to the global celebration of Climate Justice in 2015, Indian Prime Minister Narendra Modi announces to his assumed over 12 million Twitter followers, the "[o]utcome of #ParisAgreement has no winners or losers. Climate justice has won & we are all working towards a greener future" (*The Hindu* 2015). There it was: the declared victory of the radical campaigners that had worked hard globally since the activists had first gathered in the Climate Justice Summit in 2000 in The Hague to confront the global power of the oil industry and claim a payment for the ecological debt owed by the Global North to the world's poor. Here was the admission of a rich country leader, Hollande, that the economic inequality and historical injustices were at the center of climate negotiations. Moreover, almost an acceptance of the apology by one of the most affected nations in the Global South with a universal cause for the whole globe.

The Climate Justice movement (CJM) answered these niceties with protests worldwide, adding to the pre-Paris demands from a global almost 800,000 people on the streets worldwide in the Global Climate March, many under Climate Justice banners and many demanding systemic changes to the economy (350.org 2015). On December 12, 2015, activists overruled the state of emergency banning street protests by reference to the state of emergency created by unbinding and inadequate negotiation results (D12 2015).

The contradictions of the Paris agreement and preceding UNFCCC (United Nations Framework Convention on Climate Change) activities have fueled many Climate Justice campaigns, but the movement is active far in all corners of the world far beyond officialdom. For over two decades, Climate Justice has been both a rallying call for a movement and a technical term used by a very diverse group of activists, writers, analysts, NGOs and academic researchers (Dawson 2010; Bond 2012; Tokar 2014). At its base lies a normative demand to engage politically with the process of destructive global warming and thus combine the knowledge contained in climate models into the conflicts of global inequalities, past and present. Climate Justice (CJ) activists and analysts attempt to make visible inequalities that have created a situation of destructive global warming *and* the unfair burden of climate destruction on the world's poor, which will only continue to grow, if current approaches to stopping climate change are continued (Klinsky et al. 2016; Ciplet and Roberts 2017). The urgency of stopping global warming means that CJ activists work for fundamental changes to the global economy in the short term rather than a long-term promise that hinges on the promise of technological miracles (De Lucia 2016).

However, despite these strong values and continued mobilizations for solidarity and change, the movement still has no larger, explicit program for a transformation of the economy that would provide a clear guideline to reaching global Climate Justice (Bullard and Müller 2012; Bond 2018). Far from pretending to create these guidelines, this book seeks to provide a transdisciplinary approach to the way in which radical claims for Climate Justice have shaped new ways of engaging critically with local and global economies. This entails both historical, ethnographic and sociological approaches to the main actors and institutions behind these claims and a wider theoretical engagement with the political and ecological context in which the claims are made. Finally, the urgency of the cause of climate change makes it necessary to look ahead and think *with* the movement in terms of next steps. Hence the book investigates the conditions for social mobilization, the knowledge patterns and the status of political normativity through three sections: first a thorough background to the understanding where, how and by whom demands for Climate Justice have been made – what different interpretations have been prevalent and what that tells us about the current possibilities and pitfalls in moving forward. In Part II, three cases from the frontlines of recent Climate Justice campaigns and protests are analyzed. Finally, in Part III, the theoretical, empirical and historical inputs are put to work in the critical scrutiny of new paradigms for moving Climate Justice ahead.

What use is the economy to Climate Justice?

Before proceeding to the chapters' analyses, it is instructive to problematize briefly the title of the book itself. In the eyes of prominent CJ activists Tadzio Müller and Nicola Bullard the Climate Justice and the economy are not easily reconcilable phenomena:

> For all its undoubtedly widespread appeal, however, the story that it was possible to save the climate and 'the economy' at the same time was not the only one. Against and beyond this story, another one had been growing in the shadows for several years by the time the eyes of the world came to rest on Copenhagen and the UN's climate negotiations: the story of Climate Justice.
>
> (Bullard and Müller 2012, 55)

By this token, 'the economy' is equivalent to the promotion of business-as-usual of endless global GDP growth rates that green economists expect to decouple from GHG emissions at any point. Another author to place 'the economy' in scare quotes is Timothy Mitchell whose book *Carbon Democracy* provides a useful historical framing of what is at stake in the politics of energy that has caused climate change. Mitchell claims that "the economy"

> was made possible by oil, for the availability of abundant, low-cost energy allowed economists to abandon earlier concerns with the exhaustion of natural resources and represent material life instead as a system of monetary circulation – a circulation that could expand indefinitely without any problem of physical limits. Economics became a science of money; its object was not the material forces and resources of nature and human labour, but a new space that was opened up between nature on one side and human society and culture on the other – the not-quite-natural, not-quite-social space that had come to be called 'the economy'.
>
> (Mitchell 2011, 425)

Using scare quotes both Bullard, Müller and Mitchell remind their readers that they take 'the economy' to be a historically contingent construction. To Mitchell, this construction can be dated to the end of Second World War after which the transition from "a coal-based energy system to a predominantly oil-based one" was completed (Mitchell 2011, 245). Economics as "the science of money" developed GDP as a statistical simplification of all economic activities in society (Backhouse 2002). Despite fierce discussions in the 1970s over the scientific soundness of assuming a limitless amount of burnable fossil fuels available to global societies, neo-classical economists succeeded in defending the paradigm of continued GDP growth as the way forward for both poor and rich countries (Mitchell 2011; Schmelzer 2016). Mitchell accounts for the way, in which the 1970s oil crisis paved the way for "the elaboration of new modes of government. Not just the oil crisis, but almost any conflict between rival political claims, according to this new technology of rule, was to be grasped – and governed – as a matter of simple supply and demand" (Mitchell 2011, 323).

So we are warned of the power of this historical construct: For a large number of institutions and powerful political actors, working from the assumption that an entity such as 'the economy' exists has effectively suppressed knowledge of both resource limitations, ecological systems and the value of the commons. This is the reason why climate change the much-debated report by economist Nicholas Stern could resonate with world leaders by calling climate change a "market failure on the greatest scale the world has seen" (Stern 2007). This has prompted a large number of publications and policy-papers on "the Green Economy" as the new gospel (Kenis and Lievens 2016). Moreover, this is the reason why the same world leaders have asked economists to solve one layer of market failure with the implementation of a new market for trading CO_2 and other atmospheric pollutants (Bond 2018; Jacobsen 2018).

Indeed, it would seem that the recognition of the abstract phenomena of 'the economy' can easily lead to an approach that is more about upholding the historical structures that led to climate change than about creating solutions. Nonetheless, this book starts from the observation that most CJ activists do not relate to 'the economy' as a historical construct, but as a real arena for transforming societies to combat global warming. The struggle for Climate Justice has led to economic demands with consequences that would make any neo-classical economists bite her tongue: a moratorium on oil exploration and the immediate end to all public and private fossil investments, the public financing of millions of climate jobs, the payment of rich countries' climate debt and democratic ownership of energy production. Far from presenting these demands as a part of a distant utopia, the activists and organizations behind them have ceaselessly attempted to find concrete ways of igniting the change towards their realization. Discussions of economic categories, phenomena and developments are not only about rejecting 'the economy' as such but also about starting an economic transformation through specific interventions and programs. It is the economy in this sense – an arena for Climate Justice Demands and Debates – into which the book's chapters provide new insights.

Structure and main arguments of the book

Part I of the book provides an overview of the key economic issues for the Climate Justice movement (CJM), the way they have evolved over time and what main challenges lie ahead. While placing these developments in both theoretical and historical contexts, the aim is not to explain the organizational fluctuations of the movement, but rather to provide a clearer understanding of the main economic problems and arguments that have shaped global initiatives by different organizations that define themselves as part of the CJM.

The book's first chapter provides a historicization of economic issues, demands and ideas in the formation of a CJM in the 1990s. The main arguments and discursive innovations from early debates are subsequently traced in the political statements resulting from activist summits and gatherings in the name of Climate Justice in the 2000s. By focusing on the most debated publications central to the first definitions of climate change used for mobilization and political critique, the aim is to make visible the economic language of the movement's own organizations and leading authors. This includes a critical analysis of the tensions between different types of economic argumentation as they have developed. Based on this historical account, the chapter discusses recent tendencies to deradicalize economic Climate Justice demands by downplaying anti-capitalist and systemic criticisms in favor of arguments to change economic systems from within.

In Chapter 2, Rikard Warlenius investigates different notions of debt for the CJM in great historical and theoretical details. Ecological debt emerged as an important concept for the global movement for environmental justice in the 1990s. It provided an economic framing for addressing both the long-term aftermath of colonial atrocities, the looting of resources and more recent debt crises in the Global South. Ecological debt meant that the sides of who owes who would be reversed in real economic terms as part of the balance of monetary debt built up in the Global South since the 1970s. Warlenius points out, however, that as historical carbon emissions began to be part of the debt-questions, the arguments concerning forms of repayment have lost their immediate economic context. Climate change necessitates both a long-term restoration of the atmosphere and shorter-term funds for adaption, which points more to future conditions for a just global solution rather than the back looking settlements. As an effect calls for climate debt function more as a way of radicalizing local struggles than actual economic demands for the CJM.

Providing a counterweight to the conclusions on economic deradicalization as the CJM has moved further into a combination of divestment and local blockades, Patrick Bond argues in Chapter 3 for the necessity of stronger mobilization around financial disruption to collaboration between the fossil industry and nation states. Building on Chapter 2's insights into ecological debt, Bond proceeds with a broader analysis of currently available tools for changing the politics of natural capital in a direction that can become a tipping point for Climate Justice demands. Existing forms of ecosystem pricing have traditionally been criticized by Climate Justice organizations, but Bond argues that the notion of natural capital is one part of the "eco-modernist" rhetoric that CJ activists will have to win to their side. As opposed to Carbon trading, which according to Bond can never become a weapon for the CJM, Bond argues that a radicalization of the measurements of natural capital is necessary in the short run to counter runaway emissions and to create a basis for further mobilization.

Part II provides three case studies of how the economic problems and opportunities are approached in campaigns for Climate Justice. Sam Bliss and Leah Temper's Chapter 4 explains how the indigenous Unist'ot'en people of British Colombia have successfully hindered the building of a pipeline for shale gas from the Alberta Tar Sands. Through a detailed analysis of the methods and values behind the direct action, it becomes clear that the Unist'ot'en resistance is grounded in both long-term local economic infrastructures and a global outlook at destructive patterns of industrial capitalism. As part of the blockade, the Unist'ot'en have set up a permanent camp with a local ecology-based economy that develops legal and cultural ownership of areas sought out for pipelines. As the chapter concludes, the camp is a lasting expression of the values that prompt the Unist'ot'en to "aim towards a structural transformation of colonial and capitalist systems of domination of nature and subjugated peoples".

In Chapter 5, Georges Alexandre Lenferna investigates the origin, development and current influence of the divestment campaign globally. With insights into both the strategy of activists, the effect of financial stigmatization and the wider debate on divestment efficiency, the chapter is able to explain how it has become central to Climate Justice over the last 15 years. While highlighting the links to earlier divestment campaigns, Lenferna also underlines the ability of CJ divestment campaigners to augment their case by applying financial arguments entailed by the carbon bubble of unburnable fuels. Increased awareness of the proportions of the carbon bubble influences both the financial sector and the movement itself, with more activists getting involved, expanded campaigns against the banking sector and bolder claims for transformative social change. Lenferna discusses different lines critiques of the divestment movement before concluding that the success of creating a large core group of focused activists seems to have great potential for supporting wider and more globalized Climate Justice campaigns.

Chapter 6 is a case study of the South Africa campaign for One Million Climate Jobs (OMCJ) and provides insights into the possible synergies between organized labor and Climate Justice ideas. Emanuele Leonardi shows how the challenge of Climate Justice to carbon trading, as discussed in Part I, has formed the basis for a collaboration with labor resistance to change the political understanding of solutions to climate change in South Africa. As a theoretical framework, Leonardi reinterprets Ulrich Beck's notion of *definition power* in the context of ecological crises and argues that the unionist concept of the just transition has challenged market-based policies through the OMCJ. Leonardi discusses the dependency of the OMCJ on supportive state policies and concludes that the case provides insights into the dangers of losing the strong Climate Justice commitment in a process of institutionalization.

Part III provides discussions of emerging paradigms for thinking economically about Climate Justice. Gerda Roelvink investigates how the emerging tradition of community economies can be brought into closer contact with the Climate Justice. While local and community-oriented sentiments have been part of environmental social movements for decades, Roelvink argues that new forms of collective action have a more direct engagement with changing the economy from the bottom-up. Taking a posthumanist approach to economic theories and patterns of practice, Roelvink discusses the expansions of the Marxist and other revolutionary approaches necessary for acting timely and efficiently on climate change. Based on a number of cases from community economies, Roelvink provides a theoretical basis for an economic ethic with roots in radical approaches to farming, soil care, and collective learning. As part of this discussion, Roelvink provides examples of Australian indigenous communities whose greater emphasis on connectivity with the environment resonates with the Unist'ot'en experiments with expanding blockades in the direction of independent local economies investigated in Chapter 4.

Ulrich Brand intervenes critically in the debate on degrowth as an economic paradigm for Climate Justice in Chapter 8. Arguing that recent growth-critical intellectual debates have overlooked issues of domination and power central to Climate Justice, Brand discusses how Feminist and Marxist contributions can be activated to advance the understanding of necessary societal transformations in the face of climate change. In his critique of existing economic theories of degrowth, Brand seeks to provide a stronger understanding of the material conditions for democracy that can encompass both the Global North and South. Brand concludes that this should involve a clearer critical approach to class-, race- and gender-specific domination internationally and provides concrete plans for new patterns of production, housing and agriculture in a post-growth world.

Finally, in Chapter 9 Brian Tokar discusses the activist-theoretical tradition of social ecology as a paradigm for economic Climate Justice. Tokar introduces the origins of social ecology as both a philosophy and a form of political activism through a reading of the works of US social theorist Murray Bookchin since the 1960s. Bookchin pioneered a modern version of growth-critical ecological philosophy, which challenged Western enlightenment notions of nature-domination and the naturalization of stratified hierarchical societies. As a political program, Bookchin argued against strong states and a communalism of self-managing municipalities that could spread as a global challenge to capitalism. Tokar provides a number of historical and present cases of social movements from both the US, Europe and the Middle East who have been directly inspired by Bookchin's books before discussing the strengths, weaknesses and necessary updates of social ecology to serve as a decisive support for Climate Justice.

References

350.org. 2015. "350.org – Global Climate March: Report." https://350.org/global-climate-march/ (accessed 7 December 2017).

Backhouse, Roger. 2002. *The Penguin History of Economics*. London: Penguin.

Bond, Patrick. 2012. *Politics of Climate Justice: Paralysis Above, Movement Below.* Scottsville, South Africa: University of Kwazulu-Natal Press.

Ciplet, David, and J. Timmons Roberts. 2017. "Climate Change and the Transition to Neoliberal Environmental Governance." *Global Environmental Change* 46: 148–156. doi:10.1016/j.gloenvcha.2017.09.003.

D12. 2015. "D12 - Paris." http://d12.paris/ (accessed 7 December 2017).

Dawson, A. 2010. "Climate Justice: The Emerging Movement against Green Capitalism." *South Atlantic Quarterly* 109 (2): 313–338. doi:10.1215/00382876-2009-036.

De Lucia, Vita. 2016. "The Climate Justice Movement and the Hegemonic Discourse." In *Routledge Handbook of the Climate Change Movement*, edited by Matthias Dietz and Heiko Garrelts (pp. 66–83). London: Routledge.

Kenis, A., and M. Lievens. 2016. "Greening the Economy or Economizing the Green Project? When Environmental Concerns Are Turned into a Means to Save the Market." *Review of Radical Political Economics* 48 (2): 217–234. doi:10.1177/0486613415591803.

Klinsky, Sonja, J. Timmons Roberts, Saleemul Huq, Chukwumerije Okereke, Peter Newell, Peter Dauvergne, Karen O'Brien, Heike Schroeder, Petra Tschakert, Jennifer Clapp, Margaret Keck, Frank Biermann, Diana Liverman, Joyeeta Gupta, Atiq Rahman, Dirk Messner, David Pellow and Steffan Bauer. 2017. "Why Equity Is Fundamental in Climate Change Policy Research." *Global Environmental Change* 44: 170–173. doi:10.1016/j.gloenvcha.2016.08.002.

Mitchell, Timothy. 2011. *Carbon Democracy*. London: Verso.

Schmelzer, Matthias. 2016. *The Hegemony of Growth: The OECD and the Making of the Economic Growth Paradigm*. Cambridge: Cambridge University Press.

Stern, N. H. 2007. *Stern Review: The Economics of Climate Change.* London: HM Treasury.

Tokar, Brian. 2014. *Toward Climate Justice: Perspectives on the Climate Crisis and Social Change.*

The Hindu. 2015. "Paris Agreement a Victory of 'Climate Justice', Says Modi-," December 13. www.thehindu.com/news/national/paris-agreement-a-victory-of-climate-justice-says-modi/article7983268.ece (accessed 7 December 2017).

Acknowledgments

This project has been made possible with the support of a postdoc grant from the Danish Research Council for Communication and Culture. I would like to thank my former colleagues at the Copenhagen Business School's Department of Management, Politics and Philosophy for advice and support on shaping this book project in its initial stages. My gratitude to Professor Mike Hulme for hosting my stay at King's College and for organizers and participants for the opportunity to discuss the project at the 2016 "Alternative Futures and Popular Protest" Manchester. My present colleagues at Roskilde University's Department of Communication and Arts have welcomed me with curiosity, patience and important input in the work's final phases. Patrick Cockburn has helped me tremendously at all stages of thinking, writing and editing. Conversations with Gregers Andersen have stimulated ideas and perseverance all along. Lastly, but mostly, I thank Astrid and Dag for keeping me calm when times are turbulent.

Part I
The Climate Justice movement
Formation and critical economic debates

1   Climate Justice as anti-corporate economic mobilization

Stefan Gaarsmand Jacobsen

Introduction

A few years after the most extensive week of climate protests in history, during the UN Climate Summit in Copenhagen (COP 15), two leading figures of the coalition behind the protests looked back thinking that their movement had

> failed to establish an anti-capitalist CJ [Climate Justice]-discourse that was visible and understandable beyond the subcultures of activists and policy-wonks, and thus failed to provide a visible alternative to despair; failed to establish a new "pole of attraction" that would substantially reconfigure the political field around climate change; and failed to do anything to significantly advance the fight for climate justice. In some sense, the *global* CJM [Climate Justice Movement] remained something more of a potential than a reality.
>
> (Bullard and Müller 2012, 57)

If attracting activists and grassroots support from all over the world to debates and large street gatherings, while almost completely disrupting the UN negotiations was not enough, the quotation signals the extreme ambition of this global CJM. The "People's Climate Summit" in Cochabamba in 2010, had seen the demands of CJ protesters adopted by South American state leaders, gathering thousands of people to discuss a radical agenda. And only two years away was the 2014 People's Climate March, which would break all previous records for mass climate protest. In terms of numbers and friends, CJ was on the rise. Central figures to the CJM like Müller and Bullard, whose ambition was much larger than simply mobilizing resistance to the COP meetings, were left feeling that the movement was lacking, and insufficient in validating their ambitions. In fact, the development of the CJM from the late 1990s until 2009 had imbued activists and campaigners with a feeling of real progress in mobilizing for an anti-corporate and democratic global economic agenda to stop climate change. This chapter claims that a genealogy of the concept of CJ as an activist tool can explain why radical economic demands form the core of many activists' approaches to CJ, and why more reformist economic programs gradually replaced these demands.

The CJM has been recognized and analyzed as part of the global deliberations on climate change in the fields international political economy and political ecology (Roberts and Parks 2009, Newell and Paterson 2010, Parks and Roberts 2010, Hajer and Versteeg 2012, Martinez-Alier *et al.* 2014, Leach and Scoones 2015). My claim, however, is that more attention to the development of economic ideas taking place *within* the movement provide important new insights into the dynamics of climate politics from both a historical, and a contemporary point of view. The aim is to trace the role of economic issues, demands and ideas debated during the 1990s, and to explain how these relate to subsequent popular mobilization for CJ globally. I do this in two steps: first, by locating these issues in widely debated publications central to the first definitions of climate change used for mobilization and political critique. Second, by tracing these debates in the political statements resulting from activist summits and gatherings in the name of CJ. However, while drawing on the thorough studies of the development of the movement (Bond 2012, Tokar 2014), I remain narrowly focused on innovations and conflicts over the problem, as stated by Müller and Bullard above, of creating galvanizing economic strategies and alternatives at the global level. This means that I am focused on the development of what political economist Bob Jessop has called "economic and ecological imaginaries" as part of understanding the cultural sense-making in debating economic alternatives that are both galvanizing for global mobilization and realistic solutions in the face of climate science (Jessop 2012).

I approach this set of problems by way of conceptual and discourse analysis of the economic logic and global strategy (Koselleck 2002, Dryzek 2013, Jacobsen *et al.* 2017). This implies a close attention to the actual concepts used by actors, how they are utilized, and in which cultural and political contexts they stimulated debates and struggle (Hadden *et al.* 2014). Rather than applying theories that see climate mobilization as inherently prone to de-politicization or utopianism (Harvey 1996, Swyngedouw 2011), I analyze the CJ economic programs as an ongoing and constructive arena for tackling the problem of de-politicization of the global political economy (Bond 2012, Reitan and Gibson 2012, Martinez-Alier *et al.* 2016).

While the main parts of the chapter's historical analyzes are focused on economic debates since 1999, when CJ was first used as a concept by campaigners, two previous inputs are central to understanding subsequent developments. The first is the report, "Global warming in an unequal world: a case of environmental colonialism" published in 1991 by Delhi-based think tank Centre for Science and Environment (CSE). While there is wide agreement in the literature on the conceptual framework in the report (Shue 1993, Martinez-Alier 2014), I highlight specific economic critiques that became part of the CJM in the late 1990s, of which the resistance to carbon trading became most salient to subsequent debates.

Second, a summit of the People of Color Environmental Leadership (PoCEL), also in 1991, moved the hitherto localized struggles for environmental justice to a global arena, providing a link between urban activists and indigenous groups in North and South America. As the CJM took shape in the early 2000s, this summit's declaration became an explicit model for posing justice-claims in the face of climate change, making the context and content of the document important for analyzing the ways in which more holistic and systemic economic notions of CJ were debated in subsequent decades.

From this outset, I focus on the "invention" of CJ as a concept for radical climate change mobilization. Apart from sporadic academic theories mentioning the concept of CJ since the late 1980s (Warlenius 2017), 1999 was the first year it was used and defined as the focal point of grassroots organization on climate issues. The context was the publication of the report "Greenhouse Gangsters vs. Climate Justice" (GGCJ) by the San Francisco-based organization Transnational Resource and Action Center (TRAC) and its subsidiary resource office Corporate Watch (CW). Campaigners from these organizations took a pivotal role in the protests against the politics of the COP 6 meetings in 2000 in The Hague, inspiring the radical grassroots network Rising Tide (RT) to adopt both the concept of CJ and its economic underpinnings in their statements. I analyze and contextualize subsequent political statements that emerged from activist gatherings that explicitly sought to expand the CJ program and resulted in the formation of a number of networks and initiatives. I analyze how the central presence of economic demands began to diverge and transform in a different direction while retaining core phrases and demands going back to 1999.

The role of this economic CJ became increasingly conflictual ahead of the 2009 COP 15 in Copenhagen, with CJ demands exposing the continued inefficiency and cynicism of the negotiators from the Global North. From a moment of crisis, economic demands diverged dramatically away from the main focal points of preceding economic CJ debates. While the 2010 People' Summit in Cochabamba intermixed anti-capitalist CJ ideas with both a socialist and indigenous framework, North American NGOs converged around emerging campaigns for divestment. The International Trade Union Confederation (ITUC) emerged among radical demands, reinterpreting the notion of a "Just Transition," which, although part of the original definition of CJ in 1999, has become a vehicle for what I call a de-radicalization of economic CJ demands.

I conclude by briefly discussing whether this tendency toward de-radicalization should be interpreted as a brief hiatus for radical CJ demands or a more permanent approach to grassroots climate activism.

Climate Commons and climate markets

In 1991, leading Centre for Science and Environment (CSE) analysts, Anil Agarwal and Sunita Narain, were taking stock of the 1980s UN-focused debates, stating that "the concept of *sustainable development demands that human beings collectively do not produce more carbon dioxide and methane than the earth's environment can absorb.*" The question was how "*this global common—the global carbon dioxide and methane sinks—be shared amongst the people of the world?*" (Agarwal and Narain 1991, 9, emphasis in the original). This was before the establishment of the United Nations Framework Convention on Climate Change (UNFCCC) in 1992. However, in the report, the unequal historical starting point did not provide CSE with any reason for optimism:

How can we visualise any kind of global management, in a world so highly divided between the rich and the poor, the powerful and the powerless, which does not have a basic element of economic justice and equity?

(Agarwal and Narain 1991, 1)

The background to this claim was the recent publication of reports on climate change by US-based World Resource Institute (WRI) and Brussels-based International Energy Agency, which both presented databased climate scenarios that placed the main burden for cutting greenhouse gas (GHG) emissions on the developing world (ibid.). Making no distinction between poor countries' "survival emissions" and rich countries' "luxury emissions," the WRI calculations was hiding an immoral stance according to CSE (ibid., 3). This lead the authors to mock the "newfound interest in the so-called *Our Common Future* and future generations," referring the UN Brundtland Report from 1987, and to alert "Third World Environmentalist" not to get "taken for a ride by this 'highly partisan one worldism'" (ibid., 2). Instead, "Third World leaders" had to propose an "agenda that responds to the economic, political, cultural and resource realities of the Third World" (ibid., 17). The opposition to this path was identified as a form of Western "environmentalism" that might be keen to discuss "Green Economics," but less able to make the political leap to dealing with "the true cost" of rich countries' consumption (ibid.). Thus, the relations between the North and South was taken to be inherently conflictual on questions of economy and resources.

Concretely, Narain and Agarwal claimed that the WRI allowed "no distinction between those countries which have eaten up this ecological capital by exceeding the world's absorptive capacity and those countries which have emitted gases well within the world's cleansing capacity" (ibid., 6). To correct this, CSE presented detailed data to underpin a model for per capita GHG allowances given the historical inequalities. This would amount to the ability to share the atmosphere's GHG sink as a "global common should be shared equally on a per capita basis," which in turn was argued to be the only way to aspire to "lofty ideals like global justice, equity and sustainability" (ibid., 9). In practical terms, CSE proposed a trading scheme for permissible emissions given the size of remaining global GHG sinks, citing the literature on the "tragedy of the commons" to support a market-based solution.

The CSE report presented an argument for the historical responsibility of rich countries, which became both academically cited (Shue 1993) and politically negotiated by the main global NGO climate hub, Climate Action Network (CAN), in the late 1990s, without gaining support in the UNFCCC (Hadden 2015, 98). However, whereas the CSE had presented historically calculated per capita GHG permissions and markets as a package in 1991, Agarwal later stated that carbon trading was perhaps "an obstacle for a zero-carbon energy transition, rather than a solution to the global warming problem" (Agarwal 2001, 10). Significantly, the economic notions of market-based solutions and disproportionate historical per capita rights became the two opposite poles for the CJM in 1999.

Globalizing environmental justice

In 1991, more than 600 delegates from most parts of the US and Canada gathered for the PoCEL. Building on local environmental struggles among Black and Hispanic groups in the US as well as indigenous groups in South America (Martinez-Alier *et al.* 2016), the summit was more programmatic and universal in its character. Resulting in 17-point *Principles of Environmental Justice* and a brief Declaration of Cooperation, the summit created a platform for providing a critical language as well as a tentative political program and strategy.

The historical context of the 1991 summit reflects an ambition to organize around environmental justice and a critical stance towards a perceived underlying structural racism in the approach of the "group of 10" main US environmental organizations (Sandler and Pezzullo 2007, 3).[1] A closer analysis of the overall framing and content of the declaration reveals an emphasis on critical economic issues. The declaration's brief preamble explains the necessity of a new coalition based on environmental justice in order to work to

> re-establish our spiritual interdependence to the sacredness of our Mother Earth; to respect and celebrate each of our cultures, languages and beliefs about the natural world and our roles in healing ourselves; to ensure environmental justice; to promote economic alternatives which would contribute to the development of environmentally safe livelihoods; and, to secure our political, economic and cultural liberation that has been denied for over 500 years of colonization and oppression
>
> (PoCEL Summit 1991)

The coupling between spiritual beliefs and a new economic direction is striking and represents a break with both radical economic thinking and mainstreamed environmentalism of the time (Reitan and Gibson 2012). Very generally, the approach juxtaposes the potential economic and cultural liberation with the existing economic models guiding a colonialized world system. Clearly, this approach is in many aspects compatible with the notion of "environmental colonialism" suggested as a framework by CSE. Nonetheless, the approach in the *Principles* is not referring to "traditional methods" of production and "survival emissions" in the more technical argumentation of the latter, but pursuing a much more profound approach. As such, the first principles underline again the "sacredness of Mother Earth," expanding the consequences to include "interdependence of all species, and the right to be free from ecological destruction" (PoCEL 1991).

Other principles alternate between sustainability and justice for either "all peoples," "the planet" or "all living things," but the general coupling between recognizable political struggles of "land use" and "health care" remain intertwined with the broader environmental and spiritual concerns.

Several points the *Principles* mirrored the central role of were "economic alternatives" and "economic liberation," concerning both material conditions in questions of land use and "renewable resources," but also in the "economic self-determination" of people and the "rights of all workers" for a safe and healthy work environment.

Identifying a common enemy, Principle 14 states that "Environmental Justice opposes the destructive operations of multi-national corporations" (ibid.). The latter aligns the delegates' approach with the alter-globalization movement's critique of corporate power during the 1990s. However, while a number of the points about local sovereignty seem radical in terms of political economy, the 17th and final point of the declaration provides a form of a moderate antidote:

> Environmental Justice requires that we, as individuals, make personal and consumer choices to consume as little of Mother Earth's resources [...] and make the conscious decision to challenge and reprioritize our lifestyles to ensure the health of the natural world for present and future generations.
>
> (ibid.)

The individualization of the approach to solutions forms a contrast to the systemic and holistically based criticism of corporatism and colonial traces in modern economies. Further, the declaration does not discuss markets, capitalism or market-mechanisms, pointing to an overall positive evaluation of smaller-scale economies' function with a benevolent type of consumer behavior. The approach of the declaration is a deliberate attempt to form alliances between traditionally, relatively separate activist issues of environmentalism, animal protection, religion, justice and economy. The holistic approach seems to have provided a broad enough platform to start developing ideas on climate change, even though climate change was not an explicit part of the program in 1991—as opposed to CSE.

Defining Climate Justice as a global radical strategy

In 1996 TRAC started CW as an "internet and resource center," but later, after a name change to "Corpwatch," CW replaced TRAC as the organization's name (Corporate Watch 1997). CW's critical reports succeeded in drawing attention to Nike's production facilities in East Asia, corporate control over the internet and the concept of greenwashing (ibid.). Along with other prominent networking organizations on the Left, such as Adbusters, CW provided critical reports of the cheap and dangerous labor sustaining large brands, which received a lot of attention after the "Battle of Seattle" during the World Trade Organization (WTO) talks in 1999 (Klein 2000, McGuigan 2010). However, CW's work to provide activists with critical resources about "the corporate planet" included an ecological critique that was not a part of the leftwing mainstream rallying at the time.

Editorial coordinator at CW, Joshua Karliner, published the book *The Corporate Planet: Ecology and Politics in the Age of Globalization* in collaboration with leading environmental NGO Sierra Club in 1997. It documented a number of high-profile campaigns against Exxon, Chevron and other major oil companies organized by Sierra Club, Greenpeace and other major NGOs in Africa and North and South America (Karliner 1997). Parts of Karliner's research became central to the GGCJ report from 1999, providing comprehensively researched insights into the political and ecological landscape left by large oil corporations worldwide.

GGCJ uses several pages to define the concept of CJ, weaving together a number of critical strategies into a common program. While acknowledging that "it remains true that each of us should consume the least resources possible," the importance of lightbulbs and efficient cars is challenged with the claim that "each of us can join the effort to hold corporate climate culprits accountable for their role in what may well be the largest environmental justice issue of all time" (Bruno *et al.* 1999, 3). Alluding to the struggles of local environmental justice campaigns against large polluting companies, the authors coined another important concept of the "false solution," whereby, "Climate Justice provides an alternative to the 'solutions' corporations have proposed to the climate problem—false solutions which are divisive, inequitable and unjust" (ibid.).

CW's previous experience of revealing the poor working conditions behind top American brands is utilized to make claims about the discrepancies between the oil industry's green campaigns and their plans to continue pollution despite scientific warnings (ibid.). This was long before mainstreamed revelations from researchers and journalists of the industry's sophistication in furthering climate denial (Oreskes and Conway 2010), so the report's stance against any corporate negotiations is an attempt at making sharp distinctions between economic actors in the fight against climate change. In contrast, the CSE had proposed a "Green Rating Project" in 1997, betting on the effectiveness of "increased voluntary improvement and disclosure by industry" in collaboration with the United Nations Development Program (UNDP) (CSE 1999, 46). CW commented on the increasing presence of corporations in the UN system with great skepticism and were outspoken critics of Kofi Annan's UN Global compact from 2000 onwards (CorpWatch 2000). Nevertheless, GGCJ cites Narain and Agarwal's work directly on technical issues and adopts several of the points from previous CSE work (Bruno *et al.* 1999). Furthermore, GGCJ adopted a partial definition of CJ that conforms with the approach of CSE:

> Climate Justice means that while all countries should participate in the drastic reduction of greenhouse gas emissions, the industrialized nations, which historically and currently are most responsible for global warming, should lead the transformation.
>
> (ibid.)

From this broad definition, GGCJ goes on to argue that "[u]ltimately, Climate Justice means holding fossil fuel corporations accountable for the central role they play in contributing to global warming" (ibid., 3). The question of national emissions is reframed as a "blame game" that risks obscuring the political work for "global equity." Pointing to the inadequacies of the Kyoto protocol "any interpretation of equity, the U.S. should double, triple or quadruple the reductions of almost all other large countries, even the wealthiest nations of Western Europe" (ibid., 17). However, the authors go on to stating that "in simple numerical terms China, India, Brazil and a few other developing countries must become part of the solution if climate change is to be prevented." While this could easily be interpreted as a similar approach to the WRI, so heavily criticized by CSE, GGJC attempted to combine a defense of historical responsibilities with a radical agenda to unite the Global North and South against a common enemy in a time of urgency. The authors stress the mounting problems in the "numerical terms" stating that "emissions are still growing, with an increase of 11% between 1990 and the year 2000" (ibid.). Although the overall normative assessment placed responsibility for leading the transformation with US corporations and governments, the report implicitly points to limits for reductions deemed realistic in terms of consumption by US citizens. "By any interpretation of equity, the U.S. should double, triple or quadruple the reductions of almost all other large countries" (ibid., 17).

As a way out of oversimplified and extreme national accounting, the direct impediments for the necessary transformation are "oil companies, along with the international financial institutions," who "are pushing the development of fossil fuel-based economies on these countries" (ibid., 17). The strategy for rapid and sustained action to curb climate change is, therefore, to direct a radical critique against the corporations profiting directly from any tardiness in the transition away from fossil fuels.

Just solutions and the Just Transition

Bridging these the approaches, CW argued for a dual approach that encompassed both a global financial flow and local workplace questions of labor. The continued support for fossil fuel extraction from the World Bank and WTO necessitated a global CJ struggle for securing finances for equity. In addition, on the local or national level, CJ would foster "a just transition for these constituencies to a healthier and more just environment to work and live in" (ibid., 3).

The concept of the Just Transition places the report firmly in the economic debate between North American unions and the environmental justice movement that had been taking place since the 1970s. The authors highlight bases of union support and resistance to finding new ways of stopping polluting industries. Of the former, the report emphasizes the adoption in 1997 of Just Transition as official policy among a number of Canadian union groups and the growing support in the US for a similar scheme. Importantly, the report focuses on existing, nascent attempts at forming alliances between environmental justice groups, indigenous and international union networks. This means that the authors found great potential for expanding this collaboration into a cooperation on CJ, going from instances of local struggles and solutions to global ones (ibid., 25). As I will elucidate below, this only became mainstream union politics from the late 2000s, and with a much less radical economic approach than the potential CW had seen.

As an extension of the strategic expansion of the meaning of the Just Transition, the focus in the report's final part is on the democratization of production and resources in the energy industry:

Regulating not just how a company produces something, but rather what that company produces is an important step toward greater democratic control over corporations. When applied to climate change this approach might manifest itself in government requirements that oil companies invest truly significant amounts of money in developing ecologically sound energy and employment alternatives.

(ibid., 23)

A Just Transition concretely requires new sources of finance for both jobs and alternative energy resources. However, it is clear that the authors more generally see the status of the corporations in the US—their status of personhood, their access to government bodies and subsidies—as a systemic problem that withholds a sustainable transformation of society (ibid., 24).

As part of the argumentation for higher levels of democratic control, GGCJ mention the "Cool the Planet" campaign based at "many universities across the US" and aiming to "pressure their schools to divest their holdings in members of the Global Climate Coalition" (ibid., 23). "Cool the Planet" was announced in 1999 as part of Ozone Action, a Washington corporate-critical organization addressing "two atmospheric threats: global climate change and stratospheric ozone depletion." As ratification of the Montreal protocol had spread to most major economies by the end 1990s (Downie 2013), the focus on climate change became stronger for Ozone Action, providing information campaigns and supporting the "Cool the Planet" group to organize divestment campaign on 35 Universities US-wide (CoolthePlanet 2000). In August 2000, "Cool the Planet" claimed that the

student divestment campaigns dismantled the leading corporate lobbying group fighting solutions to global warming, the Global Climate Coalition (GCC), by forcing corporations like Ford Motor Company, General Motors, Texaco, Daimler Chrysler, and Southern Company to defect from the GCC. This spelled out the biggest student victory over dirty corporations since the Home Depot Campaign.

(ibid.)

The next step for "Cool the Planet" and Ozone Action was to organize a delegation of students to go to the COP 6 meeting in The Hague. As we shall see in the following section, this delegation became part of the first CJ gathering to explicitly present itself under the banner of a CJ campaign. This adds to the centrality of divestment, specifically, and economic issues, more generally, in the development of a radical US approach to climate change (Lenferna 2018). However, it would be almost another decade before divestment became a centerpiece for CJ mobilization, as I will return to below.

While on the one hand, the authors of GGCJ are eager to provide solidarity with environmental justice campaigns with a local and "on the ground" approach, they highlight the necessity of a universal approach to ending the dominance of the oil industry. As such, the calls from organizations worldwide for a moratorium on all new oil exploration receives strong support, while the other end of the spectrum measures to "oppos[e] destruction […] at every step of the production and distribution process" (ibid., 3). Among the groups mentioned behind these claims are "the Oilwatch Network, Environmental Rights Action, Greenpeace, Rainforest Action Network, Project Underground, Institute for Policy Studies, Acción Ecológica" (Bruno *et al.* 1999, 27). The moratorium is an idea fostered in concrete struggles against oil companies, but the GGCJ interprets it on a global scale as a "long-term necessity for society to wean itself eventually off of fossil fuels." This is an attempt at making a connection between the point of extraction and the power of fossil markets and marketing highlighted throughout the report (ibid., 16, 18, 20, 22, 26). Following this logic, a market-based solution as per the Clean Development Mechanism (CDM) is thoroughly rejected, marking a very different path for economic justice in relation to climate change than what had been proposed by CSE.

Climate Justice becomes activism and system critique

According to the account of CW, the publication of GGCJ led to a wider "Climate Justice Initiative," which included the coordination of the "First Climate Justice Summit in The Hague in conjunction with the Kyoto Protocol meetings [COP-6 in 2000]" gathering "500 environmental justice leaders" (CorpWatch 2001). The driving role of CW is confirmed by research literature (Roberts 2007, 294, Tokar 2014). However, the success of the two-day CJ summit seems to have deeply dependent on the organizing activities during the full duration of the COP by Rising Tide (RT)—a newly formed London-based radical network. Referring directly to the research and conceptualization of GGCJ, RT was the center point for direct action in the name of CJ (Tokar 2014). An activist pamphlet gathered by anonymous activist editors before and after the COP 6, quoted an RT spokesperson for pointing out the importance of making a strong connection between climate change and economic concepts:

> Actions will peak at the UN climate conference in November in The Hague, The Netherlands. […] A lot of people are realising inequality and climate change are both consequences of the current economic system. Different activist movements are converging.
>
> (*Dissenting voices—Climate Talks* 2000)

The activities during the COP 6 placed CW ideas on CJ in the context of a larger activist success that drew upon increased knowledge about the dangers of climate change and a widespread critique of the interplay between multilateral negotiations, corporate power and the proposed economic mechanisms (Parks and Roberts 2010). Jennifer Hadden *et al.* (2014) documented that the number of contentious events (counting 29) and separate protests (counting 5) surrounding The Hague COP meeting had only been surpassed by Copenhagen (with 77 and 9 respectively) until 2012. Hadden argues that contentious activities at The Hague in 2000 can be interpreted as a strong case of inter-movement spillover because of the adoption of protest techniques from the protest against the WTO meeting in Seattle in 1999 (Hadden *et al.* 2014). From the analysis of the ideas gathered and disseminated in GGCJ, it is clear that this spillover also rested upon an active reconceptualization of the struggles taking place politically, scientifically and environmentally since the early 1990s.

Central to the creation of the RT network ahead of the COP 6, was the agreement reached around a "political statement" among a large number of activists and NGOs, including Friends of the Earth and many other environmental justice organizations (Roberts and Parks 2009, 395). This included a number of principles, in which the emphasis of economic mechanisms echoed CSE and GGCJ in the disbelief of global *management* of atmospheric CO_2 concentrations in a way that would include economic justice:

> Rising Tide is a coalition of groups and individuals committed to a grassroots approach to fighting climate change. The coalition believes that the official United Nations (UN) negotiations are failing to resolve the climate change crisis. Instead, global equity and the environment are being marginalised by the dominance of corporate interests.
>
> (Rising Tide, quoted in *Dissenting voices—Climate Talks* 2000)

RT advocated for the payment of the "ecological debt" owed by "historical polluters" who are "responsible historically for its [climate change] causes" (ibid.). Apart from rich countries not considering historical responsibility, RT's reason for skepticism towards the management lay with the poverty of the ambitions. RT claimed that "a minimum of 60% immediate reduction" of carbon emissions was necessary in the short term and criticized the official assessment of Kyoto projections to provide a reduction of 5.2% 2010–2012 (ibid.). The statement fears that "any solution proposed by the UN will be undermined by the process of economic globalisation." These processes are clearly seen as increased by the assertion that "transnational corporations are over-represented" at the UN meetings at the expense of "'Developing' nations, island states, local communities [&] indigenous peoples" (ibid.).

In summary RT supported a moratorium on fossil fuel exploration, a curbing of over-consumption and a "per capita allocation of carbon emissions for everyone" (ibid.). RT listed as main problems nuclear energy, carbon trading and the misuse of the carbon in trees as an offsetting mechanism. The resistance to carbon trading as a new way of creating or upholding large profits was central to the direct actions of RT during the COP 6. A group of activists broke into the conference center hosting the negotiations of the national delegations in an act of transgressive activism, which included: paint bombs, climbing rafters and minor sabotage (Hadden 2015, 147). The messages delivered were directed against carbon trading and the influence of a corporate logic over the process. Reports from activist mention spoken messages as "there is no such thing as a market-based solution to a market-based problem," and spread of banners and flyers reading "profits of doom" and "Carbon trading = profit, yes—future, no" (*Dissenting voices— Climate Talks* 2000).

Overall, it is clear that the economic critique of ongoing negotiations on global climate policy was a strong point for political mobilization in 2000. While a number of the organizations behind RT were anti-capitalist in their individual aims, the communication and protests made public around the mobilization for CJ focused specifically on resistance to the activities of large transnational oil and gas corporations worldwide.

As for the outcome of this turn to activism, it is important to note the argument against the *current economic system*, quoted above, was from inside the RT organization. The notion of system failure was coming to the fore in the early 2000s, linked both the economic and ecological frames of understanding. While the notion of system analysis and ecosystems had been central to 1970s and 1980s debates on limits to growth and ecological stability (Behrens III *et al.* 1972, Holling 1973), the systemic effects were still mainly regarded as a result of the problematic influence of corporate profit interests into political negotiations. However, while exposing the "false solutions" and complex trading systems in an ecological context, key actors were keen to engage with the question of how to provide better answers. CW's Joshua Karliner interviewed different actors after the summit:

> "By resisting new oil projects in their lands," observes Ivonne Yanez, of Oilwatch International, an Ecuador-based network fighting oil development in the tropics, "people like the Cofanes in Ecuador, the Ijaw in Nigeria and the U'wa in Colombia are going forward faster than our governments in creating a true Clean Development Mechanism."
>
> (Karliner 2000)

The message was that the most radical ideas for *true* solutions would come from groups and regions with strong environmental justice movements and close encounters with the methods and pollution of the oil companies. For Oilwatch, this had resulted in the broad scheme for a moratorium on oil; an idea that was further developed into national policy with the Yasuní-ITT project launched in 2007, as discussed below.

Apart from on-the-ground experiences, CW's reports also showed optimism for data-driven opposition to large corporations and fact-based removal of false solutions from the planning within the COP system. This was a question of the types of knowledge that should guide the negotiations and the economic side of the solutions:

> climate conference delegates continue to ignore the issue of curtailing oil production and exploration, despite the fact that just burning all current oil reserves will most likely lead to ecological catastrophe. Statistics show that, when burned, the oil a company like Shell produces is responsible for

as much CO2 as the entire Central American region. And Exxon Mobil's production accounts for nearly as many emissions as all of Africa, according to data from environmental groups.

(Karliner 2000)

The use of statistics in strengthening arguments for the connection between specific economic activities and the proportions of ecological destruction was part of a broader tendency for CJ organizers to campaign around research results produced by political ecologists cooperating with local environmental justice organizations (Martinez-Alier 2014).

Bringing the economy back to the roots

The ideas discussed in The Hague during the Climate Summit marked the beginning of similar discussions globally with the establishment of the "International Climate Justice Network." The spokesperson for the network was Amit Srivastava who had been CW staff until becoming part of the India Resource Centre in 2002, indicating the continuity of the initiatives (International Climate Justice Network 2002). Following debates in an expanded group of international organizations during the preparatory negotiations in Bali 2002 for the World Summit on Sustainable Development in Johannesburg that year, a set of *Climate Justice Principles* were published online. The organizations gathered included CW, Friends of the Earth, Greenpeace, Indigenous Environmental Network, OilWatch, Uruguayan NGO World Rainforest Movement as well as organizations from India, Kenya, South Africa and Malaysia (ibid.). The release of the principles stated explicitly that they "Adopted using the 'Environmental Justice Principles' developed at the 1991 People of Color Environmental Justice Leadership Summit" as a blueprint (ibid.). This underlined the connection to Environmental Justice (EJ) movement, but significantly expanded them to both encompass a global perspective and the technical sides of climate change, which had not been part of the 1991 summit. However, the conceptual framing around the PoCEL principles underlines the fact that indigenous groups in the Global North were aligning themselves with groups in the Global South, sharing both the spiritual reference to Mother Earth and a radicalized approach promoting emissions equity, and opposing corporate power in the negotiations and the pollution from growing fossil-based production.

The principles contained 18 sets of problem statements related to climate change in a preamble, of which more than half mention economic categories as production, consumption, inequity livelihoods, banking, finance, markets and corporations. The focus of the preamble's problem analysis is the vulnerability of local communities, women, youth, indigenous peoples as well as general health issues and the heightened frequency of disasters in the Global South especially (ibid.). The 27 principles provide further definitions of CJ to provide an answer to these problems, and the result can largely be read as a political program emerging on the basis of PoCEL, CSE's 1991 report, Oilwatch's work for a moratorium and CW's attempt to provide a global framework.

Principle no. 2 underlines the "need to reduce with an aim to eliminate the production of greenhouse gases," directly connected to no. 10 calling for "a moratorium on all new fossil fuel exploration and exploitation." No. 4 argues for the necessity of a "principle of common but differentiated responsibilities" to address climate change democratically. The concept of "ecological debt" is mentioned in no. 8, as a demand to "extractive industries […] liable for all past and current life-cycle impacts relating to the production of greenhouse gases." Significantly, neither nation states nor the Global North are mentioned directly although ecological debt is asserted, in principle no. 9, as a right to "receive full compensation, restoration, and reparation for loss of land, livelihood and other damages." Therefore, there is less importance placed upon what was termed the "blame game" in GGCJ, but does not in itself provide a radicalized approach to sustainable financing that could transcend national competition and interests. That is, the principles insist ecological debt caused by "industrialized nations" of the Global North, but the payment hereof is held unspecified, thus open for further sophistication, following the CW's arguments in 1999.

In contrast, Principle 13 is very clear in its opposition to "any market-based or technological solution to climate change, such as carbon-trading and carbon sequestration, should be subject to principles of democratic accountability, ecological sustainability and social justice." While no. 11 and no. 15 calls for the implementation of "clean, renewable, locally controlled" energy sources that do not "externalize costs to the environment and communities, and are in line with the principles of a just transition." Finally, in no. 26, the emphasis on consumer choices and lifestyles has survived as a principle from the PoECL, but has been expanded with an emphasis on clean, renewable, low-impact energy."

Following the publication of the Bali principles, the India Climate Justice Forum held in October 2002 during the COP 8 in Delhi reiterated many of its ideas. A final statement, "Delhi Climate Justice Declaration" presented a shorter version of the principles that largely resembled the preamble of the Bali Principles. Absent was the framing around protection of Mother Earth, but the economic questions of equity, unsustainable production and consumption, food sovereignty and market-principles dominate the short text. The final point, which was original compared to the Bali Principles, even repeats and dramatizes the rejection of "the market based principles that guide the current negotiations to solve the climate crisis: Our World is Not for Sale!" (ibid.).

The context for the production of the principles, however, was more grass-roots oriented than Bali and according to CW "1500 participants from 17 states in India and over 20 countries, and comprising mostly of farmers, fishworkers, the poor, Indigenous Peoples, Dalits, youth," joining a "Climate Justice Summit" (CorpWatch 2002). Furthermore, there were large protests surrounding the negotiation area. CW reports that more than 5,000 people joined a rally through the streets of Delhi from the Gandhi memorial to the site of the UN negotiations. Photos from the event show banners demanding "Climate Justice," making it the first major public rally for CJ demands (Khastagir 2002).

Professionalization against CDM and re-radicalization

Having established the notion of CJ globally, it increasingly became clear to different actors that there were conflicts the CAN (Hadden 2015, 26). And furthermore, that these conflicts were mainly about the interpretation of economic mechanisms in the Kyoto agreement, which was to enter into operation by the mid-2000s. According to Hadden, CAN leadership interpreted the dissatisfaction from organizations supporting the ideas behind CJ was mainly about organizational asymmetries behind North and South in terms of decision making (ibid.).

The conflict over the CDM was stepped up in 2004 with the establishment of the Durban Group for Climate Justice that gathered around the "The Durban Declaration on Carbon Trading" issued the same year. Among the most visible organizers and contributors was Amsterdam-based NGO Transnational Institute (operating through a newly founded branch called the Carbon Trade Watch), and the Indigenous Environmental Network. The signatories included organizations from all continents, a testament to the efforts made earlier by CJ declarations to claim a truly global presence of the anti-carbon trade arguments, with 168 organizations and another 150 individual academics, politicians and organizers signing.

The statement was a full-on attack of the CDM and "similar private sector trading schemes" that were deemed "total waste of time when the world has a critical climate crisis to address" (*Durban Declaration on Carbon Trading* 2004). The reference of the time frame signals a sensitivity to the reports on concentrations of GHG in the atmosphere from climate scientists. The projections of the needed reductions to keep the atmospheric concentration of CO_2 below 350 ppm were beginning to indicate the necessity of a sharper global decline after a few years of unprecedented increases of emissions from China.

The Durban Group remained active for several years after, organizing a world tour of experts as late as 2008, which included original signatories such as Carbon Trade Watch and researchers such as Patrick Bond and Larry Lohmann, testifying to the advanced level economic analysis behind the initiative (Rising Tide North America 2008). It further marked a professionalization of the battle against carbon trading as the Kyoto Protocol began to be enforced in 2005.

The need for continuous organization around broader principles for a large number of organizations arguing for CJ, became clear with the creation of the *Climate Justice Now!* (CJN!) network, formed in Bali during the COP 13 in 2007. A political statement was issued with much fewer individual points and a more fundamental approach to changing basic economic conditions in facing the threat of climate change. The brief problem statement used the language of GGCJ to protest against "false solutions" that included "trade liberalisation, privatisation, forest carbon markets, agrofuels and carbon offsetting." The culprit was "rich industrialised countries" and the direct reference to fossil corporations used earlier was not present. Rather than the tiptoe approach to the "blame game," one of the statement's main demands is a call for "huge financial transfers from North to South, based on the repayment of climate debts" by "redirecting military budgets, innovative taxes and debt cancellation" (Climate Justice Now! 2008). This was a direct approach to national budgets and fiscal systems of rich countries—an innovation in terms of previous CJ statements.

Echoing earlier CJ programs, however, was an aim to hinder new oil explorations, but the rhetoric of the moratorium was replaced by a more stringent demand to keep "fossil fuels in the ground" and investing instead in "energy-efficiency and safe, clean and community-led renewable energy" (ibid.). Finally, the references to "personal and consumer choices," visible already in PoCEL in 1991, is replaced by the aim of "radically reducing wasteful consumption," especially in the North, but also among "Southern Elites."

Copenhagen COP: system change and anti-capitalism beyond Kyoto

The principles seem to have been sharpened on economic, financial and fiscal rhetoric as a response to the UNFCCC's declared intention to give the Kyoto Protocol an overhaul in the 2009 meeting in Copenhagen. Leading up to the meeting, a Northern European coalition of activists founded the *Climate Justice Alliance* (CJA). Organized mainly by Danish autonomist and left radicals, the meeting place for the CJM was the Klimaforum [Forum for climate], which was inspired by the approach of RT and the organization of Climate Camps in the UK since 2000 (Warlenius 2017). Focus was on enlarging the scope of climate action in the face of increasing urgency and less on technical Kyoto mechanisms (Pleyers 2013, 252)

In contrast, the CAN NGO negotiation leadership continued to engage in deliberations to improve the CDM. This was partly prompted by the influx of campaigners from large organizations as Oxfam and World Wildlife Fund (WWF) who had taken an increasing interest in climate change since the implementation of the Kyoto Protocol and the increased focus on financing mechanisms for adaption. The new players in CAN were more alert to the worries of negotiators to substantiate and improve Kyoto than the radical agenda that CJN! had developed in 2007 with reference back to CW's work in the late 1990s. Since 2008, CAN activities had de facto functioned with two parallel tracks, a situation which became an open fight concerning formulations for the COP 15 text in 2009 (Hadden 2015, 30). The argumentation against the CAN agenda by a CJN! participant underlined the continuity in the position since the first CJ summit in The Hague:

> It was a strategic mistake of the environmental movement in the past to work on issues separately, rather than to make a *systemic critique*. But it's hard because we need to come up with something that trade unions, farmers and indigenous peoples can all agree on.
>
> (CJN interviewee in Hadden 2015, 31, my emphasis)

The emphasis on the systemic problems in the search for real solutions became central in Copenhagen. CJN joined with CJA to gather between 60,000 to 100,000 protesters outside the conference center of the COP 15 in December 2009 with centrally distributed signs demanding "System Change, not Climate Change" (Nulman 2015). This was also the title of the final statement of the protesters of the conference, issued by CJN after the final text of the COP 15 was released. Apart from an analysis of the shortcomings of the negotiations and a call for resistance against repression, the text repeated the 2007 original CJN principles with the exception of the "[h]uge financial transfers from the global North to the global South" that, while still based on "climate debt", should further be under "democratic control." This indicates the strengthening of previous notions of democratization of the economic processes of distribution dating back to GGCJ. Furthermore, in contrast to the 2007 text, the 2009 statement included a critique of "capitalist enclosure of commons" (Climate Justice Now! coalition 2009). According to the statement, the COP "itself demonstrated that real solutions, as opposed to false, market-based solutions, will not be adopted until we overcome the existing unjust political and economic system" (ibid.).

The background to the sharpened anti-capitalist critique and calls for a system change, are found in the activist run-up to the CJ campaigns in 2009. One of the most visible activists in the preparation of the 2009 Copenhagen protests was Tadzio Müller, a German activist with roots in communist circles and a neo-Marxist approach (Dietz 2014, 299). In an essay on the social justice movement's history of victories and defeats from 2008, Müller sought to explain the special potential of the CJM. "Against the usual timelessness of anticapitalist politics" that he saw becoming the norm of the hopefully defeated activists in protests from Seattle to G8 meetings globally, "climate change poses the issue of urgency" (Müller 2008). Müller attempted to provide an understanding of the increasing destruction of eco-systems with relation to the effectiveness of anti-capitalist social movements, arguing for activists to "forget Kyoto" and remain focused on providing "non-capitalist solutions to climate change" from below (ibid., see also Passadakis and Müller 2009).

The market-based solutions were thus transposed from being the main problem for the CJM—judged by persistence in the statements detailed opposition to CDM and other proposed trading mechanisms—to being a symptom of a destructive economic system. While Müller became a voice for a neo-Marxist system's critique in the Global North, the concept of Mother Earth was being re-interpreted to support radical economic demands in the Global South.

Mother Earth vs. capitalism

Indian author and activist Vandana Shiva had become one of the strongest voices for environmental global justice in the late 1990s. Having been a leading global organizer and activist against the increasing power of transnational Western agricultural corporations in poor countries since the 1980s, she placed the local struggles for justice and common ownership into a wider framework of globalization and capitalism in her 1990s writings (Harms and Powalla 2014). In 2005 Shiva published *Earth Democracy* (*ED*), which, although specifically applying concepts of CJ, became an important book for the global CJ movement. In the preface of the 2016 edition, Shiva states that she wrote the original in the aftermath of 1999 and the "battle of Seattle", "because those promoting corporate globalization repeatedly said that the anti-globalization movement knew what it was against, but not what it was for." (Shiva 2016, 1). *ED* was proposed as an alternative through a number of principles that were pitted in sharp contrast to economies of globalization:

> The dominant economy goes by many names—the market economy, the globalized economy, corporate globalization, and capitalism, to name a few—but all these names fail to acknowledge that this economy is but one of the three major economies at work in the world today.
>
> (Shiva 2016 [2005])

In contrast "[i]n Earth Democracy every being has equal access to the earth's resources that make life possible" by recognizing two other major systems, namely "nature's economy and the sustenance economy" (ibid.). Shiva proceeded with detailed accounts of these economies, which included a critique of the ways in which principles of scarcity and the politics of "disembodied, decontextualized market" were detrimental to "the environment and peoples' lives" (ibid.). In a long-term historical narrative, Shiva argues that the logic behind the enclosure of the British Commons has transformed through colonial practices to latter-day capitalism and financialization of resources. "Globalization is, in fact, the ultimate enclosure of our minds, our hearts, our imaginations, and our resources" (ibid.).

While in fact, there are a number of overlaps between the rhetoric found in CSE's 1991 report on "environmentalism colonialism" and the dangers of mismanaging "vital global commons," Shiva provides a harsher critique through her rejection of marketization and commodification of resources and pollution, as well as the growth paradigm. With its direct address to social movements (e.g. Shiva 2016), it provided a language of political economy of environmentalism that became central to CJ in the Global South.

Shiva came further into further the global spotlight as an outspoken supporter of the Yasuní-ITT project in Equador. The longstanding notions of a global moratorium on new oil from Oilwatch and Acción Ecológica had resulted in a strong local campaign to stop any plans of extraction in the oil-rich region of Yasuní (Bond 2009). Their intense work to support local indigenous group and develop a national strategy had been part of the background for the CJM's slogan to "keep the oil in the soil" (Tokar 2014, 30). The idea of the initiative, officially supported by Ecuadorian president Rafael Correa since 2007, was to counter the economic pressure to extract fossil resources by setting up a global UNDP controlled fund that could compensate the state financially (Martin 2015). After negotiations in the run-up to COP 15 in 2009 in Copenhagen, the failure of the COP to reach binding target gave the concrete nature of Yasuní-ITT a further push towards institutionalization in 2010 (Martin 2015, 122). Thus, Yasuní had global attention in its disruptive nature to the global oil economy with hopes that a small-scale project could become a model for the world. At the time, this could seem like a decisive move from the economic ideas in the CJ statements since the 2000s to a direct influence in real-world fossil politics.

Shiva was invited by Ecuadorian authorities to take part in the campaigning for Yasuní and she became a voice for the initiative along with ex-minister of finances under Correa, Alberto Acosta, to further an economic language that had the aim of providing a sufficiently profound basis for a "post-petroleum" society. In 2000, Acosta had published a book with NGO Acción Ecológica called "El Ecuador Post Petrolero," providing economic arguments for a moratorium that was similar to the CJ statements in its critique of Kyoto and the CDM (Martin 2015, 128). In an interview in 2009, Acosta pointed out that

> We, the ones that planned this [Yasuní-ITT Initiative], are questioning the system [of carbon trading]. We are talking about a postextractivist economy, post-petroleum. We are looking for a different kind of organization of the society.
>
> (Acosta in ibid., 121)

The notion of attacking "the system" of certain economic schemes was coherent with the broad lines of CJ mobilization, but both Acosta and Shiva have attempted to go further in arguing for an economic approach that diverted from the "anthropocentric" foundation of politics of growth, development, and extraction. Acosta has stated, "[w]e will be forced to move from the current anthropocentrism to [...] a socio-biocentrism [...] that should be translated into a new kind of socialism" (Acosta [2012] in Guillién 2014, 198). Exchanging the reference to socialism with the anti-corporatism of the late 1990s, Shiva argued in a subsequent edition of *ED* that "corporate anthropocentrism urgently needs an antidote. The Rights of Mother Earth and Earth Democracy give us an opening to reclaim human freedom and the freedom of life on earth" (Shiva 2016). Acosta has since endorsed the indigenous concept of sumak kawsay or Buen Vivir (Escobar 2015), signaling a belief similar to Shiva's that the spiritual side of the concept of Mother Earth can co-exist with a radical economic program.[2]

To appreciate the historical tensions and developments in how the relationship between economic and environmental issues was addressed in the Global South, and India in particular, it should be noted that the 1990s mission statement of CSE consisted of a diametrically opposing approach. For CSE "[e]nvironmental issues are seen in an *anthropocentric* perspective" seeking societal changes through "appropriate governance systems, human-nature interactions, and the use of science and technology" (CSE 1999, my emphasis). The basic beliefs among these key thinkers and collectives, providing input for the CJM within two decades, are strikingly different.

However, the question is of course whether this coupling of Mother Earth and anti-capitalism provided a basis for the further concretization of economic demands. Certainly, the rhetoric of Mother Earth was applied as part of the radical answer to the failure of the COP 15 in Copenhagen when Bolivian president Evo Morales made calls for an alternative summit for a more radical agenda. The resulting People's Conference on Climate Change and the Rights of Mother Earth

(PCCCRM) was held in Cochabamba in April 2010 with over 200 civil organizations from both the Global North and South (PCCCRM 2017), but seemingly without a clear backing from prominent former CJ summit participants like Oilwatch, Acción Ecológica, Greenpeace, Indigenous Environmental Network or Carbon Trade Watch (PCCCRM 2010). The conference's activities gatherings resulted in an extensive "Peoples Agreement," a proposal for "Universal Declaration of the Rights of Mother Earth" along with a number of resolutions from separate workshops.

The Declaration itself ended with a long list of holistically oriented and biocentric definitions of the rights of Mother Earth with a call to "promote economic systems that are in harmony with Mother Earth." On the other side of the coin, the Agreement singled out the "capitalist system" and its imposing "logic of competition, progress and limitless growth" as the main problem for previous negotiations on climate change (PCCCRM 2010). The long-standing CJ issue of per capita emission rights was included and reformulated as the claim that to achieve "balance with nature, there must first be equity among human beings" (ibid.).

However, although parts of the economic diagnosis were shared with previous CJ declarations, the approach to solving the problems diverged. The visibility and initiative of Evo Morales moved the rhetoric away from decentralized democratic projects against corporate economic power and towards globalized models of approaches used by sovereign states. Concretely, the Agreement's suggestions of holding a global referendum with the aim of agreeing on necessary reductions and the creation of a Climate Justice Tribunal for past and present violations, seemed to Tadzio Müller, participating in the PCCCRM, as unrealistic and symptoms of pure rhetoric (Müller 2010).

Judging from the documents and the main organizing parties, it seems that despite the overall shared ambitions of promoting climate debt and providing new economic systems, the PCCCRM cannot be regarded as a continuation or extension of CJ Summits that were initiated in 2000 in The Hague. Going into the following COP negotiations after 2010, Morales succeeded in appearing as the "Climate Justice figurehead" and managed to stay popular both nationally and internationally even though neither his politics nor the *Agreement* pointed towards CJ demands of keeping the oil in the ground (Müller 2010, Russell *et al.* 2012). However, even if the Bolivian government's report of participation of over 35,000 people from 142 countries should be taken cum grano salis, the event marked both a strengthening in the unified front of South and North American climate activists, and the beginning of a division. For example, while extensive, the grassroots alternative gatherings to the COP 16 in Cancun 2010 separated into four camps with a general bifurcation into those who supported the "progressive statism" led by Morales, Correa and Venezuelan President Chavez, and those insisting on a more radical approach (Russell *et al.* 2012).

Just Transition and divestment as de-radicalization

Although the Bolivian delegation succeeded in getting the Cochabamba Agreement acknowledged in the COP 17 in Bonn, the following years saw key CJ organizers express a sense of lost momentum (Bullard and Müller 2012). The struggle against the CDM and other trading mechanisms had not resulted in a clear victory, although the doubts to its efficiency in existing forms was increasingly part of the mainstream academic debate and media coverage (Harvey 2012). The Ecuadorian plea for the international community to provide funding for Yasuní was far from met, leading president Correa to begin planning for extraction of the resources in the area (Martin 2015). In turn, Acosta, Shiva and several other activist leaders had begun legal action against British Petroleum (BP) in Ecuador and proposed to push forward with a moratorium without global funding (ibid.). What was initially proposed as a CJ Tribunal in the Cochabamba declaration was re-invented as a "Tribunal for the rights of Mother Earth" under the leadership of Alberto Acosta in 2014. It focused mainly on local environmental struggles, including a lamentation of the fall of the Yasuní initiative and a critique of Reforestation-schemes (REDD), and was thus less focused on systemic economic issues in relation to CJ ('Global Alliance for the Rights of Nature' 2014).

At subsequent COP meetings in Doha (2012) and Warsaw (2013), the visibility of CJ Activists and Organizers decreased (Hadden *et al.* 2014, 144). However, the COP 19 in Warsaw saw an important protest from inside the negotiations that provided insights into the status of the economic framing of CJ. In the run-up to Warsaw, CAN had begun to combine their work on compensation for climate destruction with rhetoric of the CJM, stating that "[t]ackling loss and damage is about climate justice" and emphasizing that "those who are mainly responsible for climate change to act here in Warsaw" (quoted in Allan and Hadden 2017, 610). Although loss-and-damage-mechanisms remained unclear and unbinding, this was a step in the direction of clear economic rights to vulnerable states globally. However, the lack of a sufficiently strong outcome from the COP negotiations on the issue of loss and damage lead to the walkout from the Warsaw COP of a large number of NGOs and representatives—though not CAN as a whole.

Citing the press statement of the walkout parties, Cassegård and Thörn (2017) point to the fact that while CAN still seemed divided, the International Trade Union Confederation (ITUC) had taken over as the main broker between the more and less radical NGOs and campaigners:

> The Warsaw Climate Conference, which should have been an important step in the just transition to a sustainable future, is on track to deliver virtually nothing.
> (Walkout press release in Cassegård and Thörn 2017, 39)

Instead of arguing for CJ, the key concept became the less politically charged "Just Transition" that had been pushed in COP negotiations since 2009 by ITUC (ibid.). Looking back at GGCJ, there was an invitation for unions to join the CJM. Now that the call had been heard, however, it was in a form that calmed NGOs rather than galvanize them.

The focal points for the CJ campaigns in the Global North also changed direction in terms of the fundamental economic critique raised. In an attempt to renew focus on the rising CO_2 emissions, long-term climate writer and activist Bill

McKibben co-founded 350.org in 2007 as a response to climate scientist James Hansen's claim that the safe limit for atmospheric levels of CO_2 was 350 parts-per-million (McKibben 2007). 350.org had been campaigning globally since 2008 but without a visible presence at the CJ Summits (350.org 2008). Throughout the 2000s, McKibben answered the question of how to reach this goal with a curious return to a belief in market-based climate efficiency. In a 2008 essay, he argued that "[m]arkets are powerful. Let's think about why they've failed [in solving global warming] here and how to make them work. And there's a one-word answer: information" (McKibben 2008).

McKibben's main argument concerns the urgency of the task of finding realistic solutions by channeling scientific knowledge into the political system. This means that debates about changing "our basic economic framework" are irrelevant since that would be as unrealistic as the movement "sign[ing] on to some new nature religion that would turn protecting the planet into some kind of Eleventh Commandment" (ibid.). Although McKibben was mainly testing out ideas and pointing to the paradox of supporting economic growth, the idea of the "quick market" was part of his argumentation in the 2000s (Steinberg 2010). Furthermore, with his rejection of a spiritual component to the change, it is hard to see how his ideas would be compatible with the CJM that had applied Mother Earth-inspired notions for a new economy since the 1990s.

Nonetheless, within half a decade 350.org was to be at the center of global attention on radical climate action, applying the concept of CJ while re-inventing the approach to grassroots economic climate activism with a divestment campaign (Lenferna 2018). The 2012 "Do the Math" tour in the US was a success in terms of bringing together a science-based perspective with the concrete economic tool of divestment, which pointed at a moralization of the economy without changing the "basic economic framework," in coherence with McKibben's earlier statements. The focus was on whether investments went to renewables or fossil fuels rather than any historical questions of responsibility.

The rapid growth and global expansion of 350.org behind the divestment campaign, allowed McKibben to call for a "People's Climate March" in New York in 2014. McKibben wrote the invitation in the *Rolling Stone*, providing a critical stance to the Obama administrations inaction and seeking to form new alliances by appealing to Unions. Invoking the concept of the "Just Transition," McKibben called for signs stating "CLIMATE/JOBS. TWO CRISES, ONE SOLUTION" (McKibben 2014). 350.org's turn away from McKibben's former "quick markets" approach was signaled when capitalist-critical writer Naomi Klein joined the board of directors in 2011 (Klein 2011) and her work seems to have brought 350.org significantly closer to the sentiments of the CJM, in general, and indigenous protesters, in particular (Klein 2014).

This alliance was cemented with the cooperation between 350.org and Grassroots Global Justice (GGJ) in setting up The People's Climate March that gathered over 300,000 people in New York in one of the largest marches to that date. GGJ organized across indigenous groups (including Indigenous Environmental Network), radical unionists, minorities and people of color, and the network had since 2011 called for "No War, No Warming, Build an Economy for the People and the Planet" (GGJ 2014). However, apart from referring to Martin Luther King Jr's program against poverty, racism and militarism, the question of how to build this economy remained elusive. Picking up the pieces from the dispersed US networks for CJ, GGJ had used the name "Climate Justice Alliance" to plan for the People's Climate March (ibid.). This accounts for the presence of slogan, from the CJ organization pre-COP 15 in Copenhagen, "system change, not climate change" in public statements and banners reported in both North and South America (350.org 2008). So, although the references to the PoCEL and the environmental justice movement at large were kept intact by GGJ, the development of these principles in the direction of climate debt, per capita emissions rights, false solutions, democratization of corporations and any anti-capitalist strategies were omitted from major statements (GGJ 2014, 350. org 2014, Climate Justice Alliance 2014).

In terms of an economic program, what seem to unite the different organizations was a broadened concept of "Just Transition," which has been appearing in both GGJ's and 350.org's statements since 2011 (350.org 2011, GGJ 2014). This concept had been invoked in the context of the CJM since GGCJ's proposal for unions to expand its meaning from environmental issues to climate change. In 2014, the meaning of the Just Transition had expanded for both radical campaigners and large union networks, to recognize it as a description of the way forward for CJ. During a public interview in 2015 Dallas Goldtooth, spokesperson for Indigenous Environmental Network and the blockade of the Dakota Access Pipeline, said that it was important to highlight "not only what we are fighting against, but also for we are fighting for—and that is just transition" (democracynow.org 2015). As direct actions and blockades have increasingly occupied activists, the development of an economic framework for popular economic power—in this North American context—has been "outsourced" to the international cooperation of unions. ITUC's role in global climate negotiations has increased further since its key diplomatic role in Warsaw 2013 and its ambitions were signaled with the creation of the *Just Transition Centre* in 2016 with a highly professionalized leadership (Just Transition Centre, Interview in Bonn 2017).

Concluding remarks

With the developments within the CJM since 2012, my historical account provides an explanation for Bullard and Müller's assessment of the movement's shortcomings: It made sense to be disappointed in the lack of further political mobilization against a fossil-fueled economy given the efficiency of mobilization in the preceding decade. The question remains what we can learn from the specific development.

It is clear that CW's early economic conceptualization of CJ had displayed a potential for global mobilization by moving the debate on environmental debt away from national accounting and towards a structural critique of the power of the fossil industry. CW drew upon both past mobilizations for environmental justice and emerging conceptions of climate debt to reformulate economic demands with the aim of broader mobilization for CJ. While CSE had provided a rather deterministic view of NGO inefficiency and North–South economic conflicts, CW provided counterarguments by placing responsibility with multinational corporations that had many enemies in the Global South and among minorities in the North America. Further, the attempt at providing economic solutions that explicitly rejected the efficiency of individual consumer choices elevated the debate to a systemic level, which increasingly attracted the forces behind successful environmental justice movements since the 1970s (Dawson 2010).

For CW, the ways out of climate inaction implied a move from regulation of companies to democratic control of production, especially in the energy sector. CW's suggestion to place the trust in the union-based conceptions of a Just Transition made sense in a late 1990s context, when radical demands and global solidarity was part of union rhetoric. Similarly, the ambitions for mobilizing on a global scale against technical trade agreements were supported by the resistance to the WTO in Seattle in 1999 and subsequent alter-globalization campaigns (Pleyers 2013).

When it came to creating a global platform for CJ mobilization, the PoCEL's work to transgress national borders in the name of environmental justice became pivotal for cooperation between activists in the Global South and North. The combination of a biocentric focus on Mother Earth with radical demands for ending fossil fuel exploration seems to have provided support for the global network of Oilwatch. The centrality of oil abundance for any neo-classical conception of the economy cannot be overrated (Mitchell 2011, Malm 2015), making it both necessary and effective to place a project like the Yasuní-ITT in the context of new systemic economic thinking as Shiva and Acosta have done.

However, as the CJM has grown in reach and numbers, the demands for fundamental economic changes have become difficult to maintain. There seems to be a number of factors at play. The attempt at finding a common economic program in the Just Transition has proven to be a two-edged sword, providing a positive language while risking an economic approach out of tune with the urgency of climate change action. Although reinventing of ITUC as an international platform in 2006 and entering the COP negotiations, the power balance between unions and corporations is increasingly uneven in the context of the global climate debate. This means that broadly speaking, ITUC interprets the Just Transition more as a protection of jobs than a clear roadmap for large-scale transformation and global solidarity (Stevis and Felli 2014).

On the other hand, there seems to be more to explore for a global CJM in a new conceptualization, a biocentric economy and the concept of Buen Vivir (Martinez-Alier et al. 2014, Escobar 2015). It is less clear, however, if the window for a convergence with radical groups in the Global North has closed. My participatory observations at the CJ Summits in Paris 2015 and Bonn 2017 have pointed to a clear anti-capitalist rhetoric from the leaders within the Indigenous Environmental Network that runs counter to the tendency in the official communication of coalitions such as GGJ and CJA. Similarly, Trade Unions for Energy Democracy has, since 2012, made a push from within union circles with a radically transformative economic agenda (Sweeney 2014).

The radical demands for democratic control of energy and production, however, seems to be staying alive as a subculture to the new mainstreamed version of CJ. The history of the origins of CJ shows us, however, that the right combinations of marginalized radical economic ideas have the potential of starting waves of activism.

Notes

1 Audubon Society, Environmental Defense Fund, Friends of the Earth, Izaak Walton League, National Parks and Conservation Association, National Wildlife Federation, Natural Resource Defense Council, Sierra Club, Sierra Club Legal Defense Fund, and The Wilderness Society.
2 Shiva and Acosta joined forces in formulating a radicalization of the Yasuní-ITT initiative when Correa started backing the project as the financial target for the trust fund had been met in 2010.

References

350.org, (2008). Step it up goes global [online]. Available from: http://web.archive.org/web/20080430171114/http://www.350.org:80/4/ [Accessed 28 Nov 2017].
350.org, (2014) *350.org* – PHOTOS: Largest climate march in the history of Latin America. [online]. Available from: https://350.org/photos-largest-climate-march-in-the-history-of-latin-america/ [Accessed 29 Nov 2017].
Agarwal, A., (2001). Making the Kyoto protocol work: ecological and economic effectiveness, and equity in the climate regime. CSE Statement, New Delhi.
Agarwal, A. and Narain, S., (1991). *Global warming in an unequal world: a case of environmental colonialism.* Centre for Science and Enviroment, New Delhi.
Allan, J.I. and Hadden, J., (2017). Exploring the framing power of NGOs in global climate politics. *Environmental Politics*, 26 (4), 600–620.
Behrens III., W.W., Meadows, D.L., Meadows, D.H., and Randers, J., (1972). *The limits to growth: a report for the Club of Rome's project on the predicament of mankind.* New York: Universe Books.
Bond, P., (2009). Repaying Africa for climate crisis: ecological debt as development finance alternative to carbon trading. *In*: S. Böhm and S. Dabhi, eds. *Upsetting the Offset: The Political Economy of Carbon Markets.* London: MayFlyBooks.
Bond, P., (2012). *Politics of climate justice: paralysis above, movement below.* Scottsville, South Africa: University of Kwazulu-Natal Press.
Bruno, K., Karliner, J., and Brotsky, C., (1999). Greenhouse gangsters vs. climate justice. San Francisco: CorpWatch.
Bullard, N. and Müller, T., (2012). Beyond the 'Green Economy': system change, not climate change? *Development*, 55 (1), 54–62.
Cassegård, C. and Thörn, H., (2017). Climate justice and movement mobilization. *In*: C. Cassegård, L. Soneryd, and H. Thörn, eds. *Climate Action in a Globalizing World: Comparative Perspectives on Environmental Movements in the Global North.* London: Routledge.
Climate Justice Alliance, (2014). Climate Justice Alliance statement to world leaders, 2014 [online]. Available from: www.ourpowercampaign.org/people_s_climate_justice_summit_2014 [Accessed 29 November 2017].

Climate Justice Now! coalition, (2009). Climate Justice Now! statement: call for 'system change not climate change' unites global movement. *Links International Journal of Socialist Renewal* [online]. Available from: http://links.org.au/node/1427 [Accessed 27 Nov 2017].

Climate Justice Now!, (2008). Climate Justice Now! statement [online]. Available from: www.carbontradewatch.org/take-action-archive/climate-justice-now-statement-4.html [Accessed 1 Dec 2017].

Cool the Planet, (2000). Stop global warming and hit the bad guys where it hurts… [online]. Available from: http://web.archive.org/web/20000815053236/http://cool.policy.net/about [Accessed 6 Nov 2017].

Corporate Watch, (1997). Welcome to Corporate Watch! [online]. Available from: http://web.archive.org/web/19970330200256/http://www.corpwatch.org:80/trac/about/about.html [Accessed 25 Oct 2017].

CorpWatch, (2000). Letters to Kofi Annan blasting the global compact corporations [online]. Available from: www.corpwatch.org/article.php?id=961#july20 [Accessed 1 Dec 2017].

CorpWatch, (2001). Climate Justice Initiative Campaign profile [online]. Available from: http://web.archive.org/web/20040820200307/http://corpwatch.org:80/article.php?id=919 [Accessed 1 Jan 2017].

CorpWatch, (2002). Delhi Climate Justice Declaration [online]. Available from: www.corpwatch.org/article.php?id=4648 [Accessed 1 Dec 2017].

CSE, (1999). *Director's Report 1997–99*. New Delhi: Centre for Science and Environment.

Dawson, A., (2010). Climate Justice: the emerging movement against green capitalism. *South Atlantic Quarterly*, 109 (2), 313–338.

democracynow.org, (2015). Indigenous climate activists: Paris 'police state' is the reality frontline communities live with. *Democracy Now!* [online]. Available from: www.democracynow.org/2015/11/30/indigenous_climate_activists_paris_police_state [Accessed 1 Dec 2017].

Dietz, M., (2014). Debates and conflicts in the climate movement. *In*: M. Dietz and H. Garrelts, eds. *Routledge Handbook of the Climate Change Movement*. London: Routledge, 292–307.

Dissenting voices – Climate Talks, (2000). The Hague.

Downie, D., (2013). Stratospheric ozone depletion. *In*: P.G. Harris, ed. *Routledge Handbook of Global Environmental Politics*. London: Taylor & Francis, 373–387.

Dryzek, J.S., (2013). *The politics of the earth: environmental discourses*. Oxford: Oxford University Press.

Durban Declaration on Carbon Trading, (2004). [online] Available from:www.fern.org/sites/fern.org/files/media/documents/document_3614_3622.pdf [Accessed 13 Nov 2017].

Escobar, A., (2015). Degrowth, postdevelopment, and transitions: a preliminary conversation. *Sustainability Science*, 10 (3), 451–462.

Global Alliance for the Rights of Nature, (2014). Rights of Nature Tribunal – Lima [online]. Available from: https://therightsofnature.org/lima-2014-tribunal/ [Accessed 1 Dec 2017].

Grassroots Global Justice Alliance (GGJ), (2014). It takes roots to weather the storm the people's climate march 2014: a climate justice story. [online]. Available from: http://ggjalliance.org/sites/default/files/The Peoples Climate March 2014 %7C A Climate Justice Story.pdf. [Accessed 28 Nov 2017].

Guillén, M. A., (2014). The buen vivir in Latin America: an alternative development concept challenging extractivism in Ecuador. *In*: E. Ehmke and F. Khayaat, eds. *Socio-Economic Insecurity in Emerging Economies: Building New Spaces*. London: Routledge.

Hadden, J., (2015). *Networks in contention*. New York: Cambridge University Press.
Hadden, J., Thank, I., Byrd, S., Reitan, R., Smith, J., Tarrow, S., and Yeo, A., (2014). Explaining variation in transnational climate change activism: the role of inter-movement spillover explaining variation in transnational climate change activism explaining variation in transnational climate change activism: the role of inter-movement spi. *Global Environmental Politics Backstrand Levi and Murphy*, 14 (2), 7–25.
Hajer, M. and Versteeg, W., (2012). Voices of vulnerability. *In:* J.S. Dryzek, R.B. Norgaard, and D. Schlosberg eds., *The Oxford Handbook of Climate Change and Society*. Oxford: Oxford University Press, 82–95.
Harms, A. and Powalla, O., (2014). India – the long march to a climate movement. *In:* M. Dietz and H. Garrelts, eds. *Routledge Handbook of the Climate Change Movement*. London: Routledge, 179–193.
Harvey, D., (1996). *Justice, nature and the geography of difference*. Oxford: Blackwell.
Harvey, F., (2012). Global carbon trading system has 'essentially collapsed.' *The Guardian*, 10 Sep.
Holling, C.S., (1973). Resilience and stability of ecological systems. *Annual Review of Ecology and Systematics*, 4 (1), 1–23.
International Climate Justice Network, (2002). Bali Principles of Climate Justice [online]. Available from: www.indiaresource.org/issues/energycc/2003/baliprinciples.html [Accessed 1 Dec 2017].
Jacobsen, S.G., Thorup, M., Bek-Thomsen, J., and Christiansen, C.O., eds., (2017). *History of economic rationalities: economic reasoning as knowledge and practice authority*. New York: Springer.
Jessop, B., (2012). Economic and ecological crises: green new deals and no-growth economies. *Development*, 55 (1), 17–24.
Karliner, J., (1997). *The corporate planet: ecology and politics in the age of globalization*. San Francisco: Sierra Club Books.
Karliner, J., (2000). Climate justice summit provides alternative vision. *CorpWatch*. Available from: www. corpwatch. org, 21 [Accessed 6 Nov 2017].
Khastagir, N., (2002). A human face to a human problem: climate justice summit [online]. *India Resource Center*. Available from: www.indiaresource.org/issues/energycc/2003/humanfacehumanproblem.html [Accessed 26 Nov 2017].
Klein, N., (2000). *No logo*. London: Flamingo.
Klein, N., (2011). Joining 350.org: the next phase [online]. Available from: www. naomiklein.org/articles/2011/04/joining-350-org-next-phase [Accessed 1 Dec 2017].
Klein, N., (2014). *This changes everything: capitalism vs. the climate*. London: Allen Lane.
Koselleck, R., (2002). *The practice of conceptual history: timing history, spacing concepts*. Stanford, California: Stanford University Press.
Leach, M. and Scoones, I., (2015). Mobilizing for green transformations. *In:* I. Scoones, M. Leach, and P. Newell, eds. *The Politics of Green Transformations*. London: Routledge, 119–133.
Lenferna, G.A., (2018). Divestment as climate justice: weighing the power of the fossil fuel divestment movement. *In:* S.G. Jacobsen, ed. *Climate Justice and the Economy: Social Mobilization, Knowledge and the Political*. London: Routledge.
McGuigan, J., (2010). Naomi Klein, no logo: taking aim at the brand bullies. *International Journal of Cultural Policy*, 16 (1), 50–52.
McKibben, B., (2007). Remember this: 350 parts per million. *Washington Post*, 28 Dec.

McKibben, B., (2008). The greenback effect. *Mother Jones*, (May/June) [online]. Available from: www.motherjones.com/environment/2008/05/greenback-effect/ [Accessed 19 Nov 2017].

McKibben, B., (2014). A call to arms: an invitation to demand action on climate change. *Rolling Stone Magazine*, May 21.

Malm, A., (2015). *Fossil capital*. London: Verso Books.

Martin, P., (2015). Leaving oil under the Amazon : the Yasuní-ITT initiative as a postpetroleum model? *In*: T. Princen, J. Manno, and P. Martin, eds. *Ending the Fossil Fuel Era*. Cambridge: MIT Press, 374.

Martinez-Alier, J., (2014). Climate justice: two approaches. *EJOLT*, 57–62.

Martinez-Alier, J., (2014). Global environmental justice and the environmentalism of the poor. *In:* T. Gabrielson, C. Hall, and J.M. Meyers, eds. *The Oxford Handbook of Environmental Political Theory*. Oxford: Oxfrod University Press.

Martinez-Alier, J., Temper, L., Del Bene, D., and Scheidel, A., (2016). Is there a global environmental justice movement? *The Journal of Peasant Studies*, 43 (3), 731–755.

Martinez-Alier, J., Anguelovskı, I., Bond, P., Del Bene, D., Demaria, F., Gerber, J.F., Greyl, L., Haas, W., Healy, H., Marín-Burgos, V., Ojo, G., Porto, M., Rijnhout, L., Rodríguez-Labajos, B., Spangenberg, J., Temper, L., Warlenius, R., and Yánez, I., (2014). Between activism and science: grassroots concepts for sustainability coined by environmental justice organizations. *Journal of Political Ecology*, 21, 19–60.

Mitchell, T., (2011). *Carbon democracy*. London: Verso Books.

Müller, T., (2008). The movement is dead, long live the movement! *Turbulence - Ideas for Movement*. [online] Available from: www.turbulence.org.uk/turbulence-4/the-movement-is-dead-long-live-the-movement/index.html [Accessed 13 November 2017].

Müller, T., (2010). From Copenhagen to Cochabamba: caminamos preguntando 2.0? *Notes From Below*. [online] Available from: https://notesfrombelow.wordpress.com/2010/05/17/from-copenhagen-to-cochabamba-caminamos-preguntando-2-0/ [Accessed 14 November 2017].

Newell, P. and Paterson, M., (2010). *Climate capitalism, global warming and the transformation of the global economy*. Cambridge: Cambridge University Press.

Nulman, E., (2015). *Climate change and social movements: civil society and the development of national climate change policy*. Basingstoke: Palgrave Macmillan.

Oreskes, N. and Conway, E.M., (2010). *Merchants of doubt: how a handful of scientists obscured the truth on issues from tobacco smoke to global warming*. New York: Bloomsbury Press.

Parks, B.C. and Roberts, J.T., (2010). Climate change, social theory and justice. *Theory, Culture & Society*, 27 (2–3), 134–166.

PCCCRM, (2010) Partners | World People's Conference on Climate Change and the Rights of Mother Earth [online]. Available from: https://pwccc.wordpress.com/partners/ [Accessed 1 Dec 2017].

PCCCRM, (2017). Partners | World People's Conference on Climate Change and the Rights of Mother Earth [online]. Available from: https://pwccc.wordpress.com/partners/ [Accessed 1 Dec 2017].

People of Color Environmental Leadership Summit, (1991). Principles of Environmental Justice [online]. Available from: www.ejnet.org/ej/principles.html [Accessed 1 Dec 2017].

Pleyers, G., (2013). *Alter-globalization: becoming actors in a global age*. Cambridge: Polity, 2, 336.

Passadakis, A. and Müller, T., (2009). 20 theses against green capitalism. *The Anarchist Library* [online]. Available from: https://theanarchistlibrary.org/library/tadzio-muller-

and-alexis-passadakis-20-theses-against-green-capitalism [Accessed 14 November 2017].

Reitan, R. and Gibson, S., (2012). Climate change or social change? environmental and leftist praxis and participatory action research. *Globalizations*, 9 (3), 395–410.

Rising Tide North America, (2008). Members of Durban Group For Climate Justice on Carbon Trading Speaking Tour this Winter – Rising Tide North America [online]. Available at: https://risingtidenorthamerica.org/2008/01/members-of-durban-group-for-climate-justice-on-carbon-trading-speaking-tour-this-winter/ [Accessed 26 Nov 2017].

Roberts, J. T., (2007). Globalizing environmental justice. *In:* R. Sandler and P.C. Pezzulo, eds. *Environmental Justice and Environmentalism: The Social Justice Challenge to the Environmental Movement.* Cambridge, Massachusetts: The MIT Press, 285–307.

Roberts, J.T. and Parks, B.C., (2009). Ecologically unequal exchange, ecological debt, and climate justice: the history and implications of three related ideas for a new social movement. *International Journal of Comparative Sociology*, 50 (3–4), 385–409.

Russell, B., Pusey, A., and Sealey-Huggins, L., (2012). Movements and moments for climate justice: from Copenhagen to Cancun via Cochabamba. *ACME*, 11 (1), 15–32.

Sandler, R.D. and Pezzullo, P.C., (2007). *Environmental justice and environmentalism: the social justice challenge to the environmental movement.* Cambridge, Massachusetts: MIT Press.

Shiva, V., (2016). *Earth democracy: justice, sustainability and peace.* London: Zed Books.

Shue, H., (1993). Subsistence emissions and luxury emissions. *Law & Policy*, 15 (1), 39–60.

Steinberg, T., (2010). Can capitalism save the planet?: On the origins of green liberalism. *Radical History Review* 2010 (107), 7–24.

Stevis, D. and Felli, R., (2014). Global labour unions and just transition to a green economy. *International Environmental Agreements: Politics, Law and Economics*, 15 (1), 29–43.

Sweeney, S., (2014). Climate change and the great inaction. *Rosa Luxemburg Stiftung*, [online]. Available at: www.rosalux-nyc.org/climate-change-and-the-great-inaction/ [Accessed 14 Nov 2017].

Swyngedouw, E., (2011). Depoliticized environments: the end of nature, climate change and the post-political condition. *Roy. Inst. Philos. Suppl. Royal Institute of Philosophy Supplement*, 69, 253–274.

Tokar, B., (2014). *Toward climate justice: perspectives on the climate crisis and social change.* Porsgunn: New Compass Press.

Warlenius, R., (2017). Asymmetries: conceptualizing environmental inequalities as ecological debt and ecologically unequal exchange. PhD diss., Lund Univeristy [online]. Available at: http://pqdtopen.proquest.com/pubnum/3685917.html.

2 Climate debt

The origins of a subversive misnomer

Rikard Warlenius

Introduction

In the 2000s, the climate change debate was politicized and radicalized largely through the formation of the climate justice movement (CJM). From the establishment of the United Nations Framework Convention on Climate Change (UNFCCC) in 1995, over the adoption of the Kyoto protocol in 1997, and into the 2000s, the climate discourse was focused on geopolitical controversies and techno-managerial concerns mainly over the Kyoto trade mechanisms. But through the interventions of grassroots campaigning, a wide array of social, economic and environmental justice issues emerged, ranging from economic distribution, ethnic rights and gender equality to critical views on development and global trade policies (Bedall and Görg 2014; Ciplet, Roberts, and Kahn 2015, 169–170).

The main predecessor to the CJM was the environmental justice movement (EJM), which grew in 1980s and 1990s. This historical link is quite established (Dawson 2010; Schlosberg and Collins 2014; Harlan *et al.* 2015). Less recognized and analyzed is that this shift – from environmental justice to climate justice – also, gradually led to another shift of focus. One of the most central concepts of the founding movement was *ecological debt*, which now morphed into one of the most important concepts and policy demands of climate justice, e.g. *climate debt*.

In this chapter, some clues as to how and why these shifts occurred are given. It attempts to add to the growing literature on the CJM by comparing it to its forerunner, and by focusing on the discursive transition from ecological to climate debt.

Climate debt – basically the idea that climate change is caused by rich people while mainly harming people that are poor, and therefore, the former should take the burden of mitigation and adaptation costs – is at the very core of climate justice. This is for instance clear in Anne Petermann's (2009) definition: "Climate justice is the recognition that the historical responsibility for the vast majority of greenhouse gas emissions lies with the industrialized countries of the global north", whereas peasants, indigenous peoples, women and so on, have been disproportionaly affected. "These are also the people least responsible for climate change" (ibid; also quoted in, e.g. Bond 2014).

While there are some scolarly works on the development of the ecological debt concept, such as Martínez-Alier (2002), Paredis *et al.* (2008) and James Rice's (2009) review of the NGO argument on ecological debt, very little has been said about climate debt, and nothing scholarly, to my knowledge, on the shift of focus from ecological to climate debt. As part of my PhD dissertation (Warlenius 2017a), I therefore made a thorough review of the CJM's statements on climate debt. In order to allow for a comparison and to be able to follow the shift, I used a similar methodology that Rice had previously done: a Toulmin model argumentation analysis of the most in important movement statements on the matter. In the dissertation and a separate paper (Warlenius 2017a), all the methodological nitty-gritties are discussed in detail; in this context I will merely summarize both Rice's and my studies synoptically, while focusing more closely on the results and potential explanations for this shift.

Environmental justice and ecological debt

In the 1970s and 1980s, grassroots environmental movements – often communities in direct struggle with states and businesses over their very means of livelihood – became a worldwide phenomenon. As noted by Martínez-Alier (2002, ch. 1), the traditional discourses of the environmental movement – "the cult of the wilderness" and "the gospel of eco-efficiency" – were now challenged by a third current, often called the "environmental justice movement" or to use his own label, "the environmentalism of the poor". Emblematic examples were the Chipko "tree-hugger" movement in India, and Chico Mendes' environmental and trade union struggles in the Brazilian Amazon, prior to his assassination in 1988.

The very name – EJM – originated from the U.S. There, grassroots- and ethnic minority-based environmentalism formed in the in the 1970s and 1980s. With roots in the civil rights movement, it developed struggles against "environmental racism", i.e. the tendency to place polluting industries and to dump hazardous waste close to poor, often ethnically stigmatized communities. A number of reports by activist scholars such as Bullard (1990) and Bunyar and Mohair (1992) exposed the significant extent of this tendency. These local initiatives held a national meeting in Washington in 1991, and a manifesto, Principles of Environmental Justice, was adopted. In contrast to "sustainable development", the designation itself indicates that environmental problems are not only a matter of economic development but have power dimensions related to class, gender and ethnicity – and, as would soon be emphasized, to international relations between so-called cores and peripheries in the world system.

The concept soon spread through various networks, movements and international organizations. The seminal Rio Earth Summit in June 1992 is best known for the adoption of environmental conventions on climate change, biodiversity and desertification, but it was also the scene of a convergence of radical grassroots movements and activists from over the world: the International NGO Forum. Bullard recalls that "we found that some groups had translated the Principles [of Environmental Justice] into Portuguese and were circulating the document to local community leaders" (Claudio 2007). If the EJM can be divided into a U.S. branch and an international one (cf. Harlan *et al.* 2015), Rio was the inauguration of the second.

One of the core concepts and central demands of this burgeoning movement soon became (the repayment of) the ecological debt. The concept did not emanate from the U.S. and was not mentioned in, e.g. the Principles of Environmental Justice; rather, it was a Latin American contribution to the movement. Debates about it had aroused there in the late 1980s (Gudynas 2008), and one of its first written expressions was *"deuda ecológica"* (Robleto and Marcelo 1992): a critical interjection into the negotiations at the Earth Summit in Rio, where ecological debt was referred to as "the vital heritage of nature ... that has been consumed and not returned to it" (my translation). One of the many documents adopted by the NGO Forum in Rio was the *Debt Treaty*, which stated that "planetary ecological debt of the North ... is essentially constituted by economic and trade relations based on the indiscriminate exploitation of resources, and its ecological impacts, including global environmental deterioration, most of which is the responsibility of the North" (quoted in Paredis *et al.* 2008, 3). The treaty also demanded that pressure be put "on international organizations for the establishment, by the end of 1995, of a system of accounting of planet Earth in order to quantify the cumulative debt of the Northern countries which results from the resources they have levied and the destruction and waste produced in the course of the last 500 years" (ibid., 25).

The ecological debt concept was surfing atop three important waves that all converged in Rio, 1992: the coming-together of an international EJM, the commemoration of 500 years of colonial plundering of the Americas (Columbus 'exploration' of 'India' in 1492) and the global movement for the cancellation of the third world (financial) debts. While the developing South had to this point been framed as being indebted to the North, the concept of ecological debt effectively reversed the direction of the arrow of arrears. Framed through an ecological debt discourse, degradation to both environmental and social ecologies of the South constituted an unpaid account of ongoing Northern accrual. Thus framed, the Global North became historically reprobate; a debtor (Warlenius *et al.* 2015).

The following years' calls for environmental justice and ecological debt repayment were often in tandem with calls for financial debt cancellation and grew through side events and networking opportunities at conferences, and through being mentioned in publications. A key actor was the Ecuadorian NGO *Acción Ecológica* (AE), which launched the statement "No More Plunder: They Owe Us an Ecological Debt" in Johannesburg in 1999. That same year, Friends of the Earth International (FOEI) started a campaign on ecological debt. Together, AE and FOEI launched the NGO network Southern People's Ecological Debt Creditors Alliance (SPEDCA), with the aim to push for the "international recognition of the ecological debt, historical and current" (Paredis *et al.* 2008, 4). Not long after, the European Network for the Recognition of the Ecological Debt (ENRED) – an alliance of ecological "debtors" sympathetic to arguments for recognition of the concept – was formed.

At the peak of the Jubilee 2000 Debt Campaign for the cancellation of Southern countries' financial debts, the brochure *Who Owes Who? Climate Change, Debt, Equity and Survival* (Simms *et al.* 1999) was published. The brochure was one of the first publications in which the idea of a carbon (or climate) debt was formulated, and an attempt was made to quantify the historical carbon debt of the North in comparison to the external debt facing the South. *Who Owes Who?* marked a shift in focus from the concept of ecological debt to that of climate debt.

Climate justice movement and climate debt

UNFCCC was adopted in Rio in 1992, but it took until 1995 before it was ratified and the first Conference of the Parties (COP) took place in Berlin. Two years later the Kyoto Protocol, with binding emissions targets for industrialized countries, was adopted and attached to the convention. Yet, after the victory of George W. Bush over (but with fewer votes than) Al Gore in the 2000 U.S. presidential election, the protocol was in danger. The talks at COP 5 in The Hague in November 2000 collapsed, and in March 2001 Bush decided to pull the U.S. out of the Kyoto protocol and tried to convince other states to do the same. In the following COP, in Bonn in 2001, a rescue operation was launched mainly by EU and the protocol survived. These conflicts drew attention to climate change, and after Al Gore's hugely successful *An Inconvenient Truth* in 2006 and his Nobel Prize, shared with IPCC in 2007, climate change definitely became the top environmental issue.

Both mainstream and anti-hegemonic environmental movements now focused on climate policies, both domestically and internationally. In the U.S., a CJM grew out of the EJM. As a notion, "climate justice" goes back at least to publications by Edith Brown Weiss (1989) and Henry Shue (1992). A pioneer in terms of movement use was the San Francisco-based Corporate Watch, which published "Greenhouse Gangsters vs. Climate Justice" (Bruno, Karliner, and Brotsky 1999) in the run-up to the 2000 COP in The Hague, where they also arranged a seminar called Climate Justice Summit (Roberts and Parks 2009, 394–395). Later, a number of groups attached to the U.S. EJM formed a network focusing on climate change and in 2004, adopted the Climate Justice Declaration. Their main concern was how marginalized and often ethnic minority communities are the most vulnerable to changing climate patterns and also tend to be disproportionally affected by *policies* aimed at mitigating or adapting to climate change (Abate 2010; Stephenson 2014).

Harlan *et al.* (2015) refer to this as the U.S. CJM, as opposed to the International CJM. The latter gathers environmental NGOs based in the Global South and international networks such as Friends of the Earth International (FOEI), Northern aid organizations and the external debt cancellation network Jubilee Debt Coalition, as well as indigenous movements in both North and South America and small-farmer's movements like the *Via Campesina* network. Important allies also include Southern think tanks such as Third World Network and Focus on the Global South and autonomous leftist groups in the North, such as the British climate camp movement and the mainly Danish Climate Justice Alliance (CJA) (Russel 2012).

The crystallization of the international CJM was also triggered by The Hague 2000 Climate Justice Summit. In August 2002, the Bali Principles of Climate Justice were adopted by, e.g. Corporate Watch, Friends of the Earth International, Greenpeace, Indigenous Environmental Network, Oilwatch, Third World Network and World Rainforest Movement. What would become key pillars of the climate justice discourse – its emphasis on equality between countries and social groups, its scepticism towards "false solutions" such as carbon trading and techno-fixes, its call for the recognition and repayment of the ecological (later climate) debt, and its promotion of "real" solutions, such as reducing the use of fossil fuels, food sovereignty and respect for indigenous rights – were all visible in the declaration (International Climate Justice Network 2002). Interestingly, both the Bali Principles of 2002 and the U.S. Climate Justice Declaration of 2004 devote paragraphs to the recognition of "a principle of ecological debt". Thus, the term ecological debt is still used, but the concept is defined in terms of climate impacts. In similar phrasings, both demand that fossil fuel industries are held "strictly liable for all past and current life-cycle impacts relating to the production of greenhouse gases".

Another milestone for the movement was the forming of the Durban Group for Climate Justice in 2004, which adopted the Durban Declaration on Carbon Trading (2004). It prefigured the formation of the Climate Justice Now! (CJN!) network in Bali 2007, which was first and foremost the result of a growing discontent with the endorsement of the Kyoto market mechanisms by the Northern-dominated NGO network Climate Action Network (Bond and Dorsey 2010; Russel 2012, 136). Still it was ecological debt, not climate debt, that was in focus.

The Bali COP 13 decided that a major agreement for the second period of the Kyoto Protocol should be adopted in Copenhagen two years later, which sparked the largest climate related mobilizations so far. Calls for climate justice rang all over. The Southern-dominated CJN! planned civil disobedience actions in collaboration with Climate Justice Alliance (CJA), a newly set up network of mostly Danish activists inspired by the British Climate Camps, the interventionist left and the (anti) globalization movement of the 1990s (cf. Russel 2012, 134, 138), while the more mainstream environmental NGOs, churches and aid organizations formed the network *Tcktcktck – Time for Climate Justice* (ibid.). Climate justice rang in the alternative civil society centre KlimaForum 09, whose final resolution "System Change – not Climate Change" was adopted by over 300 organizations and called for the abandonment of fossil fuels within 30 years, the recognition and compensation of climate debt and a rejection of carbon trading (KlimaForum 2009).

In 2009, finally, the acknowledgement of a *climate* debt was among the strongest demands presented by the CJM. In a run-up campaign, the declaration: Repay the climate debt: a just and effective outcome for Copenhagen (TWN 2009a) was circulated and signed by 254 organizations, mainly from the Global South (TWN 2009b).

After COP 15, which was widely acknowledged as a failure, Bolivia's president Evo Morales convened the People's World Conference on Climate Change and the Rights of Mother Earth, in Cochabamba in April 2010. This initiative was supported by over 200 civil organizations as well as by states affiliated with the Bolivarian Alliance for the Americas (ALBA, comprised of Bolivia, Cuba, Ecuador, Nicaragua and Venezuela). The conference adopted a *People's Agreement* (PWCCC 2010). Bolivia submitted a proposal to the UNFCCC process in 2010 (UNFCCC 2010), based on the demands raised by the CJM in Cochabamba.

While the years 2007–2010 signalled the global breakthrough for a new, radical discourse on climate change carried by the CJM, what happened the following years is more ambiguous. CJA ceased to exist (Russel 2012, 200) and the activities of CJN! more or less vanished. Climate justice activists continued to gather at the COPs, such as in Durban 2011, Lima 2014, Paris 2015 and Bonn 2017, but in decreasing numbers. One explanation is that the growing distrust in the UNFCCC process after the Copenhagen failure shifted the attention towards local or national struggles (Tokar 2013; Bond 2014; Foran 2014). This seems to be especially true in the U.S., where strong campaigns against fossil infrastructures such as the Keystone XL pipeline and mobilizations such as the 400,000 People's Climate March in New York in September 2014 occurred. In Europe, an explanation for the decline of the CJM is that attention was diverted to new movements launched against austerity policies such as Occupy and Indignados (Mueller 2012). The attempts to reinvigorate the European movement in the mobilization for Paris COP 21 in 2015 were seriously disturbed by the ban on climate manifestations following the November 13 terrorist attacks, but around 10,000 climate justice activists nevertheless demonstrated on Champs Elysée. The last few years a strong German CJM has evolved under the campaign cry "*Ende Gelände*" ("That's it"). During 2015, 2016 and 2017, thousands of activists have gathered in various German sites for mass actions of civil disobedience against coal mines and coal power plants. The organizers are an alliance of environmental, climate and leftist organizations with some links back to CJA.

The international CJM is a convergence of several movements with diverse approaches to climate justice and climate debt (cf. Garrelts and Dietz 2013). The different movements advocate slightly different versions of climate justice. Thus, environmental NGOs tend to emphasize that remaining fossil fuels should remain unexploited and often have a history of campaigning for ecological debt recognition, sometimes in collaboration with Northern aid organizations and the external debt cancellation network, Jubilee Debt Coalition. They have close ties to indigenous movements in both North and South America and to small-farmer's movements such as the *Via Campesina* network, which bring perspectives such as spirituality and small-scale farming to the movement (Keller 2012). The Southern think tanks instead emphasize climate change effects related to global inequalities, development issues and the importance of repaying the climate debt. Especially the Third World Network tends to rather uncritically back Southern against Northern states within UNFCCC (Chatterton *et al.* 2013). Although many of the movement's positions are shared with Southern governments, notably the Latin American ALBA-states, the relation is sometimes tense. The groups that wanted to analyze the "neo-extractivism" (Gudynas 2010) of, e.g. Bolivia and Venezuela were excluded from the official People's summit in Cochabamba in 2010 (Russel 2012, 173–175; Fabricant and Hicks 2013).

The European CJA network was allied with the Southern-dominated CJN! in Copenhagen 2009, but had a different background and approach. According to Russel (2012, 134), it became clear that although the networks both favoured climate justice, "the actual content of any climate justice discourse remained highly contested". CJA developed its own discourse based on a critical analysis of "green capitalism" (Mueller and Pasadakis 2008), in which climate debt played no part. Later, two of its leading theorists, Mueller (2012) and especially Russel (2012, 180–184), developed critiques of the climate debt concept, mainly for focusing on the geopolitical level of the "North–South" divide instead of pointing to the class dimension of capitalism as a worldwide system.

The impression is that when CJA mentioned climate debt in their statements, it was mainly out of respect for their Southern allies, for whom it was a central concept. Instead, it preferred to refer to Europe's historical responsibility for climate change and global, social and environmental exploitation. CJA (2010) mentioned geopolitical inequalities and "unequal exchange via unjust trade policies". Thus, while CJA adopted much of the theories that define and identify ecological and climate debt, the non-use of these terms was perhaps a reflection of disconnection or alienation from the Southern and NGO-based discourse in which ecological debt and climate debt was central, and of identification with a classical Marxist discourse in which unequal exchange rather than climate debt is emphasized. I have elsewhere (Warlenius 2016) made an attempt to bridge this gap between Marxism and environmental justice.

Yet with the exception of CJA-type of climate justice, the differences on how climate debt is perceived are smaller than expected. In Table 2.1, six central CJM documents are placed along two axes: whether their origination was influenced mainly by Southern or Northern organizations (or roughly equal), and whether they were influenced mostly by independent NGOs or states (or roughly mixed).

Four hypotheses are tested on this scheme. First, that Northern NGOs would focus less on climate debt repayment demands than Southern NGOs. Thus, weaker versions of debt repayment are expected in the documents that are mostly influenced by Northern NGOs, i.e. 1, 2 and 5, while a stronger emphasis on debt repayment is expected in 3, 4, 6, 7. However, full reparations and compensations are demanded in practically all documents except the People's Agreement (6) and therefore, no correlation is found.

Second, one can assume that documents influenced by Southern states would have a particular interest in debt repayments. This cannot be verified through text analysis. Third, one could expect states to be more oriented toward country-to-country debt repayments, while NGOs would be more oriented toward class, gender or dichotomies based on corporations/people. With the exceptions of 1 and 2, developed countries are pinpointed as single debtors, while the picture of

Table 2.1 CJM documents according to two types of influence

	NGO	*[Mixed]*	*State issued*
Southern	3	4, 6	7
[Equal]	1, 5		
Northern	2		

Source: own elaboration of below documents

Documents:

1 *The Bali Principles of Climate Justice* (International Climate Justice Network 2002).
2 *The Climate Justice Declaration* (CJD 2004).
3 *Climate Justice Now! Founding statement* (CJN! 2007).
4 *Repay the Climate Debt. A Just and Effective Outcome for Copenhagen* (TWN 2009a).
5 *People's Declaration – System Change – not Climate Change* (KlimaForum 2009).
6 *People's Agreement* (PWCCC 2010).
7 *Submission by the Plurinational State of Bolivia to the Ad-Hoc Working Group on Long-term Cooperative Action* (UNFCCC 2010).

claimants is more scattered. Only People's agreement (6) regard climate debt as exclusively a country-to-country affair, two documents do not mention developing countries at all (1, 2), while the rest seem to regard climate debt as *primarily* a country-to-country affair. The hypothesis is not convincingly confirmed.

Finally, I hypothesize that NGOs would emphasize ecological integrity to be stronger than states, and therefore, 1, 2, 3 and 5 would be greener than 4, 6 and 7. Yet, an analysis concluded that all climate debt claims share an ecological vision; some more emphatically than others, but the expected pattern defaults. Yet, if we search the documents for the more demanding formulation to phase out fossil fuels, the hypothesis is supported. The most state-influenced (4, 6, 7) are least interested in fossil fuel phase out, while the three documents that contain such a call are all influenced by NGOs (2, 3, 5).

Noting that the core CJM demand of keeping fossil fuels in the ground is absent from the People's Agreement, Mueller (2012) contemplated that perhaps "Comrades Evo [Morales] and Hugo [Chavez] would not have appreciated that one".[1]

Ecological debt claims

Now, zooming in on the specific claims that the EJM did on ecological debt, James Rice (2009) analyzed eight relevant documents by different NGOs using Toulmin's (2003) argumentation analysis. A brief introduction to this model seems unavoidable. In the model, an argument is disentangled into six dimensions, of which four are essential here: *claims*, *data*, *warrants* and *backing*. The claim is the manifest standpoint that the sender wants the recipient to agree with. It is almost always founded in some data (facts). Responding to the question how the data support the claim, the sender needs to refer to some principles or premises. These are the warrants, which are presumed but not always expressed in the argument. If the warrants are supported by further data, it is called *backing*. In Warlenius (2017a) this example of an analysis using three components is given:

> Industrialized countries have emitted most of the carbon emissions, while developing countries are most affected by climate change (*data*). Since the one who has messed up the climate system also should clean it up (*warrant*), industrialized countries owe developing countries a climate debt (*claim*).

The documents in Rice's analysis of ecological debt are from about the year 2000, a.k.a. the peak of the global campaign for debt cancellation.[2] The most central claim identified is that the Northern development model is predicated on a "socio-ecological subsidy" imposed on Southern countries, defined as "the underpayment and, at times, explicit looting of the natural resource assets of Southern countries" (Rice 2009). There is no explicit mention of a climate debt, but one of the papers analyzed, issued by Friends of the Earth Australia, mentions Carbon Debt, which

> is based upon the same theory as that of the Ecological Debt. That is, those countries that are using more than their fair share of carbon allocation are running up a debt to those countries that are using less than their fair allocation.
>
> (ibid.)

The assumption that the carbon/climate debt is part of a wider ecological debt is repeated in several CJM statements and academic texts (Martínez-Alier 2002; Paredis *et al.* 2008; Srinivasan *et al.* 2008 to mention a few). Its position within ecological debt was, however, still quite peripheral, at least judging from Rice's analysis, where the carbon debt is reported as a *backing* data to a *warrant* (appropriation of environmental space) legitimizing the *claim* of a socio-ecological subsidy.

Rice (2009) identifies three further claims. The second is that the external, financial debt should be cancelled since it promotes the socio-ecological subsidy; the debt crisis is but the latest way to extract value and unequal exchange from the peripheries to the core. The third claim regards the levels of production and consumption in the North, which are seen as unsustainable and predicated on the socio-ecological subsidy. The fourth and final claim calls for Northern countries to begin paying back the "the accrued socio-ecological subsidy, an obligation that can be defined as an 'ecological debt'". The only concrete form of repayment mentioned is the cancellation of external debts (ibid.).

Climate debt claims

In my review of the CJM discourse on climate debt, nine documents were analyzed. They were adopted between 2002 and 2010, by a broad collection of movements except in one case, by Bolivia (which, as explained above, was a close ally of the CJM at they time). The most important claims identified are, first, that climate debt should be acknowledged. Deducing from the CJM documents, the climate debt is regarded as twofold,

> owed by developed countries [and corporations] to developing countries [and future generations] for their appropriation of the planet's capacity to absorb greenhouse gases above their fair share (an emissions debt) and for their contribution to incremental costs caused by the adverse effects of climate change (an adaptation debt).

Furthermore, both the emissions debt and the adaptation debt should be repaid in full. There are, however, some unresolved issues associated with this debt repayment. The emissions debt is considered as a restorative, physical debt, measured in tons of CO_2, and should be repaid by the over-emitting countries through sharp emission reductions that neutralize their historical, cumulative overuse and make room for developing countries to use up their fair share of total sustainable emissions. Thus, it is about restoring or "decolonizing" the atmospheric space, occupied by developed countries' emissions. The problem, indicated in the CJM documents but not directly confronted, is that such a physical restoration/repayment would take a long time. Very high levels of historical and current emissions in combination with the limited capacity of the global sinks to absorb these emissions sustainably, would result in a process of several hundreds or even thousands of years. Therefore, parts of the restorative debt would need to be swapped into a compensatory debt repayment, understood as the transfer of finance or technology that enable the same degree of "development" that the restorative, biophysical debt repayment would amount to. This would hopefully result in faster development for debtor countries and smoother transitions for creditor countries.[3]

The adaptation debt is mainly compensatory and financial already at the outset, which make it easier to conceptualize. To actually calculate it (attempted in Warlenius 2017b) is, however, practically impossible, since "the incremental costs caused by the adverse effects of climate change" are impossible to assess in advance.

The final major claim identified is that climate debt is part of the wider ecological debt, thus implying that repaying the climate debt is not enough; it is situated within a more general pattern of economic, social and ecological exploitation that also needs to be dealt with.

Comparing the two set of claims

In my dissertation these claims are compared more systematically, while here I will elaborate on the most important findings. In conclusion, the ecological debt discourse culminates around the year 2000, and is tightly connected to the Jubilee campaigns for external debt relief, while the climate debt discourse peaks about a decade later in conjunction with the Copenhagen Climate Justice Summit in December 2009 and the People's World Conference in April 2010, and is focused on a fair, historically responsible solution for the climate crisis. While climate change and climate debt were peripheral in Rice's analysis of ecological debt, the equivalent is also true; claims for external debt cancellation is mentioned in but not at the centre of the climate debt discourse.

A first, by now evident, finding is merely that a major shift in priorities occurred during this decade. An international EJM occupied with a history of unequal exchange and debt traps, morphed into a CJM focusing on a fair, redistributive and compensatory climate deal. This shift is of course mirroring larger, discursive shifts. After the heroic mobilization of the Jubilee debt movement to the 2000 Millennium Summit, the momentum faded. The EJM is and was not reducible to the debt cancellation movement, but thereafter, the relevance of one of its main demands decreased. Instead, during the course of the decade, climate change and climate change policies got more and more attention in media, in politics and successively also in the environmental movement. In a seamless way, the main focus of ecological debt shifted from legitimizing external debt cancellation to historical responsibility for carbon emissions, before finally, in the run-up to Copenhagen 2009, the term itself was shifted to climate debt.

The second finding regards the framing of the concepts, reminiscent of Rosa Luxemburg's (2003, 432) characterization of capital accumulation as both economic and expropriative. The main ecological debt claim, a socio-ecological subsidy, is defined as "the underpayment and, at times, explicit looting of the natural resource assets of Southern countries"; as the "unequal and undervalued exchange of natural resources and labor power" (Rice 2009). The vocabulary is mostly derived from (heterodox) economics – debt, subsidy, underpayment, undervalued, exchange – while "looting" refers to extra-economic processes such as of colonial violence. The framing of ecological debt, form an association to an unjust economic relation, while cases of direct expropriation exist but are exceptions. Thus, ecological debt is viewed as mainly (but not only) the result of unfair exchanges between countries. Climate debt, on the other hand, is primarily the result of the non-traded overuse of the carbon commons, imprecating adverse effects of climate change, and is referred to with extra-economic terminology, such as "appropriation" or "occupation".

While both concepts are framed within unjust power relations between North and South, there is nonetheless a difference in how this power inequality is played out: a discursive shift from intra- to extra-economic, or expropriative, framing has occurred.

A third finding regards the principle of strict liability, or what Friman and Strandberg (2014), when they examine historical responsibility proposals within UNFCCC, distinguish as a "conceptual" and a "proportional" view. The first presents a moral case for action without a direct linkage between emissions and responsibilities, while the latter defines current responsibility in direct proportion to past emissions. Transferred to the discourses of ecological debt and climate debt, the first is often seen as conceptual while the latter is proportional. One chief explanation for this difference is certainly that while the ecological debt is comprehensive, complex and difficult to quantify in any exact manner, the climate debt can be based on quite specific data and is therefore easier to calculate.

But I would also argue that this dispute is congenial with the aims and backgrounds of respective discourse. If the ecological debt concept developed into primarily serving as a tool for cancelling the external debts, its framing in economic jargon (debt, subsidy) makes sense: the aim was economic, e.g. to balance the ecological debt for the external debt. This also explains why debt cancellation is the *only* repayment measure discussed in Rice (2009), and why a conceptual view is fully satisfying; as long as it can be confirmed that the ecological debt is (at least) as large as the external debt, it will fulfil its main objective.

When the focus shifted from ecological debt to climate debt, the primary aim was no longer to set off financial debts. Thus, the economic context was largely lost since the accrual of the debt is conceptualized as primarily expropriative. The discourse also shifted to a proportional view of historical responsibility and considers the (emissions) debt repayment mainly in restorative, biophysical terms. At the same time, the very gravity of the situation forces the movement towards more pragmatic stances, such as the acceptance of compensatory debts.

This inevitably points to a further conclusion: that "climate debt" is a misnomer; a heritage from a concept that has similarities, but also important differences. For the cumulative result of an expropriation of the atmospheric commons, climate indemnity or climate reparations would be more suitable.

Yet while a misnomer, make no mistake about the relevance or subversiveness of the concept. As concluded in Warlenius (2017a):

> Climate debt is, at first sight, not very radical. It is simply asking the one who caused the mess to clean it up – a principle that is easily derived from common sense ethics and well established in environmental politics. Yet, that it would be a consensual principle is delusory: because of the magnitude of the mess and the skewness of responsibility, it would have drastic effects. The industrialized countries are of course aware of this, and have therefore resisted it forcefully. Despite massive mobilization of both movements and Southern governments, the results, in terms of influencing the UNFCCC negotiations, are bleak. There are no references to climate debt or historical liabilities in the agreements.
>
> Yet, this delusion is also the concept's major asset. Climate debt provides radical redistributive measures with a strong legitimacy which makes them difficult to oppose, at least intellectually. Perhaps, the proponents of climate debt have therefore mistaken it for an innocent proposal and underestimated the resistance it would provoke. That would be a mistake. Because in the real world, it is a bomb.

Instead of debt cancellation, I would argue that the main objective of the climate debt discourse became to enhance climate justice: to push for serious global action on climate change in a way that recognizes historical injustices and shares the burdens fairly; to push for a "decolonization" of the atmospheric commons; or, with Petermann's (2009) words, to push for a "recognition that the historical responsibility for the vast majority of greenhouse gas emissions lies with the industrialized countries of the global north".

Final considerations

In this chapter, the background of the CJM and its use of the concept of climate debt has been outlined. Because of the loss of the economic context of the preceding concept, climate debt is referred to as a misnomer. The concept is nonetheless deemed as relevant and subversive, and intimately connected to climate justice. Yet, it has also been argued that its use peaked several years ago, in 2009–2010, and one might ask why it is not still carried on the banners of marching climate activists around the world. My short reply would be that climate debt is associated with struggles for a *global*, fair solution of the climate crisis, and the hope for such a solution has – at least temporarily – faded under the heavy pressures of failed negotiations and insufficient and voluntary targets, expressed in the Paris agreement of 2015. Instead of focusing on UN summits that can't deliver, climate struggles have become more localized, for obvious and relevant reasons.

Yet, the problems have not been localized. While all emissions are local and can be fought locally, climate change is the essence of a global political problem; unlikely to be solved without international coordination and regulation.

Hopefully, and sooner rather than later, this will lead to renewed, serious negotiations on what the CJM, before Paris, used to call a *fab* deal – fair, ambitious and binding. As soon as real attempts are made at really solving climate change, I am rather confident that the issues of global justice, historical responsibilities and reparations will resurface too. The fundamental justice concerns underlying the climate debt concept will never disappear.

Notes

1 The alliance between the CJM and the nation of Bolivia faded in 2011–2012, when Bolivia's UN ambassador Pablo Solón withdrew from office and the Evo Morales government decided to construct a road through the Isiboro Sécure National Park and Indigenous Territory (Fabricant and Hicks 2013).
2 Those of Rice's sources, which are dated are from 1999, 2000, 2000 and 2006 (four are undated).
3 In Warlenius (2017b), I have calculated the climate debt of 154 countries, and their use of "debt swaps" is apparent. According to it, 3,000 MtCO$_2$ per year can be emitted sustainably globally. The U.S. alone has an emission debt of 344,000 MtCO$_2$ (in 2011). Its sustainable emissions (basically its per capita share of global sustainable emissions), is about 138 MtCO$_2$ per year. Thus even with zero emissions, it would take the U.S. some 2,500 years to repay its debt in physical terms. The climate creditors are unlikely to have that kind of patience.

References

Abate R. (2010) "Public Nuisance Suits for the Climate Justice Movement: The Right Thing and the Right Time", *Washington Law Review*, 85, 197–252.

Bedall P. and Görg C. (2014) "Antagonistic Standpoints. The Climate Justice Coalition Viewed in Light of a Theory of Societal Relationships with Nature", in Dietz M. and Garrelts H. eds. *Routledge Handbook of the Climate Change Movement*. Routledge, London, 44–65.

Bond P. and Dorsey M.K. (2010) "Anatomies of Environmental Knowledge and Resistance: Diverse Climate Justice Movements and Waning Eco-Neoliberalism", *Journal of Australian Political Economy*, 66, 286–316.

Bond P. (2014) "Justice", in Death C. ed. *Critical Environmental Politics*. Routledge, London and New York, 133–145.

Bruno K., Karliner J. and Brotsky C. (1999) *Greenhouse Gangsters vs. Climate Justice.*, Transnational Resource and Action Center, San Francisco.

Bullard R. (1990) *Dumping in Dixie. Race, Class, and Environmental Quality*. Westview Press, Boulder.

Bunyar B. and Mohair P. (1992) *Race and the Incidence of Environmental Hazards*. Westview Press, Boulder.

Chatterton P., Featherstone D. and Routledge P. (2013) "Articulating Climate Justice in Copenhagen. Antagonism, the Common, and Solidarity", *Antipode*, 45 (3), 602–620.

Ciplet D., Roberts J.T. and Khan M.R. (2015) *Power in a Warming World. The New Global Politics of Climate Change and the Remaking of Environmental Inequality*. MIT Press, Cambridge.

Claudio L. (2007) "Standing on Principle. The Global Push for Environmental Justice", *Environmental Health Perspectives*, 115 (10), 501–503.

Climate Justice Alliance [CJA] (2010) What Does Climate Justice Mean in Europe? (https://ayya2cochabamba.wordpress.com/texts-and-articles/what-does-climate-justice-mean-in-europe/) accessed 29 February 2016.

Climate Justice Declaration [CJD] (2004) *Climate Justice Declaration*, (http://www.umich.edu/~snre492/cgi-data/ejcc_principles.html) accessed 29 February 2016.

Climate Justice Now! [CJN] (2007) *Founding Statement*, (http://ccs.ukzn.ac.za/default.asp?4,80,5,2381) accessed 29 February 2016.

Dawson A. (2010) "Climate Justice: The Emerging Movement against Green Capitalism", *South Atlantic Quarterly*, 109 (2), 313–338.

Durban Group for Climate Justice (2004) *The Durban Declaration on Carbon Trading*, (http://www.whatnext.org/resources/Publications/Carbon-Trading/carbon_trading_durban_declaration.pdf) accessed 29 February 2016.

Fabricant N. and Hicks K. (2013) "Bolivia vs. the Billionaires: Limitations of the Climate Justice Movement in International Negotiations", *ACLA Report on the Americas*, Spring, 27–31.

Foran J. (2014) "What now for Climate Justice? Re-Imagining Radical Climate Justice", in International Institute of Climate Action & Theory [IICAT] *What now for Climate Justice? Social Movement Strategies for the Final Year of Struggle over the Next Universal Climate Treaty*. IICAT, Lima.

Friman M. and Strandberg G. (2014) "Historical Responsibility for Climate Change: Science and the Science–Policy Interface", *WIREs Clim Change*, 5, 297–316.

Garrelts H. and Dietz M. (2013) "Introduction. Contours of the Transnational Climate Movement Conception and Contents of the Handbook", in Dietz M. and Garrelts H. eds. *Routledge Handbook of the Climate Change Movement*. Routledge, London, 1–15.

Gudynas E. (2010) *The New Extractivism of the 21st Century. Ten Urgent Theses about Extractivism in Relation to Current South American Progressivism*, (http://www10.iadb.org/intal/intalcdi/PE/2010/04716.pdf) accessed 29 February 2016.

Gudynas E. (2008) Mas que Deuda, un Robo, (http://www.deudaecologica.org/Que-es-Deuda-Ecologica/MAS-QUE-DEUDA-UN-ROBO.html) accessed 29 February 2016.

Harlan S., Pellow D., Roberts J.T., Bell S.E., Holt W. and Nagel J. (2015) "Climate Justice and Inequality", in Dunlap R.E. and Brulle R.J. eds. *Climate Change and Society: Sociological Perspectives*. Oxford University Press, Oxford, 127–163.

International Climate Justice Network [ICJN] (2002) The Bali Principles of Climate Justice, (www.ejnet.org/ej/bali.pdf) accessed 29 February 2016.

Keller E.M. (2012) *Re-Constructing Climate Change: Discourses of the Emerging Movement for Climate Justice*. Queen's University, Kingston, Ontario.

KlimaForum (2009) *System Change – not Climate Change. A People's Declaration from KlimaForum09*, (http://klimaforum.org/declaration_english.pdf) accessed 29 February 2016.

Luxemburg R. (2003) *The Accumulation of Capital*. Routledge, London and New York.

Martínez-Alier J. (2002) *The Environmentalism of the Poor. A Study of Ecological Conflicts and Valuation*. Edward Elgar, Cheltenham.

Mueller T. (2012) "The People's Climate Summit in Cochabamba. A Tragedy in Three Acts", *Ephemera*, 12 (1/2), 70–80.

Mueller T. and Passadakis A. (2008) 20 Theses Against Green Capitalism, (https://climateactioncafe.wordpress.com/2008/12/05/20-theses-against-green-capitalism) accessed 28 November 2017.

Paredis E., Goeminne G., Vanhove W., Maes F. and Lambrecht J. (2008) *The Concept of Ecological Debt: Its Meaning and Applicability in International Policy*. Academia Press, Gent.

People's World Conference on Climate Change and the Rights of Mother Earth [PWCCC] (2010) People's Agreement, (http://www.pwccc.wordpress.com/2010/04/24/peoples-agreement) accessed 29 February 2016.

Petermann A. (2009) What is Climate Justice? (http://globaljusticeecology.org/climate-justice/) accessed 1 September 2017.

Roberts J.T. and Bradley P. (2009) "Ecologically Unequal Exchange, Ecological Debt, and Climate Justice. The History and Implications of Three Related Ideas for a New Social Movement", *International Journal of Comparative Sociology*, 50 (3–4), 385–409.

Robleto M.L. and Marcelo W. (1992) *Deuda Ecológica*. Instituto de Ecologia Politica, Santiago de Chile.

Rice J. (2009) "North South Relations and the Ecological Debt: Asserting a Counter-Hegemonic Discourse", *Critical Sociology*, 35 (2), 225–252.

Russel B. (2012) *Interrogating the Post-Political: The Case of Radical Climate and Climate Justice Movements*, PhD Thesis Department of Geography, University of Leeds.

Schlosberg D. and Collins L. (2014) "From Environmental to Climate Justice: Climate Change and the Discourse of Environmental Justice", *Wires Clim Change*, 5, 359–374.

Shue H. (1992) "The Unavoidability of Justice", in Hurrel A. and Kingsbury B. eds. *The International Politics of the Environment: Actors, Interests, and Institutions*. Clarendon Press, Oxford.

Simms A., Meyer A. and Robins N. (1999) Who Owes Who? Climate Change, Debt, Equity and Survival, (http://www.ecologicaldebt.org/Who-owes-Who/Who-owes-who-Climate-change-dept-equity-and-survival.html) accessed 29 February 2016.

Srinivasan U.T., Carey S.P., Hallstein E., Higgins P., Kerr A., Koteen L., Smith A., Watson R., Harte J. and Norgaard R.B. (2008) "The Debt of Nations and the Distribution of Ecological Impacts from Human Activities", *PNAS*, 5, 1768–1773.

Stephenson W. (2014) "Ground Zero in the Fight for Climate Justice", *The Nation*, June, 23–30.

Tokar B. (2013) "Movements for Climate Justice in the US and Worldwide", in Dietz M. and Garrelts H. eds. *Routledge Handbook of the Climate Change Movement*. Routledge, London, 131–146.

Toulmin S. (2003) *Uses of Argument* (updated edition). Cambridge University Press, Cambridge.

Third World Network [TWN] (2009a) *Repay the Climate Debt. A Just and Effective Outcome for Copenhagen*. TWN, Penang.

TWN (2009b) Repay the Climate Debt. List of Endorsements, (http://www.twnside.org.sg/announcement/sign-on.letter_climate.dept.htm) accessed 29 February 2016.

UNFCCC (2010) *FCCC/AWGLCA/2010/MISC.2. Additional Views on Which the Chair May Draw in Preparing Text to Facilitate Negotiations Among Parties. Submissions from Parties*. UNFCCC, Bonn.

Warlenius R. (2016) "Linking Ecological Debt and Ecologically Unequal Exchange: Stocks, Flows, and Unequal Sink Appropriation", *Journal of Political Ecology*, 23, 364–380.

Warlenius R. (2017a) "Decolonizing the Atmosphere: The Climate Justice Movement's Arguments on Climate Debt", *Journal of Environment and Development*. Publ. online December 9, 2017. (https://doi.org/10.1177/1070496517744593).

Warlenius, R. (2017b) "Assessing Asymmetries: The Climate Debt of 154 Countries", in Warlenius R. *Asymmetries. Conceptualizing Environmental Inequalities as Ecological Debt and Ecologically Unequal Exchange*, PhD Thesis Human Ecology Division, Lund University.

Warlenius R., Pierce G. and Ramasar V. (2015) "Reversing the Arrow of Arrears: The Concept of 'Ecological Debt' and Its Value for Environmental Justice", *Global Environmental Change*, 30, 21–30.

Weiss, E.B. (1989) *In Fairness to Future Generations: International Law, Common Patrimony, and Intergenerational Equity*. United Nations University, Tokyo.

3 Natural capital, carbon trading and climate sanctions

Patrick Bond

Introduction

To date, large fossil fuel corporations and allied states have shaped global climate politics far more than Climate Justice (CJ) activists have, as witnessed at the annual United Nations Framework Convention on Climate Change (UNFCCC) negotiations and national policy-making. Aside from the obvious lack of political will with respect to the (inadequate) scale of emissions-reduction commitments at the 2015 Paris Climate Agreement, the landmark agreement provided at least three crucial provisions that serve the interests of Big Oil (including gas and coal):

1   the prohibition of signatories being sued for their '*climate debt*' liability;
2   the ongoing endorsement of *carbon markets* especially in the high-polluting emerging markets led by China, as a route for fossil fuel corporations' offsetting of their greenhouse gas emissions;
3   the difficulty of imposing *accountability* for violation of historic and current responsibility to cut emissions, e.g. through climate-related sanctions.

This chapter updates critiques of these three areas of *status quo* policy drawn from the CJ movement since the early 2000s and proposes remedies. However, in spite of hundreds of fragmented activist initiatives across the world that Naomi Klein (2014) labels 'Blockadia' (Temper and Bliss 2018) as well as divestment strategies targeting the major fossil fuel corporations (Lenferna 2018), there has been a distinct lack of coordinated CJ social mobilization (Jacobsen 2018). If carbon-intensive businesses and the states (and their UNFCCC delegates) that they influence are not systematically confronted by such a generalized CJ movement, there is simply no hope for resolving the climate crisis.

In moving forward to such a CJ movement, it will be necessary to identify sites of alliance building with what is termed Climate Action, i.e. the mainstream of climate activism (Bond 2018). Doing so will probably require what David Harvey (1996, 401) insists is a vital strategic and intellectual task: "to reclaim for itself a non-coopted and non-perverted version of the theses of ecological modernization … [and] to radicalize the ecological modernization discourse." The possibility of consolidating local CJ initiatives into national and then global-scale struggle lies ahead and will require CJ strategists to avoid the dangers of co-optation (including within the UNFCCC) and brute repression (e.g. as was becoming evident in the US during the Obama–Trump era). At some future stage, the potential for a much more sophisticated CJ attack on fossil fuels may emerge, including the integration of what appear, at surface level, as ecological modernization strategies such as 'natural capital accounting' (Bond 2014, 2018).

First, with Donald Trump's withdrawal from the Paris Climate Agreement, the opportunity to revisit climate debt – currently prohibited from discussion, although under the rubric of 'Loss and Damage' some minor discursive concessions have been permitted – will arise. One route is through the generational justice strategies invoked by youth, including two dozen children who sued Obama and now Trump. To measure damage done by climate change requires a degree of 'pricing' the ecological processes that are, of course, priceless. This has become a major point of debate among CJ strategists as international governance of 'green economy' processes continue. The chapter introduces these debates and argues that, in the interests of CJ radicalizing the ecological modernization discourse, 'natural capital' should be included in the national accounting schemes to go beyond the traditional measurements of economic development in GDP and other capital-based indicators. Including 'natural capital,' highlighting pollution costs, and measuring resource depletion would, for example, better prove that the 'underdevelopment' of African countries is far more severe than Gross Domestic Product (GDP) indicators suggest. One reason to make the case for natural capital depletion is that in courts of law, liability for ecological debt is being increasingly accepted. Nigeria's recent $11.5 billion claim against Shell for a 2011 oil spill includes more than $5 billion to compensate fisherfolk.

Second, there is a need to avoid recourse to emissions trading and other vehicles by which nature is put up for sale. There is indeed a danger that natural capital accounting will degenerate into promotion of payments of 'fees' for pollution: the damage continues, but with an ongoing payment. The strategy known as 'Payment for Ecosystem Services,' promoted by the more neoliberal of ecological modernizationists, represents this sort of parallel danger: commodifying the environment.

Third, the CJ movement has generally been focused on micro-politics, and only in late 2017 did Trump's withdrawal from Paris lead to some activists demanding that the US State Department vacate the UNFCCC negotiations (in Bonn, Germany) (Pan African Climate Justice Alliance 2017). There is an urgent need to go further, so as to impose the kind of accountability system that Paris signatories ignored, given that the Agreement – like all those since the 2009 Copenhagen Accord – is voluntary, not binding. CJ activists have been encouraged by Klein (2017), Stiglitz (2017) and others (Lenferna 2017) to impose a 'people's sanctions' strategy on Trump, on allied corporations (including Big Oil) and on the US economy where that might prove effective. Consider each in turn.

Natural capital accounting as an anti-extraction, climate debt measurement tool

GDP only counts extraction of non-renewable resources (such as hydrocarbons) as a positive 'credit' in the accounts, failing to recognize that a country's depleted wealth should also be considered a 'debit.' In making such a calculation, it is clear that not only has the revenue from such resources been drawn from the earth but also it has typically taken abroad by transnational corporations. In addition, historic wealth in the form of environmental assets has also been depleted, never to be recovered: the dinosaurs and ancient living matter that gave us fossil fuels won't come back.

The resulting economic argument is that by calculating natural resource depletion associated with extraction and comparing it to reinvestment made by the corporations which do the extraction, the overall impact is net negative for nearly all of Africa and many other sites across the world (World Bank 2014). Even though the World Bank has traditionally lined up in favour of extraction, including fossil fuels, several Bank staff in the office, called Wealth Accounting and the Valuation of Ecosystem Services (Waves) group, annually calculate 'adjusted net savings.' The implications – a net decline in wealth from extraction – should be of advantage to CJ advocates, in arguing against the extractivist mode of economic activity.

Specifically, the World Bank's (2014, 10) *Little Green Data Book* concedes that "88% of Sub-Saharan African countries were found to be depleting their wealth in 2010," with a 12 percent decline in per capita net African wealth that year attributed to the extraction of minerals, energy and forest products (natural capital). With that degree of underdevelopment obvious even to an agency committed to further extraction, it is long overdue for CJ and other anti-extraction activists to add an economic logic of this sort to the existing micro-ecological, spiritual, political and social critiques. In turn, this kind of measurement of the resource curse Africa suffers can assist in one of the de-cursing processes desperately needed: ecological debt advocacy. There is an urgent need to punish polluters by considering the formal monetary liabilities – or some approximation, since nature is priceless – so that reparations to the environment and affected peoples are sufficiently financed, and so in the process an incentive is generated not to pollute in future. This is the central reason to make at least a rough monetary case for ecological debt payments within courts of law.

For example, of Nigeria's $11.5 billion claim against Shell for a 2011 oil spill, more than half is meant to compensate fisherfolk. The liability owed to silicosis-afflicted mineworker victims of Anglo American and other gold mining houses has begun to reach payment stage. The South African firms Gencor and Cape PLC had to pay $65 million in 2007 to settle asbestos lawsuits after they lost their last appeal in the UK House of Lords. Similar arguments should be made against the Multinational Corporations (MNC) most responsible for what the UN calls 'Loss and Damage' due to climate change. Ideally, over time, this strategy would develop as 'fine-and-ban,' so that as a corporation makes an egregious error, it is fined punitively for the damage done, and then nationalized and sent packing.

To be sure, there is a danger that if 'fine-and-ban' is not the local state policy, then natural capital accounting will lead instead to a 'fee' for pollution, with the damage continuing alongside ongoing payment. That would logically result from establishment of a formal market in pollution rights, such as the EU's Emissions Trading Scheme. Serious environmental activists, beginning with the Durban Group for Climate Justice in 2004, have firmly rejected these strategies to 'privatize the air.' The distinction should thus be clear, between valuing nature for ecological debt payment purposes (a fine-and-ban) on the one hand, and on the other pricing nature for market-making (a fee). As Vandava Shiva put it in a 2014 interview in South Africa, 'We should use natural capital as a red light to destruction, not as a green light' (Bond 2014).

The 'red light' strategy is an example of a potential rapprochement between two different framing strategies, emphasizing technicist analysis in the ecological modernization tradition as well as being useful to anti-extractivist campaigners who need further economic arguments against fossil fuel depletion. The simple standpoint, which has been explored in the Niger Delta and Ecuador's Yasuní National Park as amongst the world's cutting-edge struggle sites, is that oil should be left underground, *but the ecological debt that Northerners owe the Global South should be paid,* in a way that strengthens local societies, not comprador elites.

However, at the time of writing, UNFCCC negotiators had done very little to advance the climate debt concept, not since Ethiopian leader Meles Zenawi raised the demand erratically in 2009 during preparations for the Copenhagen summit (McClure 2009). Grassroots articulations of climate debt have long come from African CJ advocates, e.g. Nigerian activist Nnimmo Bassey (2011) and the general secretary of the PanAfrican Climate Justice Alliance, Mithika Mwenda. The activists demanded that Zenawi – Africa's main official voice in Copenhagen – maintain his initially strong stance on climate debt. Although Zenawi and the African Union did initially make a $67 billion annual demand for compensation, he came under severe pressure. First, French President Nicolas Sarkozy persuaded Zenawi to halve the figure just before Copenhagen, and then the US State Department (according to cables leaked by Chelsea Manning) compelled him to instead sign the Copenhagen Accord in exchange for Washington's increased financial and military support to his dictatorial regime (Bond 2012, 2017a).

In succumbing to Northern pressure, Zenawi was "undermining the bold positions of our negotiators and ministers represented here, and threatening the very future of Africa," according to Mwenda. "Meles wants to sell out the lives and hopes of Africans for a pittance. Every other African country has committed to policy based on the science" (Reddy 2009, 1). Mwenda suggested instead that the African delegation could have repeated the continent's walk-out from World Trade Organization summits in both Seattle in 1999 and Cancun in 2003, when their denial of consent caused both summits to collapse (Bond 2006). This was not unthinkable, for on September 3, 2009, Zenawi had issued a strong threat about the upcoming Copenhagen summit: "If need be we are prepared to walk out of any negotiations that threaten to be another rape of our continent" (Ashine 2009).

And in a UNFCCC meeting the month before in Barcelona, the African delegation followed through with that threat.

Doubts about staying in the UNFCCC in spite of Copenhagen's shift away from Kyoto's binding commitments were repeated broken promises of North–South climate financing. In Copenhagen, such financing was meant to have risen to a sustained figure of $100 billion annually, paid through the Green Climate Fund (Bracking 2015). But according to former senior UN officials Anis Chowdhury and Jomo Kwame Sundaram (2017),

> As of July 2017, only $10.1 billion has come from 43 governments, including 9 developing countries, mostly for start-up costs. Before Trump was elected, the US had contributed $1 billion. Now that the US has announced its withdrawal from the 2015 climate treaty, the remaining $2 billion will not be forthcoming. Moreover, the $100 billion goal is vague. For example, disputes continue over whether it refers to public funds, or whether leveraged private finance will also count. The OECD projected in 2016 that pledges worldwide would add up to $67 billion yearly by 2020. But such estimates have been inflated by counting commercial loans to buy green technology from developed countries.

In 2009, with African countries and other poor allies in the G77 relatively weak (in spite of a very strong G77 chief negotiator, Lumumba Di-Aping), the stage was set for the Global North to provide the clearest answer in multilateral climate policy to the question of who would be liable for compensating victims: blunt denial. US State Department climate negotiator Todd Stern insisted: "the sense of guilt or culpability or reparations, I just categorically reject that" (Broder 2009). Stern maintained this stance over the subsequent years and was successful in forcing it into the 2015 Paris Climate Agreement, which refused to countenance standard 'polluter pays' principles.

"The red line that US, EU and other developed countries in the Umbrella group, such as Norway have drawn for the developing countries," according to Nithin Sethi (2015), was insisting "Loss and Damage would find way its way into the core Paris Agreement only if they agree to explicitly saying that compensation and liability issues would never be raised in future." Just before the 2012 Warsaw UNFCCC summit, Sethi recalled, "A leaked US document at that time showed how it had briefed all its embassies across the world to oppose such an idea from the outset." In Warsaw, Stern warned in relation to the emerging liability narrative, "I will block this. I will shut this down." Although watered-down Loss and Damage language survived in the 2012 UNFCCC declaration's final text, Stern's ruthless defence of US interests ensured it was tokenistic.

Although any such prohibition on seeking climate debt compensation was not contained in the November 2015 draft, the final Paris Climate Agreement a month later has a clause (52, Article 8) specifying that the deal does "not involve or provide a basis for any liability or compensation." The phrasing is considered by the Global North's lawyers to be sufficient protection against climate debt claims.

As the Pan African Climate Justice Alliance (2015, 45) concluded, "Northern countries have exempted themselves from paying for the effects of climate change to future generations." A similar form of liability is also contested by Northern corporations: climate-related financial loss due to the vast reserves of 'unburnable carbon' claimed by fossil fuel corporations, even though if we are to survive, such assets should be entirely devalued, according to Carbon Tracker, a City of London watchdog.

Who are the climate debtors? The main countries emitting greenhouse gases today are China (around 10 Gigatons [Gt] of CO_2 equivalents in 2013), the US (5Gt), Europe (3Gt) and India (2Gt), together responsible for 58 percent of world emissions. Taken in absolute terms and using the year 2000 as a (random) starting point, by 2017 six countries owed at least 3 percent of the world total each: the US (33.4), China (18.1), Japan (4.8), Russia (4.0), South Korea (3.8), Saudi Arabia (3.4) and Canada (3.3). China and India emit in per capita terms at a far lower level than the Northern countries, and their leaders maintain the necessity of an upward trajectory of emissions at least through the 2020s, in order to 'develop.'

Yet recent US and European claims to be reversing their emissions rise, rely upon their corporations and consumers *outsourcing* large amounts of emissions to new production sites mostly in East Asia. According to the Intergovernmental Panel on Climate Change: "A growing share of CO_2 emissions from fossil fuel combustion in developing countries is released in the production of goods and services exported, notably from upper-middle-income countries to high-income countries" (Hawkins 2014). The amounts of such net outsourcing to China are vast, having risen from 404 million tons of CO_2 in 2000 to 1.561 billion tons in 2012.

Regardless of outsourcing, the richer countries have – by all accounts – failed to cut emissions (or plan to do so) to the extent required. By late 2015, the (voluntary) Intended Nationally Determined Contribution (INDC) statement of the G20 countries confirmed huge shortfalls in emissions cuts. According to the NGO Climate Action Tracker (2015), "None of the G20 INDCs are in line with holding warming below 2°C, or 1.5°C." The agency rated the following as 'inadequate': Argentina, Australia, Canada, Indonesia, Japan, South Korea, Russia, Saudi Arabia, South Africa and Turkey, with the INDCs of another set – Brazil, China, India, the EU, Mexico and the US – also "not consistent with limiting warming to below 2°C either, unless other countries make much deeper reductions and comparably greater effort." In other words, the Global North (including the elites of the poorer G20 countries such as South Africa) are digging themselves further into climate debt.

As Rikard Warlenius (2017) confirms, "Current climate agreements do not reflect considerations of justice or historical responsibility. Developed countries have emitted disproportionate amounts of carbon dioxide and the resulting climate change disproportionately affects poor countries." The rejection of the historical link is mainly due to the negotiating stance of Todd Stern at the 2009 Copenhagen and 2011 Durban UNFCCC summits (Bond 2012, 2016). In Paris, negotiators essentially cancelled the climate debt, in spite of Pope Francis' (2015) *Laudato Si* appeal that "developed countries ought to help pay this debt by significantly limiting their consumption of non-renewable energy and by assisting poorer countries to support policies and programmes of sustainable development."

The concept of climate debt first emerged in 1992 at the Earth Summit of the United Nations in Rio de Janeiro, in an NGO 'Alternative Treaty'. The Institute of Political Ecology in Santiago, Chile then made the case in relation to the ozone hole, followed by Colombian lawyer José María Borrero with a 1994 book on the topic. Research and advocacy were provided by the Foundation for Research on the Protection of the Environment, and then Jubilee South at its founding Johannesburg conference in 1999. That year, Friends of the Earth International and Christian Aid agreed to campaign against ecological debt default by the Global North, especially in relation to climate damage. In 2000, the concept was defined by the Quito group *Acción Ecológica* (2000, 1): "ecological debt is the debt accumulated by Northern, industrial countries toward Third World countries on account of resource plundering, environmental damages, and the free occupation of environmental space to deposit wastes, such as greenhouse gases, from the industrial countries."

Three years later, Barcelona ecological economist Joan Martinez-Alier (2003, 26) calculated ecological debt in many forms: "nutrients in exports including virtual water, the oil and minerals no longer available, the biodiversity destroyed, sulphur dioxide emitted by copper smelters, the mine tailings, the harms to health from flower exports, the pollution of water by mining, the commercial use of information and knowledge on genetic resources, when they have been appropriated gratis ('biopiracy'), and agricultural genetic resources." As for the sums of money involved, "although it is not possible to make an exact accounting, it is necessary to establish the principal categories and certain orders of magnitude in order to stimulate discussion ... If we take the present human-made emissions of carbon, [this represents] a total annual subsidy of $75 billion is forthcoming from South to North" (Martinez-Alier 2003, 28). In 2008, a partial ecological debt accounting was published by environmental scientists: $1.8 trillion in concrete damages over several decades (Srinivasan et al. 2008). Co-author Richard Norgaard, ecological economist at the University of California, Berkeley, generated a crucial finding: "At least to some extent, the rich nations have developed at the expense of the poor, and, in effect, there is a debt to the poor" (*The Guardian* 2008). The study included factors such as greenhouse gas emissions, ozone layer depletion, agriculture, deforestation, over-fishing, and the conversion of mangrove swamps into shrimp farms.

In 2009, Bolivia's UN Ambassador Pablo Solon tabled a statement for the UNFCCC:

> The climate debt of developed countries must be repaid, and this payment must begin with the outcomes to be agreed in Copenhagen. Developing countries are not seeking economic handouts to solve a problem we did not cause. What we call for is full payment of the debt owed to us by developed countries for threatening the integrity of the Earth's climate system,

for over-consuming a shared resource that belongs fairly and equally to all people, and for maintaining lifestyles that continue to threaten the lives and livelihoods of the poor majority of the planet's population ... Any solution that does not ensure an equitable distribution of the Earth's limited capacity to absorb greenhouse gases, as well as the costs of mitigating and adapting to climate change, is destined to fail.

(Republic of Bolivia 2009)

The kinds of natural capital accounting and climate Loss and Damage measurements described above are vital tools for those CJ activists aiming to radicalize ecological modernization discourse, in the interests of both compensation and disincentives against further emissions. However, aside from attempting to prohibit climate debt within the Paris Agreement, another way in which Big Oil, Global North states and allied negotiators attempted to avoid responsibility for greenhouse gas emissions is the displacement technique known as carbon trading (or, in the US, 'cap and trade').

Carbon trading as a 'false solution'

The most revealing case of an ecological modernization strategy – impossible to radicalize, but instead deserving of CJ *rejection* – is carbon trading. The most notorious advocacy on behalf of pollution trading was by World Bank chief economist Lawrence Summers in 1991, in the form of a memo to his closest Bank colleagues suggesting, in effect, that nature be privatized, to better assess costs and benefits of Bank ecological intervention. As Summers (1991) put it, "I think the economic logic behind dumping a load of toxic waste in the lowest wage country is impeccable and we should face up to that ... Africa is vastly *under*polluted."

The overall point of carbon markets is that society can 'price pollution,' simultaneously cut costs associated with mitigating greenhouse gases and fund innovative carbon-cutting projects which are, in effect, 'offsets' introduced to speed transitions to post-carbon energy, transport and other activities. After a cap is placed by the state upon total emissions, the carbon-trading strategy is that high-polluting corporations and governments can buy ever more costly carbon permits from those polluters who don't need so many, or from those willing to part with the permits for a higher price than the profits they make in high-pollution production, energy-generation, agriculture, consumption, disposal or transport.

Misgivings first arose about an earlier version of carbon trading, in the form of lowering US sulphur dioxide emissions in Southern California. This strategy was, ultimately, slower and less effective than command-and-control strategies adopted in Germany's Ruhr Valley during the early 1990s. Nevertheless, large environmental INGOs endorsed the idea when it was presented as a deal-breaking demand by US Vice President Al Gore at the COP 3 in Kyoto. Gore promised that Washington would sign the Kyoto Protocol if it included carbon markets as an escape hatch for companies that polluted too much and then desired the right to purchase other companies' pollution permits. The US Senate had already voted 95–0 against endorsing Kyoto. Even though Gore won this critical concession, there was no change in attitude on Capitol Hill, so the US never ratified the Kyoto Protocol.

In any event, these markets fell into just as much chaos as any financial casino, at a time that faith in bankers – especially faith they can fairly manage climate-related funding – was badly shaken after the 2008 meltdown. In the US, the national Chicago voluntary carbon market (strongly promoted by Gore) died in late 2010, and regional markets crashed. The European Union Emissions Trading Scheme (EU ETS) is the main site of carbon trading and has been moribund since its 2006 and 2008 peaks, when the right to emit extra carbon cost around €30/ton. The carbon price's recent low point was less than €3/ton, in the wake of oversupply, various episodes of fraud and hacking and declining interest in climate change following the 2008–09 Great Recession.

By 2017, prices remained low and the World Bank (2017) calculated the 2016 global carbon trade at just $32 billion. Of the 15 percent of world CO_2 equivalent emissions that are covered by either carbon trading or a tax, only a quarter of those carry a price above $10/ton. The Canadian, Californian, Japanese and New Zealand carbon trading systems are rare exceptions, with prices in the $11–14/ton range. (The countries with a carbon price above $25/ton have achieved this by taxation, not carbon trading: Sweden $126; Switzerland and Liechtenstein $84; Finland $66; Norway $52; France $33; and Denmark $25.)

For poorer countries, a category of UN-authorized Clean Development Mechanism (CDM) projects was created to allow wealthier countries to engage in emissions reductions initiatives in poor and middle-income countries, as a way of eliding direct emissions reductions. But reflecting the global oversupply of carbon credits, the price of CDM credits fell to less than $0.50, and in order to lower supply, after 2012 the main emerging markets (especially China, India and Brazil) were no longer allowed to issue them. China then started eight pilot carbon-trading projects at local and provincial levels, with highly volatile prices ranging in 2017 from $8/ton in Beijing down to just $0.50/ton in Chongqing. Reflecting the extreme volatility in Chinese financial markets (including stock market crashes in mid-2015 and early 2016), the Shenzhen carbon market had fallen from a Chinese high of $11/ton in early 2013 to just $5/ton by mid-2016. These prices are woefully short of making a dent in climate change, according to Joseph Stiglitz and Nicolas Stern's (2017) report to the Carbon Pricing Leadership Coalition: "at least US$40–80/ton of CO_2 by 2020 and US$50–100/ tCO_2 by 2030" are needed so as to lower the rate of emissions to keep below the two degree temperature increase targeted at Paris.

Without an ever-lowering cap on emissions, the incentive to increase prices and raise trading volumes does not exist. The overall context remains one of economic stagnation, financial volatility and shrinking demand for emissions reduction credits. The world faces increasing sources of carbon credit supply in an already glutted market, thanks to the COP negotiators' failure to mandate binding emissions cuts. But another factor remains the lax system the UN, EU and other regulatory bodies appear to have adopted. All manner of inappropriate projects appear to be gaining approval, especially in Africa (Bond 2012). As California's carbon market was renewed in 2017, a new round of complaints arose from activists about the scheme's implicit environmental racism (insofar as polluting industries in neighbourhoods of colour continue emissions because of their purchase of carbon credits).

The carbon market's failures have renewed concern about the 'privatization of the air' amongst CJ activists, given that there appears to be no way to 'radicalize the ecological modernization discourse' in this instance. Even attempting to redirect funding from emissions trading schemes has proven controversial, but there are a few CJ groups that continue to try, in both policy and practice, e.g. Green for All (in California), the Pan African Climate Justice Alliance, and some indigenous people who adopted Free, Prior and Informed Consent strategies within forestry carbon offset schemes. But opposition to 'market solutions to market problems' within climate policy has been firmly articulated by the Durban Group for Climate Justice (Lohmann 2006) and in the film by Annie Leonard (2009), *Story of Cap & Trade.* In contrast, in the Climate Action branch of advocacy, which is grounded in ecological modernization groups like WWF and Greenpeace International endorse such markets (Bryant 2016, 12–13).

Climate sanctions as popular accountability strategy during global governance failure

The Trump administration removed the US from the 2015 Paris Climate Agreement in June 2017 on the grounds that compliance will be too expensive for the world's largest economy (Trump 2017). In reality, starting with the Copenhagen Accord of 2009, Obama's State Department ensured that UNFCCC negotiations were (unlike the Kyoto Protocol) voluntary and non-binding. The Paris Climate Accord avoided accountability mechanisms, as even its chief negotiator Stern (Stiglitz and Stern 2017) bragged. Yet, in spite of Obama pledging only $3 billion (in contrast to several trillion dollars his administration spent on bailing out banks), Trump (2017) expressed misplaced concern about the Green Climate Fund "costing the United States a vast fortune," and that "massive liabilities" would result from damage done by US historic emissions.

Global-scale climate regulation had, by 2016, become generally acceptable to the US population, even if many in support also voted for Trump. In November 2016, the Yale University Program on Climate Change Communication (2016) poll of registered voters found that 78 percent supported taxing or regulating emissions, and 69 percent agreed this should happen in an international agreement. In 2009, even Trump publicly supported the Copenhagen Accord, although by 2012 he argued (on Twitter) that "The concept of global warming was created by and for the Chinese in order to make the U.S. manufacturing non-competitive" (Trump 2012). His first 100-day plan stressed resurgent climate denialism as the default policy position; infrastructure construction focusing on fossil-fuel pipelines, airports, roads and bridges; cancellation of international obligations including withdrawal from Paris and default on payment obligations to the Green Climate Fund;

retraction of shale gas restrictions; enabling the Dakota Access Pipeline and Keystone pipeline; denuding of the Environmental Protection Agency (EPA); and a (futile) attempt to 'save the coal industry.' Further privatization of public land was also imminent, including Native reservations, in search of more fossil fuels.

The retreat from Paris opens up a new opportunity for a revived strategy and tactic: *delegitimation of Trump, and sanctions against his regime and supportive US corporations more generally* (Bond 2017b). Formidable alliances could be ignited internationally with much more positive implications for climate futures than otherwise exist. Such 'social self-defence' alliances (Brecher 2017) would ideally have been forged on the day of Trump's election in November 2016. But after Trump walked out of Paris and indeed a year into his presidency, these alliances remained only *potential* political approaches, because even the most sophisticated, militant US climate activists simply did not adopt *any* strategy, aside from condemnation and defence of existing space (Funes 2017). There was no open discussion in the climate movements about how to change the balance of forces, aside from continuing to promote localized blockades against fossil fuel facilities, to defend (profoundly inadequate) state regulations and improve their enforcement, mostly via the courts, and to divest from the main fossil fuel companies and climate-destructive banks while encouraging reinvestment in clean energy.

Each of these was a necessary strategy – but a much more decisive shift in the balance of forces will be necessary to secure a climate future that transcends just survival and moves society to the potentials Klein (2014) discussed in *This Changes Everything*. Such post-capitalist visions include renewable community-owned energy, massive investments in public transport, the burgeoning of organic agriculture, compact eco-cities, a widely shared green production ethos, humane consumption (so indispensable for the survival of the Global South), and 'zero-waste' disposal so that oceans, rivers, and land may recover from the 'Capitalocene' (Moore 2013).

The failure to take advantage of Trump's regime to ratchet up pressure reflects the US Left's general weakness. In spite of the political fragility, personal foibles, administrative chaos, leadership buffoonery and shrinking legitimacy, Trump's first months in office failed to generate a sustained, unified response from the society's progressive forces. Most critiques by the local US and world Left came from specific incidents or from sectorally narrow interests. Protest marches on Washington regularly drew tens or even hundreds of thousands of women, tax justice advocates, scientists, and climate activists from January through April 2017, as well as impromptu immigrant protection rallies at airports. But these generally occurred without linkage or fusion, and without a convincing strategy for changing power relations. The most effective resistance to Trump came from either late-night comedians or competing elites.

However, there are important examples of powerful resistance, in part grounded in climate change advocacy. The main activist groups that attacked the Dakota Access Pipeline owner Energy Transfer Partners and its creditors – including Greenpeace, 350.org, BankTrack and Sierra Club – did "billions of dollars in damage" as a result of "campaigns of misinformation," according to the firm's lawsuit in August 2017 (Horn 2017). As a target of anti-corporate activism, according to 350.org's May Boeve and Brett Fleishman (2017), "Exxon is the most famous example because the company's own scientists actively studied the threat of climate change, and in response the company developed taller offshore drilling rigs in anticipation of rising sea levels. Yet while they were preparing for a warmer climate, they also funded campaigns claiming that the science was uncertain." Exxon and other fossil fuel corporations were divestment victims of $5 trillion in withdrawn stock market financing, thanks to thousands of activists in universities, pension funds, churches and other institutions (Carrington 2016).

Boeve and Fleishman (2017) recall that City of London investment analysts' Carbon Tracker had in 2012, "juxtaposed the amount of carbon the world could burn within 'safe' limits of global warming and the amount of carbon embedded in the reserves of the publicly traded fossil fuel companies – the coal, oil and gas planned for future production. It provided incontrovertible evidence that the companies intended to burn all this carbon, and against the backdrop of increased caps on doing so, thereby creating a high likelihood for a massive stock devaluation: a 'carbon bubble.' This attracted the attention of more mainstream investors, who began to rank the carbon bubble as a material risk."

How far might this divestment movement reach into Trump's own wallet, and how far can his regime be delegitimated by a wider sanctions movement? Aside from repeated 2017 polls showing Trump with less than 35 percent support within the US, Pew Research (2017) pollsters reported in mid-2017 that much of the world is strongly anti-Trump. Most opposed are Mexico, Spain, Jordan, Sweden, Germany, Turkey, Chile, Argentina, Brazil, France, Colombia and Lebanon, all recording their citizenries' support for Trump at less than 15 percent. (Only the Philippines, Vietnam, Nigeria and Tanzania record more than 50 percent, although the two most populous countries, India and China, were not polled.) Imposing sanctions on rogue regimes is a time-tested approach that has often succeeded in the past, especially in the event that Trump initiates yet another unjust US war. In this case a 'people's sanctions' strategy should put not only the President's and First Daughter's own product lines under pressure, but also tackle Trump-friendly big businesses such as ExxonMobil, Koch Industries and Goldman Sachs.

One immediate reaction to Trump's rise was a call for boycott and sanctions against his own firm and associates: Color of Change (2016) pulled Coca-Cola out of the 2016 Republican Convention sponsorship; Grab Your Wallet compelled Nieman Marcus, Belk and Nordstroms to discontinue Ivanka Trump clothing sales; Sleeping Giants forced hundreds of advertisers who supported pro-Trump alt-right websites to withdraw their financing; and Boycott Trump has a long list of targets. Encouraged by the successes, a Boycott45 (2017) campaign expanded the sanctions strategies to Trump and Kushner's tenant companies, on grounds that their $100 million in annual rental payments "enable and normalize Trump and Kushner's hateful and intolerant views and agenda, participate in Trump and Kushner's unprecedented lack of transparency to use the office of the President to enrich themselves, and strengthen Trump's political brand." High-profile Trump buildings are located not only across the US, but also in Istanbul, Seoul,

Rio de Janeiro, Toronto and Vancouver, Panama and Uruguay, Manila, Mumbai and Pune.

Boycott Divestment Sanctions' (BDS) movements have recently been effective against Israeli apartheid and during 1985–94 and can be credited with splitting white business from the South African apartheid regime, in conjunction with very strong local protest. BDS against the US could succeed *if US progressives are motivated to call for a world boycott of the US government plus key Trump-related corporations.* Implementing a BDS-Trump strategy will be an important challenge for climate activists the world over, argues Klein (2016, 2017). She was soon joined by European Environmental Bureau leader Jeremy Wates (2017): "Trump is known to like walls. Maybe a wall of carbon tariffs around the U.S. is a solution he will understand."

Indeed 25 major US corporations (including Apple, Facebook, Google, Morgan Stanley, Microsoft, Unilever and Gap) warned Trump in an open letter that "withdrawing from the agreement … could expose us to retaliatory measures" (Petroff 2017). Suddenly sanctions were discussed as a powerful, useful threat in diverse media sites like *Forbes* (Kotlikoff, 2017), *Financial Times* (Wolf 2017), *DailyKos* (Lenferna 2017), *The Guardian* (Stiglitz 2017) and *The Independent* (Johnston 2017). The credibility of sanctions was enhanced by Nobel Economics Prize Laureate Joseph Stiglitz (2006), who in a 2006 paper argued that, "unless the US goes along with the rest of the world, unless producers in America face the full cost of their emissions, Europe, Japan and all the countries of the world should impose trade sanctions against the US." In May 2017, Stiglitz co-chaired a UN-mandated commission based at the World Bank that advocated widespread, urgent adoption of carbon taxes.

Even former French President Nicolas Sarkozy had in November 2016 raised the prospect of punishment against US products as a result of Trump's climate-destructive campaign promises: "I will demand that Europe put in place a carbon tax at its border, a tax of 1–3 percent, for all products coming from the US, if the US doesn't apply environmental rules that we are imposing on our companies" (Kentish 2016). A technical policy term for such sanctions emerged: 'border adjustment taxes' or for short, border measures, which avoid World Trade Organization anti-protectionist penalties (such taxes are not a 'disguised trade restriction').

Ironically, when in 2009 Obama promoted carbon trading strategies within his ultimately unsuccessful pro-market legislative strategy, further incentives were discussed so that big corporations would agree to emissions caps. Establishment economists like the Peterson Institute's Gary Hufbauer and Jisun Kim (2009) observed that in such a context, US companies 'paying to pollute' would need additional protection from outside competitors: "border measures seem all but certain for political reasons …. many U.S. climate bills introduced in the Congress have included border measures [against] imports from countries that do not have comparable climate policies."

For CJ and allied movements to ramp up the existing initiatives will require a major unifying effort by US progressive groups, and a realization that international solidarity will be a critical force in shifting the power balance. In South Africa, Ronnie Kasrils (2015) – a leader of the underground movement and from 2004–08 the Minister of Intelligence – agrees: "BDS made apartheid's beneficiaries feel the pinch in their pocket and their polecat status whether in the diplomatic arena, on the sporting fields, at academic or business conventions, in the world of theatre and the arts, in the area of commerce and trade and so on. Arms sanctions weakened the efficiency of the SA Defence Force; disinvestment by trade unions and churches affected the economy as did the termination of banking ties by the likes of Chase Manhattan and Barclays banks; boycott of products from fruit to wine saw a downturn in trade; the disruption of sports events was a huge psychological blow; dockworkers refusing to handle ship's cargoes disrupted trade links." The strategy drove a wedge between white ('English-speaking') Johannesburg capitalists and the racist ('Afrikaner') Pretoria regime. As internal protest surged, it was the 1985 foreign debt crisis caused in part by BDS that broke the capital-state alliance and compelled South Africa's nine-year transition to democracy.

With Trump*ism* such a logical target, international solidarity to weaken that power requires a boycott of both high-profile state functionaries and key corporations in order to attack the legitimacy of profits made within a climate-denialist USA. As Public Citizen's Rob Weissman (2017) warned, the US faces "a government literally of the Exxons, by the Goldman Sachses and for the Kochs." In contrast, installing the eco-socialist governments required in the US and everywhere to generate a climate future that not only keeps the temperature within the scientifically necessary maximum and does so with *justice* at its very core will require a dramatic shift in the balance of forces. Such principles must be undergirded by further analysis of how to weaken the power structure, by the widening of delegitimation strategies beyond just Trump to major corporations, by the toughening of sanctions tactics and by the forging of international alliances urgently required to repeat the South African BDS success.

Conclusion: Reducing fossil fuel influence over climate politics

How might CJ activists most forcefully resist Big Oil and other carbon-intensive corporations, along with their purchased politicians? Indeed, Todd Stern was simply responding, as he continually reminded audiences, to the US Republican Party's veto capacity over any such climate treaty if presented to the Congress, hence driving down ambitions of a comprehensive binding treaty to a mere voluntary agreement. That veto capacity, in turn, was a function of the exceptional power of the fossil fuel lobby to purchase the service of politicians, who initially denied the existence of climate change and then when that was untenable, denied the role of greenhouse gas emissions in causing it. The primary actors included ExxonMobil, whose scientists knew about catastrophic climate change threats in the late 1970s but covered up the information and funded denialist propaganda, and two oil tycoon brothers, the Kochs, who built a far-right anti-environmental lobby including the American Legislative Exchange Council (amongst whose 40 members are the carbon-intensive US Steel, General Electric, General Motors,

3M and Phillips Petroleum). The Council's role under Trump is to remove worker, social and environmental legal protection.

Likewise, ExxonMobil – the world's fourth largest firm – rose in power in January 2017 when Trump appointed its chief executive Rex Tillerson as US Secretary of State (who in December 2017 was rumoured to be on the brink of being fired by Trump). A contract for a massive $500 billion Siberian oil drill in 2013 had earned Tillerson the Russian 'Order of Friendship,' although a year later, the deal was postponed due to sanctions that followed Moscow's Crimean invasion. The fluidity of anti- and pro-Russian forces within the White House and Congress makes it difficult to predict whether those sanctions will eventually be dropped, but regardless, the Trump White House has a vast network of corporate backers starting with Goldman Sachs bank, whose several former executives in the White House include Treasury Secretary Steve Mnuchin and economic policy head Gary Cohn. (These conditions make ExxonMobil and Goldman Sachs ideal world sanctions targets.)

Extreme corporate power can also be found in other capitals. To illustrate, another instance of malevolent global climate governance occurred at Copenhagen when Obama met privately with the leaders of Brazil, South Africa, India and China ('BASIC'), in the process jettisoning the broader UN summit process so as to privately co-sign the Copenhagen Accord (Bond 2012). An unintentional metaphor was uttered by the then head of the US Senate Foreign Relations Committee, John Kerry (2009): "It's a powerful signal to see President Obama, Premier Wen, Prime Minister Singh and President Zuma agree on a meeting of the minds. These are the four horsemen (*sic*) of a climate change solution."

The BASIC countries, which along with Russia are together better known as the BRICS, are among the world's most carbon-addicted economies. From these states, large fossil fuel firms have arisen – e.g. respectively, in the BRICS, Brazil's Petrobras; Russian oil and gas corporations Gazprom and Lukoil; Coal of India, Vedanta and ArcelorMittal; China National Petroleum and Sinopec; and South Africa's new black-owned firms Oakbay (run by the notorious Gupta family) and Shanduka (founded by South Africa's president starting in 2018, Cyril Ramaphosa), as well as the much larger Anglo American, BHP Billiton, Exxaro and formerly state-owned coal-to-oil firm Sasol (all formerly initiated at the Johannesburg Stock Exchange and subsequently relisted in other stock markets).

BRICS fossil fuel companies have enjoyed outsized influence over public policy, often at the cost of major corruption scandals. The impeachment of Brazilian President Dilma Rousseff in 2016 was due to Petrobras payoffs that motivated corrupt members of Congress to put in her place a more pliable leader, Michel Temer. Vladimir Putin had, after 2003, switched policies from opposing fossil fuel and other corporate oligarchs, to embracing them. Narendra Modi's crony capitalists have long been notorious allies (Roy 2012), and China's state-capitalist relationships have hinged on unlimited fossil fuel consumption (Smith 2017).

Together, these are the kinds of vectors that require of CJ strategists a much more nuanced and unified strategy, than has existed in past Blockadia protests and UNFCCC engagements. The climate debt owed by Big Oil, the tendency by corporations and banks to promote carbon trading instead, and the potentials for sanctions against climate change criminals – especially those associated with Donald Trump – are, in combination, a formidable set of targets. But it is in the sphere of such economic forces that CJ activists must operate, ultimately, for here we can find the most intense combinations of both power and vulnerabilities. It is up to CJ to move Big Oil from the former to the latter, so as to finally exert pressures in their own states and the UNFCC to solve climate chaos in a *just* and *effective* way.

References

Acción Ecológica (2000) "Trade, climate change and the ecological debt," Unpublished paper, Quito.

Ashine, A. (2009) "Africa threatens withdrawal from climate talks," *The Nation*, 3, September.

Bassey, N. (2011) *To Cook a Continent*. Pambazuka Press, Oxford.

Boeve, M. and B. Fleishman (2017) "Case study: The fossil fuel divestment campaign," in *State of Civil Society Report 2017*, Civicus, Johannesburg, www.civicus.org/index.php/state-of-civil-society-report-2017/essays (31 January 2018).

Bond, P. (2006) *Talk Left Walk Right*. University of KwaZulu-Natal Press, Pietermaritzburg.

Bond, P. (2012) *Politics of Climate Justice: Paralysis Above, Movement Below*. University of KwaZulu-Natal Press, Pietermaritzburg.

Bond, P. (2014) "Can natural capital accounting come of age in Africa?" *TripleCrisis*, 9 July, http://triplecrisis.com/can-natural-capital-accounting-come-of-age-in-africa-part-2/ (31 January 2018).

Bond, P. (2016) "Who wins from 'Climate Apartheid'? African climate justice narratives about the Paris COP21," *New Politics*, 60, 122–129.

Bond, P. (2017a) "Climate debt, community resistance and conservation alliances against KwaZulu-Natal coal mining at Africa's oldest nature reserve," in Engels, B. and Dietz, K. (eds) *Political and Social Impacts of Climate Change in Africa*, Peter Lang Verlag, Berlin.

Bond, P. (2017b) "Shifting the balance of forces through sanctions against Trump and US carbon capital," in Foran, J., Munshi, D., Bhavnani, K. and Kurian, K. (eds) *Climate Futures: Re-imagining Global Climate Justice*, University of California Press, Berkeley.

Bond, P. (2018) "Social movements for climate justice, from International NGOs to local communities," in Lele, S., Brondizio, E., Byrne, J., Mace, G. and Martinez-Alier, J. (eds) *Rethinking Environmentalism: Linking Justice, Sustainability, and Diversity*, Massachusetts Institute of Technology Press, Cambridge.

Boycott45 (2017) "Make Trump bankrupt again," https://www.boycott45.org/ (31 January 2018).

Bracking, S. (2015) "The anti-politics of climate finance: The creation and performativity of the Green Climate Fund," *Antipode*, 47 (2), 281–302.

Brecher, J. (2017) "Social self-defense: Protecting people and planet against Trump and Trumpism," Labor4Sustainability, January, www.labor4sustainability.org/uncategorized/social-self-defense-protecting-people-and-planet-against-trump-and-trumpism/ (31 January 2018).

Broder, D. (2009) "U.S. climate envoy's good cop, bad cop roles," *New York Times*, 11 December, www.nytimes.com/2009/12/11/science/earth/11stern.html?_r=0 (31 January 2018).

Bryant, G. (2016) "The politics of carbon market design," *Antipode*, 48 (4), 877–898.

Carrington, D. (2016) "ExxonMobil is in its climate change bunker and won't let reality in", *The Guardian*, 27 May, www.theguardian.com/commentisfree/2016/may/27/exxonmobil-climate-change-bunker (31 January 2018).

Chowdhury, A. and Jomo, K.S. (2017) "Much more climate finance now!" *InterPress Service*, 12 September, www.ipsnews.net/2017/09/much-climate-finance-now/ (31 January 2018).

Climate Action Tracker (2015) Countries, 2 October, http://climateactiontracker.org/countries/southafrica.html (31 January 2018).

Color of Change (2016) "Coca-Cola: Stop sponsoring Donald Trump," www.thepetitionsite.com/takeaction/731/873/029/ (31 January 2018).

Funes, Y. (2017) "Politicians and environmentalists react after Trump pulls US from Paris Agreement," *Colorlines*, 2 June, www.colorlines.com/articles/politicians-and-environmentalists-react-after-trump-pulls-us-paris-agreement (31 January 2018).

Harvey, D. (1996) *Justice, Nature and the Geography of Difference*. Blackwell, Oxford.

Hawkins, R. (2014) "IPCC: CO2 emissions are being 'outsourced' by rich countries to rising economies," *Public Interest*, London, 4 February, http://publicinterest.org.uk/ipcc-co2-emissions-outsourced-rich-countries-rising-economies/ (31 January 2018).

Horn, S. (2017) "Trump attorney sues Greenpeace over Dakota access in $300 million racketeering case," *Desmogblog*, August 22, www.desmogblog.com/2017/08/22/dakota-access-trump-greenpeace-racketeering?utm_source=dsb%20newsletter (31 January 2018).

Hufbauer, G.C. and Kim, J. (2009) "Climate policy options and the World Trade Organization," Economics Discussion Papers, No. 2009–20, Kiel Institute for the World Economy, www.economics-ejournal.org/economics/discussionpapers/2009-20 (31 January 2018).

Jacobsen S. (2018) "Introduction," in Jacobsen, S. (ed) *Climate Justice and the Economy: Social Mobilization, Knowledge and the Political*, Routledge, London.

Johnston, I. (2017) "World could put carbon tax on US imports if Donald Trump ditches Paris Agreement, says expert," *The Independent*, May 23, www.independent.co.uk/environment/carbon-tax-us-imports-world-donald-trump-paris-agreement-climate-change-global-warming-a7751531.html (31 January 2018).

Kasrils, R. (2015) "Whither Palestine?" Unpublished paper, May 19, Johannesburg, www.sahistory.org.za/archive/whither-palestine-ronnie-kasrils-19-may-2015-london (31 January 2018).

Kerry, J. (2009) "This can be a catalysing moment," Washington, DC, 19 December, www.politico.com/arena/perm/John_Kerry_81E6D370-E8CF-4917-A30F-C (31 January 2018).

Kentish, B. (2016) "Nicolas Sarkozy promises to hit America with a carbon tax if Donald Trump rips up landmark Paris climate deal," *The Independent*, November 15, www.independent.co.uk/news/world/europe/donald-trump-us-carbon-tax-nicolas-sarkozy-global-warming-paris-climate-deal-a7418301.html (31 January 2018).

Klein, N. (2014) *This Changes Everything*. Simon & Schuster, London.

Klein, N. (2016) "Donald Trump isn't the end of the world, but climate change may be," 10 November, Sydney, http://sydneypeacefoundation.org.au/naomi-klein-donald-trump-isnt-the-end-of-the-world-but-climate-change-may-be/ (31 January 2018).

Klein, N. (2017) "Will Trump's slo-mo walkaway, world in flames behind him, finally provoke consequences for planetary arson?" *The Intercept*, 1 June, https://theintercept.com/2017/06/01/will-trumps-slow-mo-walkaway-world-in-flames-behind-him-finally-provoke-consequences-for-planetary-arson/ (31 January 2018).

Lenferna, G. A. (2017) "Trump is withdrawing from the Paris Climate Agreement. Is it time to boycott America?" *Daily Kos*, 1 June, http://www.dailykos.com/stories/2017/

6/1/1668071/-Trump-is-Withdrawing-from-the-Paris-Climate-Agreement-Is-it-Time-to-Boycott-America (31 January 2018).

Lenferna, G. A. (2018) "Divestment as climate justice: Weighing the power of the fossil fuel divestment movement," in Jacobsen, S. (ed) *Climate Justice and the Economy: Social Mobilization, Knowledge and the Political*, Routledge, London.

Leonard, A. (2009) *Story of Cap and Trade*, Story of Stuff Project, Berkeley, www.storyofcapandtrade.org

Lohmann, L. (2006) "Carbon trading: A critical conversation on climate change, privatization and power," *Development Dialogue*, September, 48, 1–362.

McLure, J. (2009) "Ethiopian leader chosen to represent Africa at climate summit," Addis Ababa, 1 September.

Martinez-Alier, J. (2003) "Marxism, social metabolism and ecologically unequal exchange," Paper presented at Lund University Conference on World Systems Theory and the Environment, Lund, 19–22 September.

Moore, J. (2013) "Anthropocene or capitalocene? On the Origins of Our Crisis," Part 1: Excerpt from *Ecology and the Accumulation of Capital*, https://jasonwmoore.wordpress.com (31 January 2018).

Pan African Climate Justice Alliance (2015) 2015 Annual Report, Nairobi, www.pacja.org/downloads/2015-ANNUAL-REPORT.pdf (31 January 2018).

Pan African Climate Justice Alliance (2017) "Press statement at COP23," Bonn, www.pacja.org/index.php/resources/presentations?download=64:pacja-press-statement-at-cop23 (31 January 2018).

Petroff, A. (2017) "CEOs make a final urgent plea: Don't pull out of Paris accord," *CNN*, 1 June, http://money.cnn.com/2017/06/01/news/trump-paris-climate-deal-business-ceo/index.html?iid=EL (31 January 2018).

Pew Research (2017) "Global attitudes survey," Washington, DC, www.pewglobal.org/2017/06/26/u-s-image-suffers-as-publics-around-world-question-trumps-leadership/ (31 January 2018).

Pope Francis (2015) "Encyclical letter Laudato Si' of the Holy Father Francis on care for our common home," *The Vatican*, 24 May, http://w2.vatican.va/content/francesco/en/encyclicals/documents/papa-francesco_20150524_enciclica-laudato-si.html (31 January 2018).

Reddy, T. (2009) "From African walk out to sell out," *Climate Chronicle*, 18 December.

Republic of Bolivia (2009) "Submission to the Ad Hoc Working Group on long-term cooperative action under the UN Framework Convention on Climate Change," La Paz, April.

Roy, A. (2012) "Indian capitalism as ghost story," *OutlookIndia*, 26 March.

Sethi, N. (2015) "US and EU want Loss and Damage as a toothless tiger in Paris," *Business Standard*, 7 December, www.business-standard.com/article/current-affairs/us-and-eu-want-loss-and-damage-as-a-toothless-tiger-in-paris-agreement-115120700043_1.html (31 January 2018).

Smith, R. (2017) "In the wake of US climate failures, don't look to China for a panacea," *Truth-Out*, 7 September, www.truth-out.org/news/item/41873-in-the-wake-of-us-climate-failures-don-t-look-to-china-for-a-panacea (31 January 2018).

Srinivasan, U., S. Carey, E. Hallstein, P. Higgins, A. Ker, L. Koteen, A. Smith, R. Watson, J. Harte and R. Norgaard (2008) "The debt of nations and the distribution of ecological impacts from human activities," *Proceedings of the National Academy of Sciences of the United States of America*, 105, 5, www.pnas.org/content/105/5/1768 (31 January 2018).

Stiglitz, J. (2006) "A new agenda for global warming," *Economist's Voice*, 3 (7), 10 July, https://doi.org/10.7916/D8XD1BHS (31 January 2018).

Stiglitz, J. (2017) "Trump's reneging on Paris climate deal turns the US into a rogue state," *The Guardian*, 2 June, www.theguardian.com/business/2017/jun/02/paris-climate-deal-to-trumps-rogue-america (31 January 2018).

Stiglitz, J. and Stern, N. (2017) Report of the High-Level Commission on Carbon Prices. World Bank Carbon Pricing Leadership Coalition, Washington, DC, 29 May

Summers, L. (1991) "The memo", 12 December, www.whirledbank.org/ourwords/summers.html (31 January 2018).

Temper, L. and Bliss, L. (2018) "Decolonizing and decarbonizing: How the Unist'o'en are arresting pipelines and asserting autonomy," in Jacobsen, S. (ed) *Climate Justice and the Economy: Social Mobilization, Knowledge and the Political*, Routledge, London.

The Guardian (2008) "Rich countries owe poor a huge environmental debt," 21 January, www.guardian.co.uk/science/2008/jan/21/environmental.debt1 (31 January 2018).

Trump, D. (2012) "Tweet: The concept of global warming …" November 6, New York.

Trump, D. (2017) "Remarks upon leaving the climate deal," *Washington Post*, June 1, www.washingtonpost.com/news/the-fix/wp/2017/06/01/transcript-president-trumps-remarks-on-leaving-the-paris-climate-deal-annotated/?utm_term=.4a9523ca12a4 (31 January 2018).

Warlenius, R. (2017) Asymmetries: Conceptualizing environmental inequalities as ecological debt and ecologically unequal exchange, PhD thesis, Lund University, Lund, https://lup.lub.lu.se/search/ws/files/19721188/Asymmetries_Introductory_chapter.pdf (31 January 2018).

Wates, J. (2017) "EEB calls for tough response to US withdrawal from Paris Agreement," Brussels, June 2, eeb.org/eeb-calls-for-tough-response-to-us-withdrawal-from-paris-agreement/ (31 January 2018).

Weissman, R. (2017) "CorporateCabinet.org tracks Trump cabinet picks," Public Citizen, 6 January, www.citizen.org/media/press-releases/corporatecabinetorg-tracks-trump-cabinet-picks (31 January 2018).

Wolf, M. (2017) "Donald Trump's bad judgment on the Paris accord," *Financial Times*, 6 June, www.ft.com/content/eecc80f6-4936-11e7-a3f4-c742b9791d43 (31 January 2018).

World Bank (2014) *Little Green Data Book 2014*. The World Bank Group, Washington, DC.

World Bank (2017) *Carbon Pricing Watch 2017*, World Bank, Washington, DC, https://openknowledge.worldbank.org/handle/10986/26565 (31 January 2018).

Yale University Program on Climate Change Communication (2016) "Global warming policy politics," New Haven, November, http://climatecommunication.yale.edu/wp-content/uploads/2016/12/Global-Warming-Policy-Politics-November-2016.pdf (31 January 2018).

Part II

Economic Climate Justice in practice

4   The indigenous climate justice of the Unist'ot'en resistance

Sam Bliss and Leah Temper

Introduction

Western Canada holds vast energy resources in Alberta's tar sands and the shale gas formations in north-eastern British Columbia (BC). The Canadian government and the oil and gas industry want to sell these fossil fuels on international markets. To do so, they must build pipelines to connect the interior extraction sites to ports on BC's west coast. The Wet'suwet'en First Nation's 22,000-square-kilometre territory lies directly in the path of the planned energy transport corridor. Like many First Nations in BC, they have never formally ceded their land to Canada.

The Unist'ot'en Clan of the Wet'suwet'en Nation have built a blockade on their ancestral land, living in an intentional community right in the route of the planned pipelines. At various points over the past few years as many as 11 proposed pipeline projects have threatened Wet'suwet'en land. Five have already been cancelled, thanks in no small part to the Unist'ot'en occupation. One of these, Enbridge's Northern Gateway project, would have pumped half a million barrels of diluted bitumen oil a day from Alberta's tar sands to the Pacific coast. Two serious pipeline proposals linger at the end of 2017: Chevron's Pacific Trails Pipeline and TransCanada's Coastal Gaslink (Rowe and Simpson 2017). Both would transport shale gas extracted with the controversial hydraulic fracturing method – fracking – which consumes and pollutes enormous volumes of freshwater.

The geopolitical stakes are considerable. Canada under former Prime Minister Stephen Harper explicitly strived to be a global energy superpower (Dalby 2016). When the Liberal party took control in 2015, new Prime Minister Justin Trudeau banned all oil tanker traffic off the north coast of BC, effectively killing Enbridge's planned Northern Gateway project and all other plans to pipe Alberta tar sands straight west through Wet'suwet'en land to the Pacific for export. Yet when Trudeau officially rejected the Northern Gateway pipeline plans in 2016, he simultaneously approved two major oil pipeline expansions, including the fiercely contentious Trans Mountain project to send the same tar-sands oil through Vancouver to BC's southern coast, where oil tankers remain legal (Cheadle 2016). Trudeau's government also approved the $CA 11.4 billion Pacific North West liquefied natural gas (LNG) project on BC's north coast, which aimed to turn fracked gas from inland BC into a super-cold liquid for shipping to Asia (Canadian Press 2016). That project, along with two other proposed LNG facilities along the north coast, have now been cancelled, but the possibility of LNG lives on in two planned liquefaction facilities in Kitimat, BC, plus the necessary pipelines through Wet'suwet'en land and shipping terminals, which would total over $CA 50 billion altogether (Hoekstra 2017). The possibility of a tar-sands pipeline remains, too, in the event that the north-coast tanker ban is lifted: a leaked document revealed that the Pacific Trails Pipeline could be converted to carry bitumen from Alberta after five years of operation as a gas conduit (Rhyno 2014). The Trudeau government claims it is on track to meet its climate targets – which are based on the carbon emissions emanating from Canada's territory, not the emissions that result from burning Canadian fossil fuels elsewhere – and claims that the government revenues from oil and gas exports are essential for funding the transition to a low-carbon energy system. The Liberals struggle mightily to reconcile their continuation of the quest to extract and sell fossil fuels with their rhetoric of environmental protection (Wherry 2016).

The climate stakes are considerable, too. If burned, the estimated 640 billion barrels of crude oil in Alberta's tar sands would emit 275 gigatons of CO_2, about a quarter of the maximum emissions humanity can release to maintain a 50–50 chance of keeping global average temperature increase under two degrees C. Two researchers from University College London published a study in *Nature* specifying which of the world's fossil fuels can be safely extracted and consumed, and which not, in order to maximize the economic benefits of using up this limited global carbon budget (McGlade and Ekins 2015). They found that Canada must refrain from extracting 99 percent of its tar-sands oil resource, and 25 percent of its economically recoverable gas reserves, including an even higher percentage of unconventional sources like the shale gas in BC. Fracking, piping, liquefying, transoceanic shipping, and re-gasifying does not make for cheap gas. The former director of NASA's Goddard Institute, James Hansen (2012), has written that unlocking the tar sands' vast petroleum resources would mean 'game over' for earth's stable climate. Blocking the infrastructure necessary to cheaply transport these fuels to consumption centres helps keep them underground, or at least slows extraction, buying time to create the new political and economic institutions needed to transition away from fossil fuels.

Energy companies and other investors claim that they cancelled LNG plants on BC's north coast because shifts in global markets made the economics unfavourable. They do not mention the resistance to the pipelines needed to deliver the gas, much less the possibility that they will not be built at all (Scotti 2017). The Pacific Trails Pipeline (PTP) project was originally scheduled to break ground in 2012. The Unist'ot'en had expressed their will to prevent all pipelines in 2007, when industry first began studying the possibility of building the PTP. In 2009, they established a checkpoint at the Wedzin Kwah, or Morice River, entrance to Unist'ot'en territory. In 2010, they began constructing a log cabin on the precise GPS coordinates of the proposed pipeline corridors (Unist'ot'en Camp 2017a). In 2011, they escorted drillers and other PTP employees off their territory.

In 2012, the clan again evicted surveyors from their territory by presenting them with an eagle feather, the first and only traditional notice of trespass (Holland 2012). In 2015, Unist'ot'en spokeswoman Freda Huson expelled a helicopter of TransCanada, the company behind the proposed Coast Gaslink pipeline. No pipeline work has proceeded on Unist'ot'en land.

The Unist'ot'en and their allies have expanded that first log cabin into a small community. The site has become a gathering place for North America's climate justice movement, a precursor to the indigenous-led pipeline blockade at Standing Rock in 2016. The Unist'ot'en camp has held weeklong action camps each summer since 2010 for activists to connect, share knowledge, and teach each other non-violent resistance tactics. In 2013, 2014, and 2015, respectively, they began constructing a traditional pithouse, a bunkhouse for guests, and a healing centre (Unist'ot'en Camp 2017a). The first two are now complete, and in October 2017, the Unist'ot'en held a work camp to bring the healing centre closer to completion. The website of the Unist'o'ten camp (2017b) says healing is its main focus: healing intergenerational trauma in First Nations communities; healing bodies and minds by restoring traditional teachings and land-based wellness practices; and healing humans' connections within the web of life.

The Unist'ot'en camp combines resistance with alternatives. Those who have visited and participated in the community, including us authors, recognise it as a laboratory for the sort of social and ecological innovation needed to create sustainable, small-scale economic systems for a post-fossil fuel era with a changed climate (see Bliss 2015). The Unist'ot'en actively endeavour to construct a living anti-capitalist community, informed by both an ancient system of values on how to create mutually respectful relationships with the natural world and a transformative politics of decolonisation that seeks to revalue, reconstruct, and redeploy indigenous cultural practices and governance systems (Napoleon 2013).

And the Unist'ot'en resistance goes beyond the local struggle against unconsented development of indigenous land. Environmentalists and climate justice activists around the world celebrate and support its powerful act of defiance against the fossil fuel industry and the extractive settler state of Canada. More than 400 organizations and leaders in the movement, plus several thousand more individuals, have signed an online declaration of solidarity with the camp, reproving industry and government for interfering with Unist'ot'en sovereignty and the Royal Canadian Mounted Police for threatening to make mass arrests (*We Stand with the Unist'ot'en* 2015). The public support delights but does not necessarily surprise the Unist'ot'en. The oil and gas pipelines would affect everyone, says Huson. 'It impacts these people who have the same concerns we do. All our waters are connected, the globe is round, and the streams flow into the rivers, the rivers flow into the ocean' (quoted in McSheffrey 2015).

To understand how the Unist'ot'en camp is holding up billions in investment, keeping millions of barrels of oil and billions of cubic metres of gas underground, preventing countless tonnes of emissions, revitalising their relationship with the land, and protecting their sacred headwaters, this chapter will first explore the special legal context of indigenous communities within Canada and then the resistance methods of the camp. Finally, the article describes some elements of the politics and economic practices in the camp.

The legal approach

We are not interested in asserting aboriginal rights. We are here to discuss territory and authority. When this case ends and the package has been unwrapped, it will have to be our ownership and our jurisdiction under our law that is on the table.

(Delgam Uukw 1997)

The Unist'ot'en have a long history of resistance against extractivism. With the Gitksan First Nation, they blockaded logging in their traditional territory in the late 1980s, an action which culminated in the ground-breaking *Delgamuukw* court case whereby in 1984, the Gitksan and Wet'suwet'en went to court to assert their sovereignty, legal jurisdiction, and aboriginal rights over some 58,000 square kilometres of their territory (Glavin 2000). The case was a landmark in several respects. It established that the First Nations' territorial sovereignty, pending proof of surrender by treaty, is a legitimate and outstanding constitutional question that remains to be resolved by the court. The case was also significant because after initial objections, the Gitksan and Wet'suwet'en were able to use their oral histories as principal evidence in the case.

In the case of the Wet'suwet'en, oral history is transmitted at important feasts through the *Kungax*, a spiritual song, dance, or performance detailing the most important laws, history, customs, and traditional territory of a House. In the case of the Gitksan, it is through the *adaawk*. It was in the feast hall throughout their history where they would tell and retell their stories, pass on important histories, songs, crests, lands, ranks, and properties from one generation to the next, and identify their territories to remind themselves of the sacred connection they have with their lands (Borrows 1999). These histories serve as an embedded law that evolved as the result of people observing the consequences of their behaviour over time (Overstall 2004). When their behaviour is disrespectful of spirits, animals, and others, the consequences are dire and are often recorded in the *adaawk*, especially if the behaviour alters a lineage's relationship with its territory. The *adaawk* thus have a role as legal precedents that inform later conduct.

The *Delgamuukw* trial opened space for decolonialising practices, yet at the same time it revealed the limitations of Canada's justice system as a medium for the realisation of self-determination and, more broadly, for the social and environmental justice for which those in the camp and climate justice activists struggle. It demonstrated the differences between indigenous and settler cultures' conceptions of human–ecological relationships (Bedford and Cheney 2013).

The Wet'suwet'en and Gitxsan understand humans as fundamentally interconnected with ecology. The plaintiffs, Gisday Wa and Delgam Uukw, describe in their opening address a view of the world as a differentiated unity, of which humans are a part. There is no strict human–nature dualism from this perspective. They write,

> The Western world-view sees the essential and primary interactions as being those between human beings. To the Gitksan and Wet'suwet'en, human beings are part of an interacting continuum, which includes animals and spirits. Animals and fish are viewed as members of societies, which have intelligence and power, and can influence the course of events in terms of their interrelationship with human beings.
>
> (Wa and Uukw 1992)

This indigenous philosophy shapes notions about ownership and jurisdiction over land and resources (Bryan 2000). Yet the court was not able to recognise nature in the relational perspective that the plaintiffs asked: the Gitksan and Wet'suwet'en understanding of the human relationship with the natural world, and flowing from that, their understanding of property rights, was irreconcilable within the world-view of the settler society and its legal system.

Nor was the court able to extinguish its own authority. Recognising the sovereignty of the tribes would have undermined the court's ability to impose its law on occupied territory. Thus, while the *Delgamuukw* trial served to redraw the boundaries of the colonial courtroom through the use of oral history, the spellings of Gitksan and Wet'suwet'en names, and the presentation of their own maps, it also revealed the limits to the decolonisation that can happen within a courtroom when the state's authority to impose its law is what is really on trial.

More progress was made toward recognizing indigenous sovereignty over traditional territory in the 2014 *Tsilhqot'in* case, when Canada's Supreme Court ruled that any land that was never formally ceded cannot be developed without consent of those First Nations that have a claim to it (McLachlin 2014). This ruling would seem to give the Unist'ot'en the right to stop pipelines that would pass through the land they have inhabited for thousands of years. Yet Canada has repeatedly expropriated large swaths of recognised First Nations land for energy and transportation infrastructure projects. This most recent court case established the territorial sovereignty over traditional lands, but it remains to be seen what this means in practice. If the territorial sovereignty were truly recognised, would the conflict not be resolved through Unist'ot'en legal systems, according to their laws?

Confronted with the paradox of seeking remedy and justice through the colonial courts, the Unist'ot'en have disavowed a rights-based discourse. They do not appeal to what they see as an occupying power to bestow them with rights to autonomy on their own land. Rather, they assert their responsibilities to the territory and their ancestral and natural law. As Mel Basil (2014), a long-time supporter of the camp, says, 'I don't have a right to these fish – I have a responsibility to this river and I will not let that responsibility be diminished'. The following sections outline how the Unist'ot'en camp has asserted this responsibility to the land.

Direct action

There are many understandings of direct action. In Canada, one definition holds that direct action, in contrast to the official politics described in the previous section, can be understood as political mobilisation outside state institutions. This definition excludes legal action and institutionalised protest, such as petitioning, lobbying, and litigation. It includes land occupations, road blockades, resource extraction deemed illegal by the state, marches, and demonstrations (Morden 2015). Another definition understands direct action as a political tactic that legally or illegally disrupts the public interest in order to attract awareness or action to an issue or cause (Wilkes et al. 2010). Activists use direct action as a means of taking matters into their own hands when established institutions exclude them from adequate participation in the political process.

Since the 1970s, First Nations in Canada have repeatedly used the blockade as a direct action tactic (Blomley 1996). These blockades have often been intertwined with legal battles seeking recognition of Aboriginal rights and titles through the courts. It was Wet'suwet'en and Gitxsan logging-road blockades that culminated in the *Delgamuukw* decision.

Blockades resist through both instrumental and symbolic power. Instrumentally, blockades 'regulate movement where movement itself is in dispute' (Blomley 1996: 14). They physically impede the massive outflow of resources from indigenous lands, often by impeding the intrusion of extractive industry. Blockades control movement with particular effectiveness in Canada because its rugged, resource-rich terrain, sparsely populated with human communities and transport infrastructure, creates choke points where the movement of materials can be blocked. Because their territories hold vast natural resources, First Nations have privileged access to the arteries of the economy and can exercise incredible leverage over the critical infrastructures that connect mines, oil fields, sawmills, hydroelectric facilities, and other extraction sites to international markets (Pasternak 2013). Moreover, several court decisions suggest that blockades on First Nations land may be legal denials of trespass (Blomley 1996). These favourable conditions in part explain First Nations' reliance on, and success with, blockades against extractive industry.

Today, climate justice activists increasingly use blockades to obstruct the operation and expansion of fossil fuel infrastructure (Bradshaw 2015, Evans 2010, Martínez-Alier et al. 2016). Direct actions against the flow of fossil fuels slow down the rate at which they are burned, both immediately and by increasing costs. When activists get in the way of new projects with legal action, blockades, or other methods of disruption, the investments become less profitable, the infrastructures less likely to be completed. One might consider the Unist'ot'en leaders in what author Naomi Klein (2014) terms 'Blockadia', the decentralised worldwide anti-extraction direct action campaign on behalf of local environments and the global climate.

Symbolically, blockades mark out two spaces – an indigenous space and a Canadian space in the case of First Nations blockades (Blomley 1996).

Beyond blocking the flow of resources, blockades map a symbolic boundary separating extractive capitalism from its resistors.

The Unist'ot'en camp goes further; its assertion of place and control of space represents much more than a symbolic action. Beyond disrupting the flows of capitalism and denying the removal of resources from the territory, blockades can – typically temporarily but in some cases for extended periods – create a space for alternative ways of organising social life to emerge, both apart from and in contradiction to the social relations of capitalism. The Unist'ot'en fulfil their responsibility to the land not just by defending it from what they consider destructive development, but by reaffirming their sovereignty over it, renewing their traditional practices on it, and regenerating the ecosystems that inhabit it.

Asserting sovereignty

The United Nations Declaration on the Rights of Indigenous Peoples (2007) recognises indigenous peoples' inherent right to inhabit, manage, and self-govern their ancestral lands. Yet, in practice, few indigenous peoples worldwide maintain sovereignty in their traditional territories. Most have been displaced, dispossessed, colonised, conquered, or some combination of the preceding (UN Department of Economic and Social Affairs 2009). We must understand the responsibilities-based discourse of the Unist'ot'en within the context of their history of denied rights.

Canada stripped First Nations of rights to their traditional territories and to self-governance more than a century ago. The Indian Act of 1876 set up a system of band councils to govern the reserves onto which First Nations people were forcefully relocated (Harris 2011). Instead of yielding authority to band councils put in place by the Canadian government, the Unist'ot'en make decisions through their traditional system of hereditary chiefs. 'Some of the people have lost a lot of their governance systems', says Unist'ot'en spokesperson Freda Huson. 'Because we were one of the larger Wet'suwet'en communities, we were able to hang on to it' (quoted in Bliss 2015).

Energy companies have essentially ignored that the *Delgamuukw* and *Tsilhqot'in* decisions acknowledge aspects of indigenous sovereignty over unceded land like the traditional territory of the Unist'ot'en. Indian Act band councils do not have jurisdiction beyond the reserves, yet when forced to consult with First Nations, pipeline companies have persistently chosen to negotiate with band councils rather than the traditional governments whose territories their infrastructures would cross. Chevron formed the First Nations Limited Partnership with several band councils to give financial benefits, shares, employment opportunities, and contract opportunities in exchange for their blessing to build the PTP. On January 23, 2015, the Moricetown Band – the band council that claims to represent the Wet'suwet'en nation – became the sixteenth and final First Nations band along the pipeline route to sign on to the partnership (FNLP 2015). In exchange, the 16 bands will share $CA 32 million once construction begins, as well as $CA 10 million per year while the pipeline is operating. It was a leaked document from the negotiations between Chevron and the Moricetown Band Council that revealed that the PTP could easily be converted to carry diluted bitumen, or tar sands, after five years conveying fracked gas (Rhyno 2014). Only the administrative units Canada has imposed on First Nations – not their indigenous systems of hereditary chiefs – have had any official say over gas pipelines.

Inclusion of indigenous voices in decisions about oil pipelines has been even more inadequate, on the part of both industry and government. Staff from Canada's environmental ministry admitted in emails that First Nations were not involved at all in the consultation process that resulted in conditional approval of Enbridge's (now-cancelled) Northern Gateway pipeline (Tello 2015). That pipeline, which was to bring tar-sands oil from Alberta to the BC coast, generated heated opposition from many of the 50 indigenous nations whose territories it would have crossed. Perhaps First Nations were excluded from decision making because those who stood to benefit from the pipeline were not willing to hear 'no'.

Some First Nations – and all the band councils – may have agreed to the gas pipelines in part because industry representatives have told them that in the event of a spill the gas would simply evaporate. In contrast, the Unist'ot'en stand adamantly against all pipelines. They will not be bought out. By obstructing construction of the PTP and other gas pipelines, they increase the price of getting gas to market, and severely limit the markets that gas can reach. In this way, they slow down fracking, shelve the liquefaction plant projects, prevent an increase in vessel traffic, and keep carbon out of the atmosphere.

Asserting indigenous sovereignty means rejecting that of the Canadian state. Freda Huson, spokeswoman for the clan, wrote a letter 'to the illegitimate colonial governments of Canada and British Columbia, and to all parties involved in the proposed PTP project' that began: 'This letter is to issue a warning of trespass to those companies associated with the PTP industrial extraction project and against any affiliates and contractors infringing upon traditional Wet'suwet'en territory' (Unist'ot'en Camp 2012). The letter makes clear that the Unist'ot'en will interpret any further intrusion into their territory as an act of aggression against their sovereignty.

But strongly worded letters do not hold back industry and the state. The Unist'ot'en assert territorial sovereignty in the ways they always have, by regulating the flows of people and materials that enter their land.

Reimagined free prior and informed consent

The blockade in the Unist'ot'en camp is controlled via a wooden bridge across the Wedzin Kwah (Morice River), 66 kilometres up a logging road from Houston, BC. This river serves as a border between Canada and the traditional territory of the Unist'ot'en. The blockade is marked by a large, painted plywood sign that reads, 'STOP. No access without prior consent'.

To cross the bridge and enter the camp, every visitor must go through a 'reimagined free prior and informed consent protocol established by the Unist'ot'en camp collective.[1] This protocol is modified from ancient conventions that require visiting peoples to ask the chiefs and matriarchs of the hosting lands for permission to enter. This convention is still practiced today on canoe journeys and community resistance building gatherings (Unist'ot'en Camp 2017c).

The protocol entails four questions that are sent to visitors when they give notice of their arrival.

1   What is your name?
2   Where are you from?
3   Have you ever worked for government or industry that has harmed this territory?
4   How will your visit benefit the Unist'ot'en people?

In this way, the Unist'ot'en blockade is really more of a check point. It does not prevent all passage, just trespass by industry and government interests that aim to develop projects without consent.

The UN declares that states should not dislocate indigenous peoples, disrupt their traditional practices, adopt measures that may affect them, dispose of hazardous materials on their lands, use their lands for military activities, or extract resources from their lands without receiving free, prior, and informed consent (FPIC, United Nations Declaration on the Rights of Indigenous Peoples 2007). Political researcher Jennifer Franco notes, 'The "C" in FPIC is increasingly redefined as "consultation", precisely because the principle of consent, if taken seriously, does imply the right to say "no" and the power to veto' (2014: 7). According to the camp members, their reimagined FPIC reclaims a process that corporations, charities, governments, and other colonial bodies have used as a mechanism to facilitate and legitimate development projects.

The protocol is not the only traditional practice the Unist'ot'en are reclaiming and reimagining. Physically obstructing the growth of the fossil fuel economy is only half of the Unist'ot'en camp's mission. By renewing traditional practices and sharing them with visiting activists, the camp works to develop the sort of shared community needed for fighting climate change, both in building resilience against environmental disruption and in kicking the fossil fuel addiction.

The ecology of indigenous resistance

> *I am not so concerned with how we dismantle the master's house, but I am very concerned with how we (re)build our own house, or our own houses.*
> (Leanne Simpson 2011)

In 2015, all five Unist'ot'en chiefs, along with four other Wet'suwet'en chiefs, signed the Unist'ot'en Declaration, a document that seeks to clear up confusion about the camp. The Declaration mainly reaffirms the convoluted legal circumstances – that the land is unceded, the Supreme Court has recognised indigenous title, and all activity must be consented to by the Unist'ot'en – by officially enacting them as law. First, though, the new decree declares, 'The Unist'ot'en settlement camp is not a protest or a demonstration. Our clan is occupying and using our traditional territory as it has for centuries' (Unist'ot'en Camp 2015).

Huson, a member of the Unist'ot'en Clan, says the primary motivation for starting the camp with her husband Toghestiy, of the nearby Likhts'amisyu (fire-weed) Clan, was to give their people the opportunity to reconnect with the land their ancestors have lived on, and lived from, since time immemorial. Moving more people back to their territory and re-establishing traditional hunting, fish-ing, trapping, foraging, and other subsistence practices might also create a legal case against pipelines that is legitimate in the eyes of Canadian courts. The *Delgamuukw* decision, from 1997, held that indigenous title and rights are based on the customs, traditions, and practices of the indigenous people. Showing that pipelines infringe on their traditional lifeways could give the Unist'ot'en veto power. Reviving their ancestral culture requires healing – healing the people, the land, and the relationship between the people and the land.

To heal their people, the Unist'ot'en are focusing on indigenous youth. Between 1883 and 1998, the Canadian government financed boarding schools for First Nations children that were created with the explicit goal to 'take the Indian out of the child' (Moran 2014). A report released this year by Canada's Truth and Reconciliation Commission (2015) described the schools as 'cultural genocide'. Huson describes the Unist'ot'en Camp's healing centre as a direct counterpoint to this, trying to 'put the Indian back in the child' (quoted in Bliss 2015).

To heal the land, the Unist'ot'en must restore the functioning woodland eco-system that once fed them. The forests that cover their territory today are a patch-work of clear-cuts and chillingly sterile tree-plantation monoculture that's been devastated by mountain pine beetle. But the land needs far less healing than most these days: the forest mostly still stands, the wildlife remain, and the water is clean enough to drink straight from the river, as camp residents do. The ecologi-cal health needed to sustain the camp community is returning. Volunteers have created a permaculture garden that supplies food and medicine to supplement plants gathered from the broader forest ecosystem. The Unist'ot'en set traplines and hunt for mammals small and large. Residents harvest firewood for much of the camp's heating and cooking needs. Restoring these ecological interactions that include humans helps heal the relationship between the people and the land.

The Unist'ot'en camp lives lightly on the land. Nearly everything there is donated or collected from the waste streams of Western civilisation. Solar panels power a microgrid, with a row of 12-volt batteries storing electricity for when the sun is not shining. A culture of ecological frugality prevails, as draining the batteries means firing up a diesel generator, overconsuming fuelwood means working harder and felling more trees, buying goods means fuel-intensive trips to town, and wasting water means lugging more up from the river. In the winter of 2015, the camp used about 13 litres of water per person per day (Bliss 2015). Canadians outside of First Nations communities use over 250 litres a day, on aver-age (Environment Canada 2009).

Without romanticising or essentialising indigenous society, the recognition of indigenous skills and perspectives that Western culture tends to ignore can serve as an invaluable source of knowledge. Indigenous peoples tend to value long-term sustainability and resilience over growth and efficiency, perhaps because indigenous peoples learned to live prosperously within the ecological limits of their territories rather than continually colonising new areas from which to take resources. The fact that Gitksan and Wet'suwet'en Nations' hereditary Chiefs are among the oldest continually held titles of any society on the planet, according to First Nations scholar Antonia Mills, a professor at the University of Northern British Columbia, is a testament to this intergenerational vision. In contrast, it's been about fewer than two centuries since the widespread adoptions of coal and capitalism revolutionised Western society, enabling production and consumption to begin to grow like never before.

Huson expressed in a 2014 interview with the Vancouver Media Co-op that humanity's role in ecosystems is the reason for blocking pipelines, for restoring autonomy, for opposing and opting out of the unmaintainable industrial capitalist economy.

> Fish need the water, and bears eat the fish, and everything is connected and rely on each other. And if we don't sustain all of the earth including the animals – if the animals die – we will be the next ones to die because we follow suit with the animals. Everything we do on this earth today, man has learned that from animals. So why would they disrespect the animals and ruin their homelands by putting stupid pipes through this land?
>
> The whole world is messed up right now because everything is about economics. Economics, all the bottom line of how much money they can make. Yet one day that money is going to mean nothing. … All I can say to these people is you're going to be woken up when the economy collapses and the dollar doesn't mean a thing. You're going to have to fend for yourself and you're not going to survive.
>
> The ones who have always lived modestly, and grew their own food, and knew how to take care of themselves, and didn't rely on anybody else to sustain their own families, they are the only people that are going to survive.
>
> (Huson 2014)

Conclusion

The Unist'ot'en resistance is more expansive than most 'not-in-my-backyard' opposition to infrastructure projects – spatially, temporally, and conceptually expansive. The Unist'ot'en do not fight only to protect their own land and water from contamination, but against the expansion of the fossil fuel industry on behalf of all earth's interconnected ecosystems and the climate system they rely on. They do not just oppose the infrastructures threatening their land, but the extractivist disease of which those projects are a symptom, the colonialist governance institutions that enable them, and the capitalist economic system that necessitates them. They do not drive sedans home to gas-heated suburban lives after spending an afternoon resisting oil and gas development; they *live* in the way of the pipelines, in a community that is not connected to any.

'Blockadia' as a movement might need to expand its scope similarly to succeed in slowing global warming, and ultimately achieve some semblance of climate justice. It must block fossil fuel development worldwide, because the globe warms the same regardless of where carbon emissions are released. It must challenge the root of the problem: the unjust, unsustainable economic institutions that have created the climate crisis. And it must embed its alternatives in the resistance, persistently exploring new ways to relate to each other and to the rest of nature, new ways to live without the fossil fuel infrastructure the movement opposes and obstructs. The resistance to the Dakota Access Pipeline at Standing Rock illustrates these ideals: it is an indigenous-led direct action, grounded in collectively reimagined renderings of traditional ceremony, that has inspired many groups in many places to stand up to the fossil fuel industry.

Indigenous peoples have contributed little to the build-up of carbon dioxide in earth's atmosphere, yet climate change will hit them hard because their livelihoods tend to rely directly on environments whose conditions will transform quickly (UN Department of Economic and Social Affairs 2009). The Unist'ot'en living blockade reveals the underlying clash of values that pits movements of resistance to fossil fuel extraction against a capitalist growth economy that can only take nature into account by converting resources into commodities or by putting prices on ecosystem services. Indigenous demands for self-determination such as those claimed by the Unist'ot'en aim towards a structural transformation of colonial and capitalist systems of domination of nature and subjugated peoples. Such movements, in the words of Taiaiake Alfred's (1999) *Indigenous Manifesto*, are informed by 'a set of values that challenge the homogenizing force of Western Liberalism and free market capitalism; that honour the autonomy of individual conscience, non-coercive authority, and the deep interconnection between human beings and other elements of creation'.

Such pronouncements may not have much resonance within the negotiation halls of the COP summits, where the future of the planet ostensibly hangs in the balance. Yet, when one visits the camp, living off the land, picking huckleberries, eating recently hunted and smoked moose or hedgehog, one gets the feeling that this remote corner of the planet is as close as one can get to ground zero in the transformation of the global energy infrastructure.

The Unist'ot'en vision of climate justice does not depend on the state to grant rights to nature, but upon communities asserting their environmental responsibility through direct action. In the words of the camp organisers,

> Indigenous Peoples must be uncompromising and be thoughtful of how their knowledge can teach the rest of the world to degrow as a society. The Laws of the Land are Natural Laws and Indigenous Laws. These laws can be self-regulated by all, not only the Indigenous Peoples. There can still be an abundance enjoyed, but no longer at the expense of peoples whom we don't see across the world.
>
> (Unist'ot'en Camp 2017c)

Note

1 Leah Temper visited the camp in summer of 2013 and Sam Bliss visited for a week in 2015.

References

Alfred, T. (1999) *Peace, Power, Righteousness: An Indigenous Manifesto*. Ontario: Oxford University Press.

Basil, M. (2014) *Personal Correspondence*, 2014.

Bedford, D. and Cheney, T. (2013) 'Labor, Nature, and Spirituality: Human Ecology and a Left-First Nations Politics'. *Capitalism Nature Socialism* 24 (3), 204–216.

Bliss, S. (2015) 'Spending Time in a Controversial Camp That's Blocking Tar-Sands Pipelines'. *Grist* [online] 21 August. Available from <http://grist.org/climate-energy/spending-time-in-a-controversial-camp-thats-blocking-tar-sands-pipelines/> [28 November 2017].

Blomley, N. (1996) '"Shut the Province Down": First Nations Blockades in British Columbia, 1984–1995'. *BC Studies: The British Columbian Quarterly* (111), 5–35.

Borrows, J. (1999) 'Sovereignty's Alchemy: An Analysis of Delgamuukw v. British Columbia'. *Osgoode Hall Law Journal* 37, 537–596.

Bradshaw, E.A. (2015) 'Blockadia Rising: Rowdy Greens, Direct Action and the Keystone XL Pipeline'. *Critical Criminology* 23 (4), 433–448.

Bryan, B. (2000) 'Property as Ontology: On Aboriginal and English Understandings of Ownership'. *Canadian Journal of Law & Jurisprudence* 13 (1), 3–31.

Canadian Press (2016) 'Liberals Approve Controversial Natural Gas Project on B.C. Coast'. *The Toronto Star* 27 September.

Cheadle, B. (2016) 'Justin Trudeau Halts Northern Gateway, Approves Kinder Morgan Expansion, Line 3'. *The Canadian Press* 29 November.

Dalby, S. (2016) 'Geopolitics, Ecology and Stephen Harper's Reinvention of Canada'. In *Handbook on Sustainability Transition and Sustainable Peace*. ed. by Brauch, H.G., Spring, Ú.O., Grin, J., and Scheffran, J. Hexagon Series on Human and Environmental Security and Peace. New York: Springer, 493–504.

Environment Canada (2009) *Municipal Water and Wastewater Survey* [online] available from <www.ec.gc.ca/Publications/B77CE4D0-80D4-4FEB-AFFA-0201BE6FB37B/2011-Municipal-Water-Use-Report-2009-Stats_Eng.pdf> [30 November 2017].

Evans, G. (2010) 'A Rising Tide: Linking Local and Global Climate Justice'. *The Journal of Australian Political Economy; Sydney* (66), 199–221.

FNLP (2015) 'Moricetown Indian Band Joins First Nations Limited Partnership' [online] available from <www.newswire.ca/news-releases/moricetown-indian-band-joins-first-nations-limited-partnership-516510191.html> [30 November 2017].

Franco, J. (2014) *Reclaiming Free Prior and Informed Consent*. Amsterdam: Transnational Institute.

Glavin, T. (2000) *A Death Feast in Dimlahamid*. Vancouver, British Columbia: New Star Books.

Hansen, J. (2012) 'Game Over for the Climate'. *The New York Times* 9 May.

Harris, R.C. (2011) *Making Native Space: Colonialism, Resistance, and Reserves in British Columbia*. Vancouver, British Columbia: UBC Press.

Hoekstra, G. (2017) 'LNG Possibility Lives on, Even after Death of Pacific NorthWest LNG'. *Vancouver Sun* 2 August.

Holland, L. (2012) 'Statement by Laura Holland, Wet'suwet'en Nation at the Vancouver Rally in Support of the Unist'ot'en'. *Vancouver Media Co-Op* 27 November.

Huson, F. (2014) No Band Councils or Tribal Councils Have Jurisdiction over Unist'ot'en Territory [interview by B. Rhyno], 1 August 2014.

Klein, N. (2014) *This Changes Everything: Capitalism Vs. The Climate*. New York: Simon & Schuster.

McGlade, C. and Ekins, P. (2015) 'The Geographical Distribution of Fossil Fuels Unused When Limiting Global Warming to 2°C'. *Nature* 517 (7533), 187–190.

McLachlin, B. (2014) *Tsilhqot'in Nation v. British Columbia*. 34986.

McSheffrey, E. (2015) 'What You Need to Know about the Unist'ot'en – Pipeline Standoff'. *Vancouver Observer* 31 August.

Martínez-Alier, J., Temper, L., Del Bene, D., and Scheidel, A. (2016) 'Is There a Global Environmental Justice Movement?'. *The Journal of Peasant Studies* 43 (3), 731–755.

Moran, M. (2014) 'The Role of Reparative Justice in Responding to the Legacy of Indian Residential Schools'. *University of Toronto Law Journal* 64 (4), 529–565.

Morden, M. (2015) 'Right and Resistance: Norms, Interests and Indigenous Direct Action in Canada'. *Ethnopolitics* 14 (3), 256–276.

Napoleon, V. (2013) 'Thinking About Indigenous Legal Orders'. In *Dialogues on Human Rights and Legal Pluralism*. ed. by Provost, R. and Sheppard, C. Dordrecht: Springer Netherlands, 229–245.

Overstall, R. (2004) 'Encountering the Spirit in the Land: "Property" in a Kinship-Based Legal Order'. In *Despotic Dominion: Property Rights in British Settler Societies*. ed. by McLaren, J. Vancouver: University of British Columbia Press, 22–49.

Pasternak, S. (2013) 'The Economics of Insurgency'. *The Media Co-Op* [online] available from < www.mediacoop.ca/story/economics-insurgency/15610> [28 November 2017].

Rhyno, B. (2014) 'Leaked Document Reveals Chevron's Oily Intentions for the Pacific Trials Pipeline'. *Vancouver Media Co-Op* 5 August.

Rowe, J. and Simpson, M. (2017) 'Lessons from the Front Lines of Anti-Colonial Pipeline Resistance'. *Waging Nonviolence* [online] 9 October. Available from <https://wagingnonviolence.org/feature/lessons-front-lines-anti-colonial-unistoten-pipeline-resistance/> [27 November 2017].

Scotti, M. (2017) 'What Killed the $36-Billion Pacific NorthWest LNG Project?' *Global News* [online] 26 July. Available from <https://globalnews.ca/news/3625528/what-killed-the-pacific-northwest-lng-project/> [27 November 2017].

Simpson, L. (2011) *Dancing on Our Turtle's Back: Stories of Nishnaabeg Re-Creation, Resurgence and a New Emergence*. Winnipeg, Manitoba: Arbeiter Ring Publisher.

Tello, C. (2015) 'Gov't Emails Reveal Concerns over First Nation Consultation on Enbridge Northern Gateway'. *The Vancouver Observer* 23 April.

Truth and Reconciliation Commission of Canada (2015) *Honouring the Truth, Reconciling for the Future* [online] available from < www.myrobust.com/websites/trcinstitution/File/Reports/Executive_Summary_English_Web.pdf> [30 November 2017].

UN Department of Economic and Social Affairs (2009) *State of the World's Indigenous Peoples*. New York: United Nations Publications.

Unist'ot'en Camp (2012) 'Raising Resistance – Global Day of Action #nopipelines' [27 November 2012] available from <https://unistotencamp.wordpress.com/2012/11/27/raising-resistance-global-day-of-action-nopipelines/> [30 November 2017].

Unist'ot'en Camp (2015) 'Press Release: Unist'ot'en Clan Enacts Declaration as Law' [6 August 2015] available from <https://unisoten.camp/press-release-unistoten-clan-enacts-declaration-as-law/> [30 November 2017].

Unist'ot'en Camp (2017a) 'Timeline of the Campaign' [online] available from <http://unistoten.camp> [26 November 2017].

Unist'ot'en Camp (2017b) 'Healing Centre' [online] available from <http://unistoten.camp/come-to-camp/healing/> [28 November 2017].

Unist'ot'en Camp (2017c) 'Free Prior and Informed Consent Protocol' [online] available from <http://unistoten.camp/come-to-camp/fpic/> [29 November 2017].

United Nations Declaration on the Rights of Indigenous Peoples (2007, 61st session, agenda item 68) [online] available from <www.converge.org.nz/pma/DRIPGA.pdf> [29 November 2017].

Uukw, D. (1997) *Delgamuukw v. British Columbia.* 23799.

Wa, G. and Uukw, D. (1992) *The Spirit in the Land: Statements of the Gitksan and Wet'suwet'en Hereditary Chiefs in the Supreme Court of British Columbia, 1987–1990.* Gabriola, British Columbia: Reflections.

We Stand with the Unist'ot'en (2015) available from <https://docs.google.com/forms/d/e/1FAIpQLSelOzrs0bKasJXLmcEOVUaUiaOBGHToLRkDvb0sl0xjs83xNQ/viewform?c=0&w=1&usp=embed_facebook> [1 December 2017].

Wherry, A. (2016) 'Trudeau Government at Pains to Explain Pacific Northwest LNG'. *CBC News* 28 September.

Wilkes, R., Corrigall-Brown, C., and Myers, D.J. (2010) 'Packaging Protest: Media Coverage of Indigenous People's Collective Action'. *Canadian Review of Sociology/Revue Canadienne de Sociologie* 47 (4), 327–357.

5 Divestment as climate justice

Weighing the power of the fossil fuel divestment movement

Georges Alexandre Lenferna

In spring 2010, on the campus of Swarthmore College, the student group Swarthmore Mountain Justice formed one of the first fossil fuel divestment campaigns – a coal divestment campaign in solidarity with frontline communities fighting against mountaintop removal coal mining in Appalachia (Grady-Benson & Sarathy 2015).[1] Following Swarthmore, fossil fuel divestment campaigns began to emerge across the United States. In Fall 2011, Unity College became the first university to divest from fossil fuels. In 2012, in partnership with dozens of other organizations, the international climate justice grassroots non-profit, 350.org launched the *Do the Math Tour* (350.org 2012). The tour aimed to take the divestment strategy, and the science, politics, economics and questions of justice and morality underpinning it, across the United States, and then across world. The tour succeeded beyond the expectations of many involved. Hundreds of campaigns popped up across the United States, and then around the globe in Europe, Australia, South Africa, the UK, South America, and more.

By 2013, the fossil fuel divestment movement had become the fastest growing divestment movement in history (Ansar et al. 2013). By the end of 2013, just over two years after the movement began, more than 70 institutions had committed to some form of fossil fuel divestment. Then, by September 2014, the number of commitments had more than doubled to 181 entities and 650 individuals with control over approximately $50 billion in total assets (Arabella Advisors 2014). Remarkably, by the time of the Paris Climate talks in December 2015, the total had risen to over 500 institutions representing $3.4 trillion worth of assets (Fitzgibbon 2015). By December of 2016, the number had almost doubled again with over 58,000 individuals, and 688 institutions, representing over $5 trillion in assets, making some form of fossil fuel divestment commitment (Arabella Advisors 2016).

Despite the fossil fuel divestment movement's remarkable growth and success, some still claim that divesting from the fossil fuel industry is a futile gesture that has little to no tangible impact in addressing climate change. Such a view has been espoused not only by fossil fuel industry lobby groups and consultants (Davidson 2015; Peterson 2015), but also by university administrators such as Harvard's President (Faust 2013); scholars such Robert Stavins (2015), and Christian Parenti (Parenti 2013); investments professionals; and influential figures such as Bill Gates (Lenferna 2015; Richardson 2015). Many of them argue that divestment, particularly the selling of shares in fossil fuel companies, will be ineffective, for if one institution or individual divests, then another will simply buy up those stocks and it will have no tangible impacts on the fossil fuel industry, end of story.

In response to these criticisms, in this paper, I offer a sympathetic yet critical appraisal of the fossil fuel divestment movement, which demonstrates its power and potential, while also highlighting its limitations. I argue that the divestment movement has been successful in stigmatizing and exposing the injustices of the fossil fuel industry; raising broad awareness of the financially and ecologically unsustainable nature of the fossil fuel industry business model; shifting financial norms and financial capital away from fossil fuels; elevating morality and justice in climate change discourse; and helping build a broader more powerful climate justice movement. I then consider some of the divestment movement's limitations and argue that the movement can leverage the power it has built and improve upon some of its limitations through: an increased focus on direct financiers of fossil fuels, like banks; pushing for regulations of the financial sector and the fossil fuel industry; and wielding the political power created by the divestment movement to pursue policy changes and more directly politically engaged activism.

As a scholar and an advocate who has been heavily involved in the climate justice and divestment movement, my views are shaped by and indebted to many people in both overlapping movements. Alongside broader climate justice research and advocacy, I have written and researched extensively on fossil fuel divestment; been involved and helped lead divestment campaigns targeted at the University of Washington, the city of Seattle, the Seattle City Employees Retirement System, the Bill and Melinda Gates Foundation, and a range of banks. I have also worked as a research consultant for 350.org in support of divestment campaigns across the globe. As such, I do not claim to come to this from an uninfluenced perspective, but I do hope to balance personal bias with experience, research, and a survey of the literature on divestment, to critically weigh both the power and the limitations of fossil fuel divestment and the fossil fuel divestment movement.

The divestment stigma

The fossil fuel divestment movement is far from monolithic and top-down, as some fossil fuel industry funded, ideologically driven "scholars" have suggested.[2] Rather, it is a sprawling grassroots movement with many different ideological viewpoints, approaches, perspectives, and disagreements. Thus, to delineate its aims is not a straightforward task. Nonetheless, drawing on the growing literature on the movement, and the testimony of many activists, it is safe to conclude that one of the major aims of the divestment movement has been to stigmatize the fossil fuel industry.

By bringing to light the fossil fuel industry's deeply unsustainable business model, and exposing its problematic practices of spreading misinformation, harming communities, and lobbying against progress on climate change, environmental justice, and clean energy, the divestment movement aimed to unleash a wave of public revolt against the most profitable and harmful industry on the planet. The aim has been to remove the social licence of the fossil fuel industry, creating a stigma that would open the door for broader restrictive legislation and create broader shifts in political, social, moral, and even financial norms.

History shows the tactic of divestment to be effective in creating powerful stigma. Oxford University's Stranded Assets Programme released an influential report that overviewed the history of other divestment campaigns and found that stigmatization was one of their most potent effects. As their report highlighted, in almost every divestment campaign "from adult services to Darfur, from tobacco to South Africa, divestment campaigns were successful in lobbying for restrictive legislation affecting stigmatised firms" (2013, p.14). It seems unlikely that fossil fuel divestment will prove to be an exception to this trend given that it is the fastest growing divestment movement in history.

While there has not yet been a social science study to determine just how effective divestment has been in driving stigmatization, there are increasing examples, many within the fossil fuel industry itself, of increased stigmatization. Most prominent among them is Shell's CEO Ben Van Beurden warning that "societal acceptance of the energy system as we have it is disappearing" such that "trust had been eroded to a point where it starts to become a serious issue for [the fossil fuel industry's] long term future" (Geman 2017).

As Van Beurden's quote highlights, divestment is succeeding in creating a growing reputational risk for companies deemed to fall on "the wrong side of history" to use the words of divestment activists. As Hunt et al. highlight, 50–70% of a firm's value can be attributable to their name and goodwill. As such, the risk of reputational defamation from divestment can serve as "motivation for ethical behavior by high profile firms" (Hunt et al. 2016, p.71).[3]

For instance, NRG Energy Inc, a company that built a leading electricity business from coal and other conventional power plants, announced that it is aiming to reduce its carbon emissions 50% by 2030 and 90% by 2050. In making the decision, NRG's CEO stated specifically that "if divestment from fossil fuel companies becomes the issue that preoccupies college campuses around America for the next decade", then he doesn't "relish the idea that year after year we're going to be graduating a couple million kids from college, who are going to be American consumers for the next 60 or 70 years, that come out of college with a distaste or disdain for companies like [his]" (Cardwell 2014).[4]

While the fossil fuel industry's business model is deeply out of line with needed climate action, and has only made tokenistic investments in clean energy, the increased stigma is driving them increasingly to at least try and demonstrate the semblance of aligning with a clean energy, climate friendly future, even if it often does so in ways which are deeply inadequate, misleading, and tokenistic (cf. Carrington 2016). More broadly divestment is creating a stigma, which is driving broader socio-political shifts, as we will explore in section three. As the next section explores, divestment's stigma is also exposing the major financial risks that the fossil fuel industry faces, which has been significantly impacting views of whether they will be an ongoing, financially viable industry moving into the future.

Exposing the carbon bubble

Unlike previous divestment campaigns, such as those aimed at tobacco and South Africa apartheid, the fossil fuel divestment stigmatization is also aimed at exposing the financially unsustainable nature of the fossil fuel industry's collective business model. More specifically, drawing on the sophisticated work of financial analysts, divestment activists have been exposing a financial bubble underpinning the fossil fuel industry to the light of day, and bubbles, when exposed to the sun, tend to pop. As one of the prominent members of the divestment movement, Daniel Apfel, observes, "in no other situation has a financial argument been tied so tightly to a divestment case" (Apfel 2015, p.929).

The carbon bubble, now popularized by the divestment movement among other actors, refers to the realization that the vast majority of coal, oil and gas reserves of listed fossil fuel firms are unburnable if we are to act in alignment with internationally agreed upon targets of keeping global warming well below 2°C above pre-industrial levels with the safer aspirational target of 1.5°C. For instance, 60–80% of coal, oil and gas reserves of listed fossil fuel firms are unburnable to stand a likely chance of keeping warming below 2°C, never mind well below it (CTI 2013). To put a financial number on the amount of reserves that would be unburnable, Kepler Chevreux estimates that adhering to the 2°C target would result in $28 trillion in lost revenue for the fossil fuel industry in just the next two decades, with the oil industry accounting for $19.3trn, gas $4trn, and coal $4.9trn (Lewis 2014). In the longer term, Citibank estimates over $100 trillion in lost revenue by 2050 (Citi 2014). Recognition of the carbon bubble has led the likes of British Energy Secretary Ed Davey to call fossil fuels "the sub-prime assets of the future" (Godsen 2014).

Despite having enough oil, gas and, coal already either in production or being developed, to take the global temperature rise well beyond 2°C (Muttitt 2017), the fossil fuel industry was spending approximately 1% of global GDP just on developing even more *new* unburnable reserves (CTI 2013). In a tragic turn of irony that was about the same amount of money that the both the Stern Report on the Economics of Climate (2007) and the International Energy Agency (2014) estimated is required to invest in the clean economy in order to stay below the 2°C target.[5] Economist Anatole Kaletsky (2015) has referred to this as "one of the greatest misallocations of capital in history" and has argued that the proper recognition of this should lead big oil to self-liquidate and put itself out of business.

The carbon bubble has been central to much divestment activism since early on in the movement, and particularly since the publication of the seminal *Rolling Stone* piece: 'Global Warming's Terrifying Math', by prominent divestment and climate activist Bill McKibben (2012). The carbon bubble often served a dual role. First, as an underlying moral reason for why investment in the fossil fuel industry's business model is immoral, as its successful fulfilment would entail climate chaos. Second, the carbon bubble served as a financial reason for not investing, for if the global community is successful in acting on climate, the fossil fuel business model would fail. As Ayling and Gunningham (2015, p.135) highlight, "the movement seeks to raise the spectre of asset stranding while at the same time, by encouraging divestment, trying to increase the likelihood of that stranding – in other words, to make asset stranding a self-fulfilling prophecy".[6]

Not only does the carbon bubble make the future of the fossil fuel industry look potentially bleak, divestment activists have also been drawing attention to evidence which illustrates that institutions who divested from fossil fuels over the last decade would have done potentially just as well financially, if not significantly better than those who hadn't. The fossil fuel industry has already been underperforming in the broader market, and is set to potentially take on significant losses, due to a combination of factors, including the rapid decrease of alternative energy costs, increasing costs of fossil fuel extraction, lower fossil fuel prices, fossil fuel price volatility, increases in energy efficiency, changing social norms, increased environmental regulation, and suppressed growth of demand for fossil fuels in key economies (Lenferna 2014a; Geddes et al. 2014; MSCI 2013; Gunther 2015; Paun et al. 2015). Recognition of these trends, driven in part by the fossil fuel divestment movement, has led to a remarkable shift in thinking about fossil free investing over the last few years, from being virtually unheard of in 2011, to over a quarter of institutional investors having begun divesting from fossil fuels, with three quarters believing divesting will not affect returns (Demasters 2017).

Apart from drawing attention to the fossil fuel industry's ecologically and financially unsustainable business model, divestment activists are also drawing significant attention to the rapid progress in clean energy technologies, shining a spotlight on what the fossil fuel industry is working so hard to keep from being widely known – that a clean energy future is increasingly preferable to the fossil fuel status quo in terms of jobs, energy access, energy costs, health, wealth, and environmental integrity (Lenferna 2018; Roberts 2015a; Supran 2015). By stigmatizing the fossil fuel industry and elevating the success and emerging economic dominance of the clean energy industry, the divestment movement is playing a significant role in influencing the sentiments that guide investments and pushing investments away from the fossil fuel industry, and into clean energy and other sectors of the market.

Even though many divestment activists argue that the aim of their campaigns is not to directly impact the financial valuation of the fossil fuel industry, recent evidence suggests that they may be doing so nonetheless. A study by the University of Waterloo's Truzaar Dordi, measured the impacts of fossil fuel divestment announcements on the valuation of fossil fuel companies. It found that divestment does have a significant negative impact on fossil fuel firm valuation. More specifically, Dordi's analysis demonstrated that announcements of fossil fuel divestment negatively impacted the share price of fossil fuel firms, demonstrating that "the financial market perceives divestment and related events to be a material threat to the performance of fossil fuel firms" (Dordi 2016, p.iii).[7] Truzaar's study provides evidence that fossil fuel divestment is materially affecting the fossil fuel industry through direct impacts on their share prices, which runs contrary to previous literature which claimed that divestment does not have significant direct impacts on fossil fuel company valuation (cf. Ansar et al. 2013). The impacts of divestment, however, are much larger than can be measured by the day-to-day fluctuations of the stock market, and instead require a broader perspective on possible impacts.

According to Nobel Prize-winning economists Robert Shiller and George Akerlof (2009), our economies and financial systems are driven significantly by emotions, psychology, and perception. These jointly make up what are referred to as animal spirits, a Keynesian term used to describe the psychological state of investors that drives economic activity in spite of uncertainty (Pilkington 2014). By changing our perceptions of the future of fossil fuel industry, and influencing investor and societal sentiment about fossil fuels, divestment has the potential to significantly shift those animal spirits. Of course, many divestment players are relatively small players in the financial world, but as Nathaniel Bullard, the Global Head of Executive Insights at Bloomberg New Energy Finance, points out, fossil fuel divestment is drawing attention to carbon asset risk and is causing much larger investors to rethink the wisdom of staying invested in fossil fuels (Adler 2014). As Bill McKibben (2016) points out, divestment efforts "have driven the necessity of keeping carbon underground from the fringes into the heart of the world's establishment" into places as diverse as the G20, the world's major churches, the Bank of England, major universities across the globe, the world's largest pension funds, and more. Similarly, Daniel Apfel highlights that "the volume of published articles that simultaneously reference the divestment campaign and the risks of investing in fossil fuels ... leads us to believe that these campaigns are beginning to influence the financial industry's thinking on climate change" (Apfel 2015, p.932).

Divestment does not only impact the current valuation of fossil fuel companies but also its potential to leverage capital for future expansion. According to a research report from HSBC Bank, substantial divestment would create "less demand for shares and bonds, [which] ultimately increases the cost of capital to companies and limits the ability to finance expensive projects, which is particularly damaging in a sector where projects are inherently long term" (Paun et al. 2015, p.19).[8] This ability to limit finance is a crucial element of climate action, given the need to prevent new investments in fossil fuel infrastructure, and avoid the social, financial, and political lock-in they create (Erickson et al. 2015). This provides a stark rebuttal to Christian Parenti's (2013) claims that divestment will be unable to materially injure fossil fuel companies, slow their rate of extraction, or keep unburnable reserves in the ground. Additionally, these impacts may most determinately affect the financing of fossil fuels that most need to be kept in the ground. As Ansar et al. (2013, p.131) highlight, the oil and gas sector make up about 11% of the S&P 500, it has a broad range of shareholders, and is highly liquid. As such, they argue that the financial impacts of divestment will likely be most hard felt in more expensive and marginal projects in the oil and gas sector, as well as in the coal sector, given that it is much smaller, financially vulnerable, and fragmented. This points to somewhat of an alignment between the ethics and economics of divestment, insofar as coal and marginal oil and gas projects that are more resource, greenhouse gas, and capital intensive are the sectors of the fossil fuel industry that are least compatible with staying within the carbon budget (McGlade & Ekins 2015; Lenferna 2017a).

The fossil fuel industry has attempted to obscure the truth about the impacts that the divestment movement is having on them, as part of their broader offensive against the fossil fuel divestment movement (Carrington 2015; Ayling 2017). For instance, the World Coal Association (2014) wrote a report which argued that "divestment does nothing to affect the demand for or use of fossil fuels". However, their public relations poker face was belied by a February 2015 filing with the Securities and Exchange Commission by Peabody Coal, at the time the largest member of the World Coal Association and the largest private coal company in the world. In Peabody's filing, where they are legally required to be honest about the potential risks they face, Peabody acknowledged (in bold print) that the divestment movement was a threat:

> Concerns about the environmental impacts of coal combustion, including perceived impacts on global climate issues, are resulting in increased regulation of coal combustion in many jurisdictions, unfavorable lending policies by government-backed lending institutions and development banks toward the financing of new overseas coal-fueled power plants and divestment efforts affecting the investment community, which could significantly affect demand for our products or our securities.
>
> (Peabody Energy Corporation 2015, p.29)

Not long after issuing their concerns about the divestment movement, Peabody, along with much of the U.S. coal industry, went bankrupt, leaving behind a trail of pollution, debt, and lost jobs, in contrast to handsomely rewarded executives who cashed out while riding the company into the ground (Lenferna 2017b). While the decline of the coal industry cannot, of course, be attributed to divestment alone, it provides an example of the way that divestment might contribute to a perfect storm of factors, which can significantly constrain and potentially (morally and financially) bankrupt an industry.

Not only are divestment activists helping moving money out of the fossil fuel industry, many are also pushing for re-investment into clean energy. Many of the early wins of the divestment movement involved commitments by institutions to invest in clean energy, as often this was seen as less controversial than divestment. For instance, at the University of Washington one of our divestment campaigns earlier wins was a commitment to increasing investments in the clean energy sector. This shift of investments out of fossil fuels into renewable energy is needed to stave off the worst effects of climate change. As the latest Intergovernmental Panel on Climate Change (IPCC) report highlights, if we are to achieve the target of keeping warming well below 2°C above pre-industrial levels, we will need to reduce annual investment in fossil fuels by at least $30 billion dollars per year over the coming decades *and* increase annual investment in low carbon electricity supply by $147 billion a year (IPCC 2014, p.27).

Beyond re-investing into clean energy, there is a growing call for reinvested funds to be dedicated to a just transition away from fossil fuels, and more broadly to investments that are beneficial to communities and people, rather than simply directed at profit (Ressler & Schellentrager 2011; Coronel et al. 2016; Healy & Barry 2017). For instance, the divest and reinvestment work of the Hip Hop Caucus, is focusing on redirecting funds in ways that concentrate on revitalizing communities, particularly the most vulnerable, as embodied in their Revitalize Vulnerable Communities project (Ali 2017). Other activists have been pushing for reforms in the way cities bank. For instance, as Oscar Abello (2017) reports, increasing numbers of divestment campaigns are asking cities to revisit public banks and financing. The City of Portland decided to divest from corporations altogether and instead reinvest its holdings into community projects (Ludwig 2017).

For those who argue that divestment of shares and equities does not address those who directly finance fossil fuels, there is a growing movement to target banks and other more direct financiers. While banks are much larger institutions than most typical divestment targets, because fossil fuels make up a relatively small percentage of a bank's investments, activists aim to stigmatize those investments and expose their poor financial prospects, to make them not worth the reputational and financial risk. While Hunt et al. (2016) note that it was surprising that the movement hadn't targeted banks much, within the divestment movement there is an increasing shift to doing just that. Targeting banks is not new either, as there is a history activists focusing on banks and other financiers (Alexander et al. 2014, p.7). For instance, the group Market Forces, targets banks, superannuation funds, and government subsidies. The move to target banks has been most prominent in Australia. For instance, activists, working alongside economic forces, have made it such that no major Australian banks would fund the Adani Carmichael coal project – what would have been Australia's largest ever coal mine (Burton 2017). This follows on a trend of a growing number of banks that are committing to reduce and/or end their financing of new coal projects, many citing pressure from divestment activists as part of their reason (Reuters 2015; Corkery 2016).

Beyond coal, a growing number of divestment movements are targeting banks for their financing of oil and gas projects. In response to divestment activist pressure, U.S. Bank recently became the first bank to commit to no project level financing of oil and gas pipelines, a step towards stopping funding pipelines altogether (Last Real Indians 2017). Similarly, Seattle, where the author is based, became the first city to commit to stop banking with Wells Fargo because of its funding of the Dakota Access Pipeline (Mapes 2017b). Local activists also organized a mass civil disobedience against JP Morgan Chase for its financing of the Keystone Pipeline (Mapes 2017a). These actions have been led by local groups such as 350 Seattle, and *Mazaska Talks*, a coalition including over 150 First Nations and Tribes of the Treaty Alliance Against Tar Sands Expansion, which are demanding that banks divest from the companies building the Dakota Access pipeline and four other proposed Canadian tar sands pipelines.

Divestment has turned the minds of communities, activists, and some of the world's youngest and brightest minds at universities across the globe, towards critically examining one of the greatest failings of the financial sector. The critical attention that the divestment movement has helped draw to the financial sector provides fertile grounds for broader reform beyond just climate justice concerns. While the divestment movement, so far, has done a lot to help redirect the investments of existing financial institutions, the political power it creates also helps open the possibility to enact changes to the financial sector itself and the rules that govern it. Looking forward, as Benjamin Richardson (2017) argues, an important and under-explored direction for the divestment movement is to harness its power to effect broader changes to the financial sector, including to how it is governed and regulated regarding climate change, the carbon bubble, and other environmental and social issues. One of the important tools it can use to effect this change, as highlighted by Benjamin Franta (2017), is through litigation.

So far, this survey of the evidence shows that divestment is having significant impacts on the financial sector and has the potential to be one factor among many others, which hastens the necessary decline of the fossil fuel industry and reinvestment into a more just, clean energy transition. However, it is important to not overly celebrate the financial impacts that divestment is having, as the global community is not decreasing fossil fuel investments and increasing clean energy investments at the speed needed to align with keeping global warming to 2°C, never mind well below it (Figueres et al. 2017; Sussams & Leaton 2017). Looking forward, it is crucial to identify what are the most powerful leveraging points in policy, politics, and economics, which can increase the rate of divestment and reinvestment to what is required to avert dangerous climate change. A significant part of ensuring that this occurs, is driving a broader moral, social, and cultural shift, which can create the necessary environment to drive forward the rapid action needed – something that the divestment movement has also been contributing to, as the next section explores.

Transformative social change

For many divestment activists, the impact of their work is intended to be much broader than just affecting financial markets. A major part of the aim of the divestment movement is to lay the grounds for what Mark and Paul Engler refer to as transformative social change, "which attempts to alter the climate of public debate to make much more far-reaching changes possible" (Engler & Engler 2016). To create the possibility of transformational change, the movement aims to transform the social, moral, and political norms around fossil fuels, clean energy, climate change, and environmental justice (Yona & Lenferna 2016; Grady-Benson & Sarathy 2015). As climate journalist David Roberts (2015b) points out, part of that shift involves both problematizing and contesting the legitimacy of the old order and envisioning a new better future.

One of the fossil fuel divestment movement's significant strengths in bringing about transformative social change, lies in its framing of the problem of climate change as a moral issue. As Ayling and Gunningham (2015, p.132) highlight, the divestment movement's arguments rely heavily and primarily on claims of morality. Part of this is a strategy both implicit and explicit, to act as a norm entrepreneur, shifting the moral norms of society so that fossil fuels and the harms they bring are increasingly seen to be immoral. As research by Yale and George Mason universities suggests, doing so is perhaps one of the most important ways to motivate many people to take climate action, as large sectors of the American public who do not currently feel that climate change is a dangerous and very present threat can be convinced of the necessity of action if the issue is presented as a moral one (Roser-Renouf et al. 2016).

The importance of moral framing is well recognized within the fossil fuel divestment movement. For instance, Fossil Free MIT's Geoffrey Supran (2015) argues that by taking climate change out of technocratic discourse and bringing the deeply moral nature of the climate crisis to the fore, divestment activists are shifting the predominate technocratic and wonky climate narrative into a moral imperative for action arguing that the fossil fuel industry, and those who oppose such action, are firmly "on the wrong side of history". Divestment activists argue that we have a moral responsibility to reject the climate instability, pollution, corruption and violence that is associated with the trajectory that the fossil fuel industry business model entails. In it stead, we have a moral responsibility to move rapidly towards the more prosperous and just future that is possible if we align our economies with needed climate action (Lenferna 2018; Ullmann 2013; Moss 2017). To quote Bratman et al., "the divestment movement aims to transform the discussion of climate change from a technocratic analysis of carbon emissions to a human-centered narrative calling for systemic change that is both social and economic" (Bratman et al. 2016, p.680).

Divestment activists are helping reshape the climate narrative as one of justice, by exposing and challenging the deep injustices, power imbalances, and inequalities underlying the climate issue, and showing the intersection between other forms of justice, such as racial, global and social justice. A broad trend within many fossil fuel divestment groups is their aspiration to work in solidarity with grassroots climate justice movements and to centre environmental justice (Bratman et al. 2016; Healy & Debski 2016; Grady-Benson & Sarathy 2015). The aim is to highlight fossil fuel divestment as not just a climate change issue, but as a climate justice issue (Schlosberg & Collins 2014). This involves looking at how the fossil fuel industry's contribution to climate change and other harms, such as air and water pollution, disproportionately impact people of colour, indigenous communities, young people, future generations, and the Global South. This broader justice-based and intersectional analysis has often helped to create a broader and more inclusive movement, bringing in those who did not traditionally view themselves as environmentalists (Bratman et al. 2016, p.682).

Divestment has also helped challenge an individualistic, depoliticized, often business-friendly sustainability politics prevalent across society, and in many higher education institutions (cf. Bratman et al. 2016; Healy & Debski 2016; Grady-Benson & Sarathy 2015). In its stead, many in the divestment movement provide an analysis that is more focused on structural, systemic, and political factors driving the climate crisis – factors which are, in many ways, more consequential than the traditional, individualistic focus on emission reductions. The more structural analysis adopted by many in the divestment movement also provides an answer to those who argue that it is hypocritical for students who are reliant on fossil fuels to argue for fossil fuel divestment (cf. Coplan 2016, p.283). For many, the aim of the movement is not about ending individual fossil fuel use in the immediate future, but rather about making the necessary systemic and structural shifts, which will allow us to move rapidly towards a low carbon future. While it is of course preferable if individuals reduce their emissions, the sorts of shifts required to tackle the climate crisis are at a much more comprehensive, structural, and sweeping scale than just individual consumer decisions can shift (Cuomo 2011; Lukacs 2017).

As Healy and Barry argue, "divestment, in calling for a full 'life-cycle' political economy analysis of energy draws attention to the full range of actors, dynamics and interests that are behind energy extraction, production and final use" (2017, p.453). Through reckoning with the political economy of the climate crisis and the fossil fuel industry, the divestment and climate justice movement together have the potential to drive significant shifts. According to Rowe, Dempsey and Gibbs (2016), the divestment movement has played a powerful role in challenging the intertwined political and corporate structures, which hold the current deeply problematic energy regime in place. Drawing on Antonio Gramsci's work in social movement theory, they argue that the divestment movement is undercutting the necessary social consent, which allows elite hierarchical power structures like the fossil fuel industry to remain in place. By doing so, they claim the divestment movement could create dramatic and unpredictable shifts to the social, legal, and economic order that props up the fossil fuel industry.

As a social science study by Schifeling and Hoffman (2017) found, within the United States the divestment movement was successful in shifting public discourse towards discussing solutions to climate change. Their study shows that the divestment movement was successful in driving what they refer to as a positive radical flank effect, where the relatively more radical demands of the divestment movement helped re-centre the U.S. climate debate towards a discussion of alternative solutions for climate change, and away from the previously more dominant framing of whether or not we should do something altogether.[9] They found, for instance, that "liberal policy ideas (such as a carbon tax), which had previously been marginalized in the U.S. debate, gained increased attention and legitimacy" as a result of the divestment movement's influence.

While it is difficult to more broadly estimate the extent of influence the divestment movement has, and could have, in driving societal shifts away from fossil fuels, when leading cultural, financial, educational, and religious institutions and investors denounce the old order and make commitments to a clean energy future, it arguably draws such a future increasingly into the realm of the possible and helps to mobilize broader action towards that goal. The power that this shift can have in addressing climate change becomes clearer if we look to the context within which divestment is situated. Increasingly, clean energy and climate action are inhibited not by being expensive or technically infeasible, rather it is held back by political obstacles from entrenched interests. This point is succinctly highlighted in the following quote from a Wuppertal Institute for Climate Environment and Energy Report entitled *Towards a Global Energy Transformation*:

> Only rarely are there immutable facts or technical conflicts that impede or even prevent the expansion of renewable energy. Instead, long-established structures and elites problematize the challenges of an energy transformation and sustain the existing system and their own (market) power with corresponding narratives. The success of an energy transformation will depend on whether a broad alliance of civil society, politics, science, and industry develops a convincing alternative and positive narratives – and implements them against resistances.
>
> (Kofler et al. 2014, p.2)

The divestment movement has become one important part of the broad alliance that is developing positive alternative visions and implementing them against the resistance of the fossil fuel industry. It is helping to highlight and erode the corrupting influence of the recalcitrant fossil fuel industry, redefine our social imaginary, develop positive alternative narratives and inspire hope about the possibility of a low carbon future. And hope, as environmental philosopher Byron Williston (2012, p.183) points out, "can cause us to turn our energies aggressively" to bringing about the desired outcome. Of course, divestment alone is not sufficient to drive the needed action, but it has proven to be a powerful tool in driving the broader cultural shifts needed to drive a rapid transition.

The limits of shareholder engagement

There are those who admit that the divestment strategy might have some power, but who worry that, by divesting, conscientiously minded investors are giving up on the possibility to continue to influence corporations through shareholder engagement. In brief, shareholder engagement entails using one's voice as shareholder to request information from and change to companies. Institutions, including non-profits, pension funds, and universities (such as the Wellcome Trust, the Seattle City Employees Retirement System, and Harvard University), have argued that instead of divesting they should retain their investments in fossil fuel companies so that they can engage in shareholder advocacy (Grady-Benson & Sarathy 2015).

When contemplating the efficacy of engagement, it is important to recognize that organizations like Ceres, As You Sow, and Arjuna Capital have been successful in using shareholder engagement in important ways. They have been working hard to help try change practices, incentives, and leadership within fossil fuel companies. The major progress that has come from their shareholder engagement, has been that fossil fuel companies are beginning to disclose how they plan to address climate change and the carbon bubble (Cleveland 2017). While disclosure is an important step in helping us understand and evaluate the fossil fuel industry, in most cases it seems that the response of those companies is to simply declare that they plan to push way passed climate change targets, claiming that the world will continue to need fossil fuels based on their own self-serving projections of the future energy mix. For instance, a recent report from ShareAction, shows that two years after BP and Shell shareholders voted resoundingly in favour of forcing the companies to make detailed disclosures about climate risks, the companies are still planning for global temperatures to rise as much as 5°C (Chapman 2017).

Apart from being wildly out of line with needed climate action, another problem with such disclosures, is that fossil fuel companies use them to shape broader discourses around energy and turn them into self-fulfilling prophecies, which serve the interests of fossil fuel companies (Muttitt 2017). Indeed, fossil fuel companies work very hard to ensure their vision of the future comes into existence by spreading misinformation, corrupting political systems, and lobbying against the sort of progress needed to act on climate change (Conway & Oreskes 2010; McKinnon 2016). Despite decades of some of the most sustained and concerted shareholder efforts on climate change, fossil fuel companies continue to flout international climate agreements, spread misinformation, and lobby against climate progress.

A recent overview of shareholder engagement efforts from 2012–2016 shows its influence to be modest and limited in reach, with the slowness of engagement posing significant limitations given the urgency of addressing accelerating climate risk (Griep 2016). Another review of shareholder engagement by Ivar Kolstad, demonstrates that many of the reasons for favouring shareholder engagement over divestment are open to challenge, such that it is possible that "the move towards more engagement reflects bureaucratic incentives and political considerations among institutional investors, rather than arguments about the effectiveness and efficiency of engagement" (Kolstad 2015, p.45).

As Surbhi Sarang (2016, p.320) and many divestment activists have pointed out, shareholder activism has principally pursued firm disclosure, but addressing climate change will require fossil fuel companies to change their fundamental business plan. However, the rules of shareholder engagement stack the deck against the sort of progress needed. The Securities and Exchange Commission (SEC) restricts shareholders from engaging with firms on operational issues and limits shareholder engagement to "requesting information and attempting to engender change in corporate policies on related issues, but does not allow shareholders to modify the business model or to engage with firms directly on the problem of keeping oil reserves in the ground". Thus, while engagement may be good at requesting information or making changes at the margin, it is not particularly effective at shifting the core business models of companies.

As Former SEC Commissioner Bevis Longstreth (2014) points out, "in regard to fossil fuel companies directly engaged in extractive activities, it is unrealistic to imagine them being swayed by shareholder arguments to get out of their core business of exploring for, extracting and selling carbon-emitting fuel". Longstreth argues that engagement may in fact provide fossil fuel companies with "the protective cover they need to stretch out the transition process to renewables for as long as they can". Thus, while shareholder engagement has played a positive role in several contexts, the balance of evidence suggests that the approach of indefinite shareholder engagement may not be sufficient either to protect investments against the rapid unfurling of the carbon bubble, or to move fossil fuel companies in the right direction in the short amount of time we have left to address the climate crisis. Indeed, after more than 20 years of engagement with fossil fuel companies, it is does not seem as if protracted shareholder engagement is up to the task of shifting the business model of the fossil fuel industry in the time we have available.

In the words of Dempsey and Gibbs, the theory of change behind shareholder engagement (and other attempts to achieve changes through polite dialogue with the fossil fuel industry) represent "a fantastical reading of political change, one where the different players can find common ground through earnest dialogue (no matter how asymmetrical the power differentials are)" (2016). Such a view of political change fails to grapple with how the fossil fuel industry uses its power and influence to corrupt climate progress, while often using shareholder engagement, corporate disclosures, and other corporate engagement arenas, as smokescreens and greenwashing forums to present the image that they are taking climate change seriously.

However, despite shareholder engagement's limitations, it is not an all or nothing game for divestment or shareholder engagement. To combine the strengths of divestment and engagement, an institution could follow the example of the Rockefeller Brothers Foundation or the Unitarian Universalist Church, who are engaging in a form of conditional divestment, where one divests all but the minimum stocks needed to engage as a shareholder. This could perhaps be coupled with conditional reinvestment if a company subsequently illustrates its compliance with needed climate action. Alternatively, researchers at Oxford and Cambridge have argued that shareholders who choose to engage could issue deadlines by which they expect companies to demonstrate their compliance with the carbon budget, which if not fulfilled would then result in divestment from non-compliant companies (Covington & Thamotheram 2015a; Covington & Thamotheram 2015b). Seemingly heeding their advice, the $14.7 billion Swedish AP4 fund made a commitment that by 2020, their pension fund will pull money from businesses that lack plans or provide inadequate proposals demonstrating their alignment with keeping global warming well below 2°C (Flood 2016).

A combined approach of divestment and shareholder engagement could provide both a carrot through shareholder engagement and the stick of divestment, which together could be more powerful than either strategy on its own. However, the strategy of indefinite engagement, may provide indefinite cover to fossil fuel companies who can then claim they are working on these issues and leach off the credibility of the organizations they are engaging with to lend themselves unwarranted legitimacy. It is also worth considering that, particularly for institutions such as churches and mission-oriented non-profits, using shareholder engagement is somewhat akin to fitting a round peg in a square hole, as the strength of their voice would come from their moral voice, something which is all but precluded from shareholder engagement.

Recognizing the urgency of the climate crisis, and the way that working strictly within the system and in partnership with fossil fuel companies has greatly slowed down needed progress on climate change, much of the fossil fuel divestment movement is informed by the insights of the likes of former dean of the Yale School of Forestry and Environmental Studies Gus Speth (2015) who points out that "we can no longer hope to address the climate crisis, or our deep social ills, by working strictly within the system". That's not to say there is no place for working within the system – or in the case of shareholder engagement, strictly in the con- fines of SEC shareholder engagement limitations – but it is to say that rigid and limited approaches like shareholder engagement are not adequate by themselves to address the scale and urgency of this crisis.

Building on the limitations of divestment

Of course, divestment also has limitations, and divestment alone will not solve the climate crisis. Thus, proportionate amounts of time should be dedicated to divest- ment, such that it does not draw too much energy from other climate change efforts. However, it is a straw-man to argue, as Bill Gates does, that divestment activists think divestment alone is going to solve the problem (Richardson 2015; Lenferna 2015).[10] Most activists are well aware that, similarly to how divestment did not by itself end South African apartheid, so fossil fuel divestment by itself will not fix the climate crisis (Massie 1997; Apfel 2015). Indeed, it is the synergy between divestment and the broader climate justice movement that can drive stronger political action.

Some, such as Scott Wisor, argue that the divestment movement is merely symbolic. As I have argued in response (Lenferna 2014b), what such an argu- ment fails to appreciate is the importance of symbolism in building transforma- tive movements (Engler & Engler 2016), as well as the broader non-symbolic effects that divestment brings about, as I have highlighted throughout this paper. As social movement theorists Engler and Engler argue, one of the most critical elements of pushing forward transformative change for a movement are its sym- bolic properties, and "how well a demand serves to dramatize for the public the urgent need to remedy an injustice" (Engler & Engler 2016). Thus, while many have argued against divestment as merely symbolic, they have failed to appreci- ate both its broader non-symbolic impacts and the power of its symbolic impacts.

Of course, any movement must complement symbolic movement building activism with concrete instrumental actions. Wisor worries that this will not occur and argues that divestment leads to complacency and inaction (cf. Wisor 2014). However, such a claim has not been empirically substantiated, and experience from divestment activists often suggests quite the opposite. In many cases the movement is a solidarity tactic, which explicitly aims to bolster broader climate action and to grow the climate justice movement. Divestment activists have also been activists and leaders within important movements, such as Shell No, and the fight against the Keystone and the Dakota Access pipelines, and in many instances divestment activists have stood in solidarity with these and other indigenous-led climate action, civil disobedience, and broader climate justice struggles movement (Yona & Lenferna 2016; Grady-Benson & Sarathy 2015).

Similarly, for those who claim that divestment activists should focus on the practice of politics and of putting in place serious policies to address climate change, there is much evidence to suggest that divestment activists and alumni are doing just that. For instance, in Washington State divestment activists played a leading role in the effort to put the first carbon tax initiative in the United States on the ballot in 2016 (Clauson 2016). More broadly, divestment activists have gotten involved in campaigns to ban fracking, end fossil fuel subsidies, put a price on carbon, encourage renewable energy, and be key organizers in the climate justice movement. What this highlights, is that to a significant extent, the divestment movement is training a generation of highly politically engaged climate justice activists.

Another critique comes from a recent analysis of the fossil fuel divestment movement by Mayes, Richards and Woods. They argue that the movement "unwittingly reproduces neoliberalizing logics by reinforcing a shift away from the state as the key corporate regulator" (Mayes et al. 2017, p.12). The authors claim that by arguing that civil society, institutions, and businesses need to step up in the face of government failure, divestment activists have endorsed if not legitimated "the reduction of state responsibility in favour of increased responsibility on the part of civil society" (Mayes et al. 2017, p.140).

Mayes et al.'s analysis deserves attention, as *some* of the organizations and individuals involved in the divestment movement have reinforced somewhat of a neoliberal logic by elevating the importance of the actions of individuals, companies and institutions, while also not properly recognizing the importance of state action in addressing climate change, or not directly advocating for such action, or at times denigrating it (Elliott 2016; Alexander et al. 2014). However, Mayes et al.'s analysis does not quite engage with the rich ways many within the divestment movement are challenging a neoliberal framing, as was highlighted in the previous section. Indeed, the Fossil Fuel Divestment Student Network specifically developed an anti-neoliberal message in its trainings on divestment and reinvestment in a just transition.[11] Additionally, their offshoot organization, Sunrise, is specifically aimed at taking back political power and pushing back against fossil fuel industry influence on the state.[12]

For many activists, far from embracing neoliberalism, one of the primary aims of divestment was to build political power in response to the failure of government to act, so as to be able to drive government and policy action. As Stephen Zunes highlights, this is an important strategic route for many movements, to first build power through activism and taking to the streets, and to then fight for policy change wielding that political power (Ross & Lowery 2017). To a certain extent, the strategy seems to be working, for as Linnebluecke et al. highlight, "grassroots support through the divestment movement is rapidly spreading worldwide, creating stakeholder-driven support for action on climate change in addition to top-down policy measures. This confluence of the organisational and policy levels", they argue, "will see greater action on climate change" (2015, p.486). Of course, there is much more work to be done, particularly in the United States with the rise of a Trump administration rapidly dismantling progress on climate change. Particularly in this context, divestment activists would do well to reassess whether divestment is the most effective lever they have for change under such rapidly shifting circumstances.

Another critique of the divestment movement has been that it has taken place predominately in the developed world, and not as much in the developing world (Ayling & Gunningham 2015, p.142). In response, it is worth considering that this is, to a certain extent, how it should be. As ethicists Stephen Gardiner (2011) and Peter Singer (2010) point out, there is a broad consensus within the climate ethics literature that industrialized countries should take the lead in addressing climate change, both in reducing their emissions and in dealing with the negative impacts created by a problem, which they have been the predominant cause. Additionally, there is an emerging consensus that such countries should also take the lead in leaving fossil fuels in the ground too (Lenferna 2017a; Kartha et al. 2016). With many developed countries falling far behind their fair share of climate action and developing countries like China and India beginning to forge ahead with climate action, the developed world needs to move much faster and more aggressively if it is to uphold its fair share of emission reductions (Höhne et al. 2017).

Nonetheless, with developing countries starting to emit more than developed countries, the divestment movement, which has at times been somewhat local and domestic in its focus, should arguably pay more attention to global climate justice questions, and the need for enabling a just transition to clean energy in developing countries (EcoEquity 2015; Kartha et al. 2016; Caney 2016). This is particularly important as fossil fuel companies are aggressively trying to push into developing country markets, under the false guise of being the answer to energy poverty (Lenferna 2016; CTI 2014). This, to a certain extent, echoes how tobacco companies pushed aggressively into less regulated markets in the developing world following stigmatization and regulation in the developed world, in part thanks to divestment efforts. This is a question that arguably merits more attention, particularly in the U.S. context where funding to assist developing countries shift to a low carbon future has been reneged on by the Trump Administration (Mathiesen 2017).

Concluding thoughts on an unconcluded movement

To conclude, divestment has served as a clarion call for a generation of activists who have grown tired of inaction, and who are leveraging a range of tools available to them to take on the most powerful industry in the world, in the hope of winning one of the most consequential struggles of our time. The movement has achieved significant victories and has grown faster than any other divestment movement in history. It has helped create a cadre of climate justice advocates, many of whom cut their teeth on divestment campaigns, and are continuing to push for climate justice.

While it is difficult to precisely estimate just how effective the divestment movement itself has and will be in driving the changes necessary to stave off the climate crisis, that is part of the uncertainty of organizing for large sweeping social changes. To quote environmental journalist David Roberts (2015b): "Social change is nonlinear and devilishly hard to predict. But it seems far from futile or pointless. It seems like an important part of the most important fight in the world".

Looking forward, many participants are considering how much they want to double down and continue to push for divestment or shift tactics to embrace different strategies or struggles. With the time left to avert dangerous climate change dangerously short, looking to what are the most effective leverage points to enact change is incredibly important. Some in the movement are aiming to build off divestment's momentum by more directly targeting financiers of fossil fuels, like banks. Others are pushing for regulation, aimed at the financial sector and/or the polluting industries that have been the target of their divestment campaigns. Others are aiming to build political power to contest political spaces and politicians more directly.

While divestment as a strategy certainly has limitations and weak points, the movement has been a powerful force to be reckoned with. It is helping to shift significant amounts of capital away from the fossil fuel industry, while revoking its social licence, potentially laying the grounds for broader more transformational change. The movement has used its power to help reshape the climate narrative, to advance meaningful climate policies and action, and to build power for broader climate justice struggles. Divestment has been a powerful tool to expose and take on one of the most powerful industries in the world, and it has had a profound and lasting impact on the global struggle for climate justice.

Acknowledgments

For their helpful discussions, comments, and/or greatly helpful work, many thanks are due to Brett Fleishmann, Stephen Gardiner, Leehi Yona, Lauren Hartzell-Nichols, Alec Connon, Stefan Jacobsen, Michael Lazarus, Trace Lane, Jess Grady-Benson, Bruce Hebert, Mike McGinn, Lynn Fitz-Hugh, Kyle Murphy, Morgan Sinclaire, Angela Feng, Sarra Tekola, Bryce-Bartl Gellar, Ben Peterson, Jess Spear, Patrick Mazza, Caitlin Piserchia, Carter Case, Kaya Axelsson, Eric Godoy, Chloe Maxmin, members of Divest UW, 350.org (especially the Seattle branch), Mazaska Talks, the Divestment Student Network, and many others in the broader climate justice and fossil fuel divestment movements. A luta continua.

Notes

1 In the 1990s, Greenpeace had attempted to convince the insurance industry that investing in fossil fuels was a bad financial investment (Ayling & Gunningham 2015). This differs from the modern instantiation of fossil fuel divestment campaigns, who, like other divestment campaigns before them, relied not only on financial arguments, but

predominately on moral arguments. There was also another precursor to the modern divestment movement, when in 2000 Ozone Action targeted corporations that were part of the Global Climate Coalition, a group of corporations who jointly opposed climate action. The campaign helped lead to the dissolution of the coalition in 2002 (Mayes et al. 2017).

2   The National Associations of Scholars, a fossil fuel-industry funded right-wing think tank, released a report arguing that the divestment movement was a top-down illiberal movement (Peterson 2015). The report's claims are deeply inaccurate and not representative of the movement at all. The author seems to have deliberately ignored an overwhelming body of evidence unsuited to her line of argument, cherry-picking and distorting evidence to suit a very narrow ideologically driven argument. (I was interviewed for the report).

3   Kiyar and Wittneben wrote a paper examining whether divestment had directly and significantly influenced the decisions of the top four energy giants in Germany. They argued that other factors played a more significant role and that divestment wasn't yet as significant a factor. However, one of the factors that they did attribute to the decisions of the energy giants was how climate change had become "one of the most financially significant concerns facing investors" as pressure is increasing on companies "as investors express concerns about regulatory uncertainty …" (Kiyar & Wittneben 2015, p.9629). As Ansar et al. and the previous sections argues, this is precisely the sort of effect divestment can have. Thus, Kiyar and Wittneben may be taking somewhat of a limited view of the effects of divestment when they claim that divestment is not having a considerable influence. Just because it is not explicitly stated by decision makers, does not mean that divestment is not having an influence, even if it is indirect.

4   While subsequent NRG leadership has reversed course on NRG's leadership on clean energy, what this quote nonetheless demonstrates is that the divestment movement can affect the broader social norms and expectations regarding the future of fossil fuels.

5   Furthermore, fossil fuel companies have been increasingly investing in high-cost, carbon-intensive fossil fuels, such as oil sands and deep sea drilling, which for reasons of both equity and economic efficiency are not burnable in a low-carbon future (McGlade & Ekins 2015; Lenferna 2017a).

6   Sarang (2016) has explored how the recognition of the carbon bubble can lead to potential lawsuits and the possible development of a legal duty for institutions to divest from fossil fuels.

7   Truzaar's study measures the impacts of divestment on the days around the announcement of divestment, employing event study methodology.

8   Additionally, HSBC recommended investors consider divesting, warning that the fossil fuel industry is at serious and growing risk of stranded assets from climate policies and unfavourable economics, including reduced demand for fossil fuels and the rapid development of renewable energy and efficiency measures.

9   Although as Bill McKibben is fond of highlighting, the true radicals in this equation are those whose business models would fundamentally undermine the climate stability upon which our societies depend.

10 Of course, the divestment movement is not monolithic, and as Robin Xu (2015) highlights, there are some activists that should be careful about exaggerating the importance of divestment and decrying other important strategies to address climate change.

11 From author's involvement in Fossil Fuel Divestment Student Network trainings, and from materials on the Fossil Fuel Divestment Student Network website: http://www.studentsdivest.org/.

12 It is also worth noting that, at times, divestment activists adopt more neoliberal or economic messaging as part of a broad strategy of communication aimed to reach and influence audiences not typically swayed by more political, justice-based or moral messaging.

References

350.org, 2012. Do the Math Tour. *350.org*. Available at: http://math.350.org/ (2 May 2010).

Abello, O.P., 2017. Amid Divestment Protests, More Cities Explore Public Banks. *Next City*. Available at: https://nextcity.org/daily/entry/cities-form-public-banks-divestment-wells-fargo (10 May 2017).

Adler, B., 2014. The Divestment Movement is Gaining Steam. What Can It Achieve? *Grist*. Available at: http://grist.org/climate-energy/the-divestment-movement-is-gaining-steam-what-can-it-achieve/ (15 December 2014).

Alexander, S., Nicholson, K. & Wiseman, J., 2014. Fossil free: The development and significance of the fossil fuel divestment movement. *MSSI Issues Paper No. 3, Melbourne Sustainable Society Institute*, (4), pp.1–16. Available at: http://sustainable.unimelb.edu.au/sites/default/files/docs/MSSI-IssuesPaper-4_Divestment_2014.pdf (31 January 2018).

Ali, M., 2017. Real Talk with Mustafa Ali: Science, Environmental Justice, and Power. *Got Science*. Available at: http://damethad.com/blog/mustafa (31 January 2018).

Ansar, A., Caldecott, B. & Tilbury, J., 2013. Stranded Assets and the Fossil Fuel Divestment Campaign : What Does Divestment Mean for the Valuation of Fossil Fuel Assets?, Oxford. Available at: www.bsg.ox.ac.uk/stranded-assets-and-fossil-fuel-divestment-campaign-what-does-divestment-mean-valuation-fossil-fuel (31 January 2018).

Apfel, D.C., 2015. Exploring divestment as a strategy for change: an evaluation of the history, success, and challenges of fossil fuel divestment. *Social Research*, 82(4), pp.913–1050.

Arabella Advisors, 2014. Measuring the Global Fossil Fuel Divestment Movement. Available at: www.arabellaadvisors.com/wp-content/uploads/2014/09/Measuring-the-Global-Divestment-Movement.pdf (31 January 2018).

Arabella Advisors, 2016. The Global Fossil Fuel Divestment and Clean Energy Investment Movement. Available at: www.arabellaadvisors.com/wp-content/uploads/2016/12/Global_Divestment_Report_2016.pdf (31 January 2018).

Ayling, J., 2017. A Contest for Legitimacy: The Divestment Movement and the Fossil Fuel Industry. *Law and Policy*, (Accepted Article). Available at: http://onlinelibrary.wiley.com/doi/10.1111/lapo.12087/abstract (31 January 2018).

Ayling, J. & Gunningham, N., 2015. Non-state governance and climate policy: the fossil fuel divestment movement. *Climate Policy*, 3062(98), pp.1–15.

Bratman, E., Brunette, K., Shelly, D.C. & Nicholson, S., 2016. Justice is the goal: divestment as climate change resistance. *Journal of Environmental Studies and Sciences*, 6(4), pp.677–690. Available at: http://dx.doi.org/10.1007/s13412-016-0377-6.

Burton, B., 2017. Adani's Telling Meltdown Over Westpac's New Climate Policy. *Renew Economy*. Available at: http://reneweconomy.com.au/adanis-telling-meltdown-westpacs-new-climate-policy-14504/ (12 May 2017).

Caney, S., 2016. Climate change, equity, and stranded assets, Oxfam America Research Backgrounder series. Available at: www.oxfamamerica.org/explore (31 January 2018).

Cardwell, D., 2014. NRG Seeks to Cut 90% of Its Carbon Emissions. *The New York Times*. Available at: www.nytimes.com/2014/11/21/business/energy-environment/nrg-sets-goals-to-cut-carbon-emissions.html (21 November 2014).

Carrington, D., 2015. Carbon Reserves Held by Top Fossil Fuel Companies Soar. *The Guardian*. Available at: www.theguardian.com/environment/2015/apr/19/carbon-reserves-held-by-top-fossil-fuel-companies-soar (19 April 2015).

Carrington, D., 2016. Oil Firms Announce $1bn Climate Fund to Clean up Gas. *The Guardian*. Available at: www.theguardian.com/environment/2016/nov/04/oil-firms-announce-1bn-green-fund-as-paris-climate-deal-comes-into-force (15 December 2016).

Chapman, B., 2017. BP and Shell Planning for Catastrophic 5°C Global Warming Despite Publicly Backing Paris Climate Agreement. *The Independent*. Available at: www. independent.co.uk/news/business/news/bp-shell-oil-global-warming-5-degree-paris-climate-agreement-fossil-fuels-temperature-rise-a8022511.html (27 October 2017).

Citi, 2014. Energy 2020: The Revolution Will Not Be Televised as Disruptors Multiply. Available at: http://tecsol.blogs.com/files/citi--rapport-énergie-08-14.pdf (31 January 2018).

Clauson, D., 2016. Washington State Millenial Lead First-Ever Citizen's Led Initiative to Put a Price on Carbon. *National Geographic*. Available at: http://yearsoflivingdangerou sly.com/learn/news/washington-state-millennials-lead-first-ever-citizens-ballot-put-price-carbon/ (31 January 2018).

Cleveland, S., 2017. Investors Pressure ExxonMobil to Plan for Climate Risks. *Ceres*. Available at: www.ceres.org/news-center/blog/investors-pressure-exxonmobil-join-peers-planning-low-carbon-future (31 January 2018).

Conway, E.M. & Oreskes, N., 2010. *Merchants of Doubt*, New York: Bloomsbury Press.

Coplan, K.S., 2016. Fossil fuel abolition: legal and social issues. *Columbia Journal of Environmental Law*, 41(2), pp.223–312.

Corkery, M., 2016. As Coal's Future Grows Murkier, Banks Pull Financing. *The New York Times*. Available at: www.nytimes.com/2016/03/21/business/dealbook/as-coals-future-grows-murkier-banks-pull-financing.html (31 January 2018).

Coronel, B. et al., 2016. *Reinvestment Toolkit*. Available at: https://d3n8a8pro7vhmx. cloudfront.net/themes/550a18732213934e51000001/attachments/original/1463103231/ ToolkitForPriorityCampaigns.pdf (1 March 2017).

Covington, H. & Thamotheram, R., 2015a. The Case for Forceful Stewardship (Part 1): The Financial Risk from Global Warming. Available at: http://papers.ssrn.com/sol3/ papers.cfm?abstract_id=2551478 (31 January 2018).

Covington, H. & Thamotheram, R., 2015b. The Case for Forceful Stewardship (Part 2): Managing Climate Risk. Available at: http://papers.ssrn.com/sol3/papers.cfm?abstract_ id=2551485&rec=1&srcabs=2551478&alg=1&pos=1 (31 January 2018).

CTI, 2013. *Unburnable Carbon 2013: Wasted Capital and Stranded Assets*, London. Available at: www.carbontracker.org/wastedcapital (31 January 2018).

CTI, 2014. Energy Access: Why Coal Is not the Way Out of Energy Poverty, London. Available at: www.carbontracker.org/wp-content/uploads/2014/11/Coal-Energy-Access-111014-final.pdf (31 January 2018).

Cuomo, C.J., 2011. Climate change, vulnerability and responsibility. *Hypatia*, 26(4), pp.690–711.

Davidson, S., 2015. A Critique of the Coal Divestment Campaign. Available at: www. minerals.org.au/file_upload/files/reports/A_critique_of_the_coal_divestment_camp aign_Sinclair_Davidson_Jun_2014.pdf (31 January 2018).

Demasters, K., 2017. Knowledge Needed To Divest Of Fossil Fuels. *Financial Advisor*. Available at: www.fa-mag.com/news/knowledge-needed-to-divest-of-fossil-fuels-32943. html (31 January 2018).

Dordi, T., 2016. An Event Study Analysis of the Fossil Fuel Divestment Movement. University of Waterloo. Available at: https://uwspace.uwaterloo.ca/bitstream/handle/ 10012/10736/Dordi_Truzaar.pdf?sequence=7&isAllowed=y (31 January 2018).

EcoEquity, 2015. *Fair Shares: A Civil Society Equity Review of INDS's*. Available at: https://decorrespondent.nl/3705/Hoeveel-klimaatactie-moeten-rijke-landen-nemen-als-ze-hun-eerlijke-aandeel-willen-doen-/408324345-fab73cb8%5Cnpapers3:// publication/uuid/A9831D33-8CB8-4A12-9357-6EFF957C05D0 (31 January 2018).

Elliott, B., 2016. *Natural Catastrophe: Climate Change and Neoliberal Governance*, Edinburgh: Edinburgh University Press.

Engler, M. & Engler, P., 2016. *This Is an Uprising: How Nonviolent Revolt Is Shaping the Twenty-First Century*, New York: Nation Books.

Erickson, P., Kartha, S., Lazarus, M. & Tempest, K., 2015. Assessing carbon lock-in. *Environmental Research Letters*, 10(8), pp.1–7.

Faust, D., 2013. Fossil Fuel Divestment Statement. *Harvard University Office of the President*. Available at: www.harvard.edu/president/fossil-fuels (31 January 2018).

Figueres, C., Schellnhuber, H. J., Whiteman, G., Rockström, J., Hobley, A. & Rahmstorf, S., 2017. Three years to safeguard our climate. *Nature*, 546(7660), pp.593–595.

Fitzgibbon, B., 2015. Divestment Commitments Pass the $3.4 trillion Mark at COP21. *CommonDreams.org*. Available at: www.commondreams.org/newswire/2015/12/02/ divestment-commitments-pass-34-trillion-mark-cop21 (2 December 2015).

Flood, C., 2016. Sweden's AP4 Pension Fund Avoids Fossil Fuels in Landmark Move. *Financial Times*. Available at: www.ft.com/content/4bfa92da-49c5-11e6-b387-64ab 0a67014c (31 January 2018).

Franta, B., 2017. Litigation in the Fossil Fuel Divestment Movement. *Law and Policy*, (Accepted Article).

Gardiner, S.M., 2011. *A Perfect Moral Storm*, New York: Oxford University Press.

Geddes, P. et al., 2014. Building a Carbon-Free Equity Portfolio, Sausalito CA. Available at: www.aperiogroup.com/resource/138/node/download (31 January 2018).

Geman, B., 2017. Shell CEO Warns of "Disappearing" Public Patience on Carbon Emissions. *Axios*. Available at: www.axios.com/shell-ceo-scared-about-disappearing- public-patience-on-carbon-emission-2307927166.html (31 January 2018).

Godsen, E., 2014. Fossil Fuel Investing a Risk to Pension Funds, says Ed Davey. *The Telegraph*. Available at: www.telegraph.co.uk/finance/newsbysector/energy/11277546/ Fossil-fuel-investing-a-risk-to-pension-funds-says-Ed-Davey.html (28 July 2015).

Grady-Benson, J. & Sarathy, B., 2016. Fossil fuel divestment in US higher education: student-led organising for climate justice. *Local Environment*, 21(6), pp.661–681.

Griep, C., 2016. Shareholder Resolutions in the Carbon Undergound 200 Companies, 2012–2016: A Complex Picture. Available at: http://fossilfreeindexes.com/2016/09/06/ shareholder-resolutions-carbon-underground-200-companies-2012-2016-complex- picture/ (31 January 2018).

Gunther, M., 2015. Sustainable Investing: Are Companies Finally Moving Money Away From Fossil Fuels? *The Guardian*. Available at: www.theguardian.com/sustainable- business/2015/sep/16/goldman-sachs-morgan-stanley-merrill-lynch-fossil-fuel- divestment (16 September 2015).

Healy, N. & Barry, J., 2017. Politicizing energy justice and energy system transitions: fossil fuel divestment and a "just transition". *Energy Policy*, 108(June), pp.451–459.

Healy, N. & Debski, J., 2016. Fossil fuel divestment: implications for the future of sustainability discourse and action within higher education. *Local Environment*, 22(6), pp.1–26. Available at: https://www.tandfonline.com/doi/full/10.1080/13549839.2016. 1256382 (31 January 2018).

Höhne, N. et al., 2017. Action by China and India Slows Emissions Growth, President Trump's Policies Likely to Cause US Emissions to Flatten. Available at: http:// climateactiontracker.org/assets/publications/briefing_papers/CAT_2017-05-15_ Briefing_India-China-USA.pdf (31 January 2018).

Hunt, C., Weber, O. & Dordi, T., 2016. A comparative analysis of the anti-Apartheid and fossil fuel divestment campaigns. *Journal of Sustainable Finance & Investment*,

795(April), pp.1–18. Available at: www.tandfonline.com/doi/full/10.1080/20430795.
2016.1202641 (31 January 2018).

IEA, 2014. Energy Technology Perspectives 2014: Harnessing Electricity's Potential, Paris. Available at: www.iea.org/etp/ (31 January 2018).

IPCC, 2014. *Summary for Policymakers.* In: *Climate Change 2014: Mitigation of Climate Change. Contribution of Working Group III to the Fifth Assessment Report of the Intergovernmental Panel on Climate Change.* Available at: http://mitigation2014.org/ (31 January 2018).

Kaletsky, A., 2015. Why Big Oil Should Kill Itself. *Project Syndicate.* Available at: www. project-syndicate.org/commentary/marginal-pricing-end-of-western-oil-producers-by-anatole-kaletsky-2015-12 (31 January 2018).

Kartha, S., Lazarus, M. & Tempest, K., 2016. Fossil Fuel Production in a 2°C World: The Equity Implications of a Diminishing Carbon Budget, Stockholm Environmental Institute. Available at: www.sei-international.org/mediamanager/documents/Publica tions/Climate/SEI-DB-2016-Equity-fossil-fuel-production-rents.pdf (31 January 2018).

Kiyar, D. & Wittneben, B.B.F., 2015. Carbon as investment risk-the influence of fossil fuel divestment on decision making at Germany's main power providers. *Energies*, 8(9), pp.9620–9639.

Kofler, B., Netzer, N. & Beuermann, C., 2014. Towards a Global Energy Transformation. Available at: http://library.fes.de/pdf-files/iez/10817.pdf (31 January 2018).

Kolstad, I., 2015. Three myths about engagement and exclusion in responsible investment. *Business Ethics: A European Review*, 25(1), pp.45–58.

Last Real Indians, 2017. No, US Bank Has Not Stopped Funding Pipelines, Yet. *Last Real Indians.* Available at: http://lastrealindians.com/no-us-bank-has-not-stopped-funding-pipelines-yet/ (31 January 2018).

Lenferna, G.A., 2014a. Fossil Fuel Divestment Report for the Seattle City Employees Retirement System, Seattle. Available at: http://bit.ly/DivestSCERS (31 January 2018).

Lenferna, G.A., 2014b. Why Fossil Fuel Divestment Is Working. *Ethics & International Affairs.* Available at: www.ethicsandinternationalaffairs.org/2014/why-fossil-fuel-divestment-is-working/ (31 January 2018).

Lenferna, G.A., 2015. Bill Gates Gives Exxon Cover: The Gates Foundation Is Deadly Wrong on Climate Change, Fossil Fuels. *Salon.* Available at: www.salon. com/2015/11/07/bill_gates_gives_exxon_cover_the_gates_foundation_is_deadly_ wrong_on_climate_change_fossil_fuels/ (31 January 2018).

Lenferna, G.A., 2016. How Africa Could Leapfrog Fossil Fuels to Clean Energy Alternatives. *The Conversation.* Available at: https://theconversation.com/how-africa-could-leapfrog-fossil-fuels-to-clean-energy-alternatives-55044 (31 January 2018).

Lenferna, G.A., 2017a. Can we equitably manage the end of the fossil fuel era? *Energy Research & Social Science*, 35, pp.217–223.

Lenferna, G.A., 2017b. Don't Believe Trump—The Fossil Fuel Era is Ending, The Real Question Is How Fast. *Medium.* Available at: https://medium.com/@AlexLenferna/ dont-believe-trump-the-fossil-fuel-industry-is-going-under-the-real-question-is-how-fast-505b116dda24 (31 January 2018).

Lenferna, G.A., 2018. Divest-Invest: A Moral Case for Fossil Fuel Divestment. In H. Shue & R. Kanbur, eds. *Climate Justice: Economics and Philosophy.* Oxford University Press. Available at: http://bit.ly/AMoralEndowment (31 January 2018).

Lewis, M.C., 2014. Stranded Assets, Fossilised Revenues. Available at: www.kepl ercheuvreux.com/pdf/research/EG_EG_253208.pdf (31 January 2018).

Linnenluecke, M.K., Meath, C., Rekker, S., Sidhu, B.K. and Smith, T., 2015. Divestment from fossil fuel companies: confluence between policy and strategic viewpoints. *Australian Journal of Management*, 40(3), pp.478–487. Available at: http://aum.sage pub.com/cgi/doi/10.1177/0312896215569794 (31 January 2018).

Longstreth, B., 2014. Climate Change and Investment in Fossil Fuel Companies: The Strategy of Engagement Won't Work. *Huffington Post*. Available at: www.huffingtonpost.com/ bevis-longstreth/climate-change-and-invest_b_6295444.html (8 February 2015).

Ludwig, M., 2017. Under Activist Pressure, Portland Agrees to End All Corporate Investments. *Truthout*. Available at: www.truth-out.org/news/item/40179-under-activist-pressure-portland-agrees-to-end-all-corporate-investments (11 April 2017).

Lukacs, M., 2017. Neoliberalism Has Conned Us into Fighting Climate Change as Individuals. *The Guardian*. Available at: www.theguardian.com/environment/true-north/2017/jul/17/neoliberalism-has-conned-us-into-fighting-climate-change-as-individuals (31 January 2018).

McGlade, C. & Ekins, P., 2015. The geographical distribution of fossil fuels unused when limiting global warming to 2°C. *Nature*, 517(7533), pp.187–190. Available at: www. nature.com/doifinder/10.1038/nature14016%5Cnpapers2://publication/doi/10.1038/ nature14016 (31 January 2018).

McKibben, B., 2012. Global Warming's Terrifying New Math. *Rolling Stone*. Available at: www.rollingstone.com/politics/news/global-warmings-terrifying-new-math-20120719 (19 July 2012).

McKibben, B., 2016. Why We Need to Keep 80 Percent of Fossil Fuels in the Ground. *Yes!* Available at: www.yesmagazine.org/issues/life-after-oil/why-we-need-to-keep-80-percent-of-fossil-fuels-in-the-ground-20160215/ (31 January 2018).

McKinnon, C., 2016. Should We Tolerate Climate Change Denial? *Midwest Studies in Philosophy*, 40(1), pp.205–216.

Mapes, L.V., 2017a. Climate Activists Shut Down Chase Bank Branches in Seattle; Arrests Made. *The Seattle Times*. Available at: www.seattletimes.com/seattle-news/climate-activists-shut-down-chase-bank-branches-in-seattle/ (31 January 2018).

Mapes, L.V., 2017b. Wells Fargo to Seattle: Take Your Money and Go Now. *The Seattle Times*. Available at: www.seattletimes.com/seattle-news/politics/letter-to-mayor-lets-city-out-of-its-contract-for-financial-services-immediately/ (31 January 2018).

Massie, R.K., 1997. *Loosing the Bonds: The United States and South Africa in the Apartheid Years*, New York: Doubleday.

Mathiesen, K., 2017. Seattle Pledges Support for Climate Fund Barred by Trump. *Climate Home*. Available at: www.climatechangenews.com/2017/06/14/seattle-pledges-support-green-climate-fund/ (14 June 2017).

Mayes, R., Richards, C. & Woods, M., 2017. (Re)assembling Neoliberal Logics in the Service of Climate Justice: Fuzziness and Perverse Consequences in the Fossil Fuel Divestment Assemblage. In V. Higgins & W. Larner, eds. *Assembling Neoliberalism: Expertise, Practices, Subjects*. New York: Palgrave Macmillan, pp.131–150.

Moss, J., 2017. The Morality of Divestment. *Law and Policy*, 39(4), pp.412–428.

MSCI, 2013. Responding to the Call for Fossil-fuel Free Portfolios. Available at: www.msci.com/resources/factsheets/MSCI_ESG_Research_FAQ_on_Fossil-Free_ Investing.pdf (31 January 2018).

Muttitt, G., 2017. Forecasting Failure: Why Investors Should Treat Oil Company Energy Forecasts with Caution. Available at: http://priceofoil.org/content/uploads/2017/03/ forecasting-failure.pdf (31 January 2018).

Parenti, C., 2013. A Worthy Goal, but a Suspect Method. *The New York Times*. Available at: www.nytimes.com/roomfordebate/2013/01/27/is-divestment-an-effective-means-of-protest/a-worthy-goal-but-a-suspect-method (31 January 2018).

Paun, A., Night, Z. & Chan, W.-S., 2015. Stranded Assets: What Next?. Available at: www.businessgreen.com/digital_assets/8779/hsbc_Stranded_assets_what_next.pdf (31 January 2018).

Peabody Energy Corporation, 2015. Annual Report Pursuant to Section 13 or 15(d) of the Securities Exchange Act of 1934. Available at: https://mscusppegrs01.blob.core.windows.net/mmfiles/files/investors/2014 peabody annual report.pdf (31 January 2018).

Peterson, R., 2015. Inside Divestment: The Illiberal Movement to Turn A Generation Against Fossil Fuels. Available at: www.nas.org/projects/divestment_report/the_report (31 January 2018).

Pilkington, P., 2014. Volatile Emotions are Driving the World Economy. *Al Jazeera*. Available at: http://america.aljazeera.com/opinions/2014/8/animal-spirits-spureconom icgrowthpsychologyofmarkets.html (31 January 2018).

Ressler, L. & Schellentrager, M., 2011. *A Complete Guide to Reinvestment*. Available at: https://s3.amazonaws.com/s3.350.org/images/Reivestment_Guide.pdf (31 January 2018).

Reuters, 2015. Bank of America's New Policy to Limit Credit Exposure to Coal. *The New York Times*. Available at: www.nytimes.com/reuters/2015/05/06/business/06reuters-banking-coal-climatechange.html?_r=1 (31 January 2018).

Richardson, B.J., 2017. Divesting from Climate Change: The Road to Influence. *Law and Policy*, (Accepted Article), pp.1–47.

Richardson, V., 2015. Multibillionaire Bill Gates Rejects Calls to Divest from Fossil Fuels. *The Washington Times*. Available at: www.washingtontimes.com/news/2015/jun/25/multibillionaire-bill-gates-rejects-calls-divest-f/ (31 January 2018).

Roberts, D., 2015a. College Students are Making Global Warming a Moral Issue. Here's Why That Scares People. *Vox*. Available at: www.vox.com/2015/4/29/8512853/fossil-fuel-divestment (29 April 2015).

Roberts, D., 2015b. What Critics of the Keystone Campaign Misunderstand About Climate Activism. *Vox*. Available at: www.vox.com/2015/11/8/9690654/keystone-climate-activism (8 November 2015).

Roser-Renouf, C., Maibach, E., Leiserowitz, A., Feinberg, G. & Rosenthal, S., 2016. Faith, Morality and the Environment: Portraits of Global Warming's Six Americas, New Haven. Available at: http://environment.yale.edu/climate-communication/files/Faith_Morality_Six_Americas.pdf (31 January 2018).

Ross, J. & Lowery, W., 2017. Turning away from street protests, Black Lives Matter tries a new tactic in the age of Trump. *The Washington Post*, (May 4).

Rowe, J., Dempsey, J. & Gibbs, P., 2016. The Power of Fossil Fuel Divestment (and its Secret). In Carroll, W.K. and Sarker, K, eds. *A World to Win: Contemporary Social Movements and Counter-Hegemony*. Winnipeg: ARP Books.

Sarang, S., 2016. Combating climate change through a duty to divest. *Columbia Journal of Law and Social Problems*, 49(2), pp.295–341. Available at: www.columbia.edu/cu/jlsp/pdf/Mar2016/Sarang.pdf (31 January 2018).

Schifeling, T. & Hoffman, A.J., 2017. Bill McKibben's Influence on U.S. Climate Change: Shifting Fieldlevel Debates Through Radical Flank Effects. *Organization & Environment*. Available at: https://doi.org/10.1177/1086026617744278 (31 January 2018).

Schlosberg, D. & Collins, L.B., 2014. From environmental to climate justice: climate change and the discourse of environmental justice. *WIRES Climate Change*, 5, pp.359–74.

Shiller, R. & Akerlof, G., 2009. *Animal Spirits: How Human Psychology Drives the Economy, and Why It Matters for Global Capitalism*, Princeton: Princeton University Press.

Singer, P., 2010. One Atmosphere. In S. M. Gardiner et al., eds. *Climate Ethics: Essential Readings*. New York: Oxford University Press, pp.181–199.

Speth, J.G., 2015. Am I a "Radical"? *The Nation*. Available at: http://www.thenation.com/article/how-i-became-radical/ (31 January 2018).

Stavins, R., 2015. Pitching Divestment as a "Moral" Crusade is Misguided. *The New York Times*, (August 10).

Stern, N., 2007. *The Economics of Climate Change: The Stern Review*, Cambridge: Cambridge University Press.

Supran, G., 2015. How Fossil Fuel Divestment Can Rewrite the Climate Narrative. *Good*. Available at: www.good.is/articles/mit-scientists-sit-in-fossil-fuel-divestment (31 January 2018).

Sussams, L. & Leaton, J., 2017. Expect the Unexpected: The Disruptive Power of Low-carbon Technology, London. Available at: www.carbontracker.org/wp-content/uploads/2017/02/Expect-the-Unexpected_CTI_Imperial.pdf (31 January 2018).

Ullmann, K., 2013. Simply, We Ought to Divest. *Inside Vandy*. Available at: www.insidevandy.com/opinion/article_21f3fd92-a3af-11e2-be92-0019bb30f31a.html (31 January 2018).

Williston, B., 2012. Climate Change and Radical Hope. *Ethics & the Environment*, 17(2), pp.165–186.

Wisor, S., 2014. Why Climate Change Divestment Will Not Work. *Ethics & International Affairs*. Available at: www.ethicsandinternationalaffairs.org/2014/why-climate-change-divestment-will-not-work/ (31 January 2018).

World Coal Association, 2014. Coal Matters: Divestment and the Future of Coal, London. Available at: www.worldcoal.org/extract/divestment-and-the-future-role-of-coal-4509/ (31 January 2018).

Xu, R., 2015. Looking Beyond Fossil Fuel Divestment: Combating Climate Change in Higher Education Combating Climate Change in Higher Education. Pomona College. Available at: http://scholarship.claremont.edu/pomona_theses/134 (31 January 2018).

Yona, L. & Lenferna, G. A., 2016. The Fossil Fuel Divestment Movement Within Universities. In G. Sosa-Nunez & E. Atkins, eds. *Environment, Climate Change and International Relations*. Bristol: E-International Relations Publishing, pp.167–179.

6 Carbon trading, climate justice and labor resistance

Definition power in the South Africa campaign *One Million Climate Jobs*

Emanuele Leonardi

Introduction

In a powerful article published a few days before the infamous Paris Agreement was signed, Patrick Bond (2015) depicted three key challenges for climate justice (CJ): explore more thoroughly its proximity to other struggles – apparently unrelated; strengthen the link amongst the myriad local, grassroots movements mobilized around the fight to global warming; jump scale from the local to the global in order to gain effectiveness. My goal in this chapter is to contribute to the first challenge. The main premise, in fact, is that it would be beneficial for the global CJ movement to establish a deeper connection with organized labor, and vice versa. Although far from being universally shared, this claim is hardly an original one. For example, Nora Räthzel and David Uzzell called for the establishment of a new field of inquiry, *environmental labor studies*, characterized by a twofold rationale: theoretically, it should assess "the way in which nature and labour are intrinsically linked and equally threatened by globalising capital"; empirically, it should shed light on "the development of environmental trade union policies worldwide" (Räthzel and Uzzell 2013: 10). From a complementary perspective, Stefania Barca – whose research on the interplay between ecology/climate change and labor represents the foundational ground of my reflection here (Barca 2012; 2014; 2016; 2017a; 2017b) – wrote that "fighting climate change is a challenge where the labour movements should be on the front line because workers are already at the front line on the war against capitalism and climate change. In addition to labour movements, Indigenous Peoples, small farming communities, the unemployed, and women of all groups are at the forefront of this front line. Therefore in organising to defend themselves, they defend humanity from ecological ruin. These types of struggles require a profound transformation of labour's traditional visions and mottos, and of those from the Left in general" (Barca 2015a: 76–77).

Against such background, this chapter argues that an important way to tighten the link between unionists and climate activists is to take into careful account the profound transformations of contemporary capitalism in the last decades. In particular, I discuss the process of cognitization of the capital–labor nexus and that of financialization through a critical revision of Ulrich Beck's concept of *definition power* (§1). Once the definition power is seen as a productive force, then it becomes possible to make sense of the attempts to turn the ecological crisis from an obstacle to valorization – as it was perceived in the 1970s – to a profitable opportunity for business, namely an accumulation strategy. Such strategy has been variously labeled as green economy, green growth or circular economy (Leonardi 2017a). However, with specific regard to global warming, I propose to name this procedure *carbon trading dogma*, which is to say an extremely entrenched – albeit empirically indemonstrable – political belief according to which climate change, although a market failure (since negative externalities were not represented into prices), can be viably solved only by a wave of further marketization (§2). This entails the usual win–win rhetoric of environmental business circles: profits go up, the planet heals, nobody is hit. Unfortunately, only the first part is true. This is why I believe that a new, deeper relationship between labor and CJ movements should start from the practical disarticulation of this dogma.

A good case in point is the South African *One Million Climate Jobs* (*OMCJ*) campaign (§3).[1] What is most interesting from my perspective is that it assumes the carbon trading dogma of the green economy – capital is able to internalize global warming in such a way that ecological protection and economic growth can go hand in hand – but immediately disarticulates and inverts it. Instead of coupling low impacts and dividends' increase, the campaign links the transition to a low-carbon economy to the erasure of unemployment, a historical and particularly dramatic plague of the South African workforce.[2] This discursive displacement is what allowed the campaign to overcome the well-known organizational barrier separating CJ claims for the reduction of social metabolism – a necessary consequence of the gradual phasing out of fossil fuels – and mostly male blue-collars' vested interest in economic growth as a driver of rising industrial employment levels. This is partly due, as Stefania Barca notes, to the fact that *OMCJ* is "a large-scale green jobs coalition which includes 'community caregivers' as its most relevant employment sector" (2015b: 398). This centrality of reproductive labor is an element of novelty that sounds extremely promising for the future of a new articulation of CJ and organized labor. Just beside these positive features, however, stands what I perceive as a limit, namely an over-reliance on the state and on public intervention. As I argue in the conclusion, my conviction is that the prefigurative dimension of the *OMCJ* campaign would benefit from a non-state-based perspective such as that provided by the notion of *common/s*.

Knowledge, finance, labor: the concept of definition power

Already in his groundbreaking *Risikogesellschaft*, originally published in 1986, Ulrich Beck suggested that class-situations, characterized by the positive logic of wealth distribution, were increasingly being substituted by risk-situations, marked instead by the negative logic of disposal/rejection. Risk-situations disclosed a radically new scenario, a sort of universal exposition to uncertainty that loosened traditional senses of belonging linked to social stratification – hence, irreducible to class analysis (Beck 1992). In the context of late modernity, social conflicts over the appropriation of wealth increasingly take the form of a battle of definitions, which is qualitatively distinct from the distributive struggles that were foundational to the welfare state up until the 1970s. Rather, such battle is linked to a kind of antagonism revolving around the production of institutionalized risks, namely social constructs whose validity ultimately rests on how deeply productive subjects conform and participate to them, on how often social actors mobilize and share them in their concrete practices. As Beck put it: "[W]*hat 'relations of productions' in the capitalist society represented for Karl Marx, 'relations of definition' represent for risk society*" (2009: 31; emphasis in the original).

Beck's analysis entails significant consequences with regard to the theoretical relationship between relations of production and relations of definition. On the one hand, in fact, there are important affinities: historical determination and constitutive politicization. On the other, however, there are also key divergences: "Relations of production manifest themselves in the domain and language of business, labor and production; relations of definition, by contrast, in the domains and languages of tradition, publicity, science, law and politics. The former concern the 'conflict logic' of the laboring society, the latter the 'conflict logic' of the discourse society" (*Ivi*: 33–34).

Although Beck acknowledges several areas of possible overlapping between the two elements – from the deregulation of labor markets to the all-pervasive rhetoric of self-entrepreneurship –, there is no doubt that he claims relations of production and relations of definition as separated by a difference in kind – rather than in degree: the two are to be understood as independent from one another. In other words: the two concepts belong to different epochs and the centrality of the latter implies the marginalization of the former.

Beck's argument is certainly compelling, but its conclusion should not be assumed – in my opinion – as logically necessitated.

In order to understand what "definition power" (*Ivi*: 32) may mean, consider, for example, financial conventions, namely crystallizations of markets' short-term expectations around 'bubbles' (the Internet, sustainability, big data, etc.). These are not virtual images from a distant universe; rather, they are valuation criteria that mold all risks, most notably collective ones, "into sellable products, formatted for the market by private actors in search of a profit" (Holmes 2010: 230). Accordingly, financial conventions constitute the contemporary form of capitalist accumulation by enacting the social control of cognitive labor power. Thus, it is my conviction that it is possible – and fruitful – to slightly modify Beck's elaboration in order to maintain the explicative effectiveness of his general framework while reaching a significantly different outcome. I propose to conceive of the relations of definition as precisely the late-modern form – better still: *post-Fordist form* – of capitalist relations of production. In order to keep producing value – an imperative in a capitalist system – labor increasingly assumes the shape of discourse. Thus, the discourse society does not substitute the laboring society: rather, it absorbs and transforms it. In this historical conjuncture, the definition power acquires a crucial and unprecedented role, that of establishing what a risk actually is, to produce it through the exploitation of social knowledge – what Marx called *general intellect* (Marx 1993) – and finally to inscribe its management within the financial realm. Otherwise put: in contemporary capitalism the definition power simultaneously imposes a shared vision of a given problem, produces it as economically valuable, and governs it by means of financial markets. This political dimension of financialization is particularly manifest in the role rating agencies are playing in the Eurozone crisis: such agencies actively dictate neoliberal social policies to sovereign states, exercising a 'destructuring power' aimed at shrinking national welfare systems in order to open up new sectors for financial penetration (e.g. private health insurances, etc.) (Lucarelli and Leonardi 2015: 111).

In order to better grasp the epochal shift conveyed by the intermeshing of relations of production and relations of definition it may be useful to recall two elements. The first is historical and concerns the emergence, from the crisis of industrial-Fordist capitalism, of *cognitive capitalism*, namely "a new system of accumulation in which the cognitive dimension of labor becomes the dominant principle of value creation, whereas the main form of capital becomes the so-called immaterial and intellectual one" (Lucarelli and Vercellone 2013: 10). From this perspective, socialized knowledge – a common/s – becomes the fundamental productive factor, such that the economy can be said to rely on the production of knowledge by means of knowledge. What is thus set in motion is a circular process, whereby the output constantly regenerates the input through relatively cheap innovation based on seemingly endless reproducibility.

The second element is economical and refers to the process of financialization namely a set of practices through which companies, institutions and individuals become completely embedded in financial transactions. The outcome of this process is an unprecedented dependence on unstable markets and volatile money for virtually everything: from food supplies to services, from education to income. Granted, finance has been a feature of the capitalist mode of production since its inception; nonetheless, the current configuration of finance is qualitatively and quantitatively unique, with a massive proliferation of sophisticated and opaque financial tools such as derivatives, Credit Default Swaps and Collateralized Debt Obligation. These technologies represent an immensely complicated and coordinated attempt to make profit out of the financial colonization of every aspect of social life: "Financialization is not an unproductive/parasitic deviation of growing quotas of surplus-value and collective savings, but rather the form of capital accumulation symmetrical with new processes of value production" (Marazzi 2011: 48). It should be noted that a new form of accumulation requires an institutional counterpart. In fact, financialization fundamentally transformed economic practices – by exercising the definition power to shape them differently – in at least three central areas: in business strategy, it privileged the logic of shareholder activism; in wage relations, it internalized workers by turning them into powerless micro-shareholders; in everyday life activities, it colonized people's imaginaries by capturing them in the debt process (from student loans to pension funds).

Carbon trading dogma

The definition power that emerged at the crossroad between the processes of cognitization of the capital–labor nexus and financialization of the economy (and its imaginary), also and deeply, affects climate governance. I propose to name such influence *carbon trading dogma*, which is to say an extremely entrenched – albeit empirically indemonstrable – political belief, according to which global warming, although a market failure (since negative externalities were not represented into prices), can be viably solved only through a wave of further marketization (Leonardi 2017b). Only carbon trading – so the dogma prescribes – can simultaneously avoid the cost of inaction,[3] profit from climate risks and improve the planet's health (Barrett 2012). Here the market functions as a site of veridiction, as Michel Foucault suggested in his biopolitical lectures from the late 1970s (2007; 2008). In fact, being an expression of the definition power, the carbon trading dogma is highly performative in that it actively (re)creates the conditions for its continuous unfolding (MacKenzie, Muniesa and Siu 2007) – or, to use Judith Butler's words, it enacts the "reiterative power of discourse to produce the phenomena that it regulates and constrains" (1993: 2). Referring to the concept of green economy – of which the carbon trading dogma is a global warming-related sub-set – Sarah Bracking remarks: "This performativity can refer to materialities which can be invoked, but which can also be dispensed with, in a large proportion of individual transactions [...] and systemically in the derivatives market as a whole. Value is instead discursively mobilized within a virtual framing of 'care' and the performativity of 'green'. But this virtuality is not without material effect – in fact far from it – in that it works to enable certain power holders to gain strategic access and control of natural resource assets and energy systems" (2015: 2339).

In the context of potentially catastrophic global warming, such a market-based regime of truth gives rise to a dogmatic equation – as discursively indisputable as it is empirically unprovable – that, elaborating on recent work by Larry Lohmann (2011), might be formulated as follows:

$$\text{climatic stability} = \text{reductions in } CO_2 \text{ emissions}$$
$$= \text{carbon trading} = \text{sustainable economic growth}$$

The strength of this dogma is demonstrated not only by the insistence with which climate policymakers invested in carbon markets despite their irrelevant – if not negative (Gupta 2014) – ecological impacts, but also by the increasing difficulties encountered by market actors in justifying the narratives of green economy and sustainable growth. Yet, the circular structure of the carbon trading dogma makes any alternative unthinkable: as every religious belief, the confirmation of its truth, claims is already contained in its fundamental assumption: since there is no effective politics outside of the market, global warming is solvable only in so far as it is possible to make a profit out of it. It is treated as a self-evident truth that 'Climate stability equals surplus value production', as shown one more time by the outcome of the 21st UNFCCC Conference of the Parties – the *Paris Agreement* (Moreno, Fuchs and Speich Chassé 2016).

Two elements should be emphasized to connect the carbon trading dogma to the definition power (in its revised form): first, it is worth considering how the very visibility of climate change relies on complex, contested and always re-negotiable knowledge infrastructures. As Paul Edwards (2010: 17) argued:

> Instead of thinking about knowledge as pure facts, theories, and ideas – mental things carried around in people's heads, or written down in textbooks – an infrastructure perspective views knowledge as an enduring, widely shared socio-technical system. Knowledge infrastructures comprise robust networks of people, artefacts, and institutions that generate, share, and maintain specific knowledge about the human and natural worlds.

From this perspective, to experience a global warming event as such presupposes the infrastructural support of climate science. In other words, linking a weather-related event – no matter how extreme – to climate change requires a massive mobilization of the general intellect in its diverse forms (various knowledge-factories such as universities, think tanks, activists' counter-narratives, etc.). Obviously, this dependence on knowledge does not make climate change any less concrete or material, both in the individuation of its multiple causes and in the destructiveness of its heterogeneous effects.

Second, the pervasiveness of financial systems has not spared climatic alterations; in fact, carbon trading mobilizes complex hybrid instruments (simultaneously financial *and* environmental), such as weather-derivatives and CAT bonds (catastrophe bonds).[4] Moreover, carbon markets share with the financial sphere a constitutive attitude towards *instability*: the complexity of procedures for producing, measuring and exchanging carbon commodities (such as European Union Allowances or Certified Emissions Reduction) closely resembles the opaque trade in derivatives (Layfield 2013). What needs to be emphasized is that in both cases, such instability does not result from the imperfect application of otherwise correct protocols. Rather, it is a necessary condition for the production of these particular commodities.

Just transition and the One Million Climate Jobs *campaign in South Africa*

As anticipated in the Introduction, the carbon trading dogma is not an unassailable fortress, a struggle-proof monolithic entity. Rather, it is the expression of the 'green' elites' hegemony over global warming policy – a hegemony constantly put to question by various instances of the global CJ movement. To expand the effectiveness of such a global movement, I believe it is key to include organized labor. A relevant concept to achieve such inclusion is that of *Just Transition* (JT), which is now official policy of the International Trade Unions Council (ITUC). According to ITUC executive Anabella Rosenberg, this concept is a

> tool the trade union movement shares with the international community, aimed at smoothing the shift towards a more sustainable society and

providing hope for the capacity of a green economy to sustain decent jobs and livelihoods for all [...] JT is a supporting mechanism of climate action, and not inaction. JT is not in opposition to, but complements environmental policies. This comforts the idea that environmental and social policies are not contradictory but, on the contrary, can reinforce each other.

(Rosenberg 2010: 141)

As Stefania Barca notes, however, the specific meaning of this notion depends on the actors' more general political stance: "Within a common tendency [within labor environmentalism] to adopt a JT framework, important differentiations persist in the way of interpreting it: from a simple claim for jobs creation in the green economy, to a radical critique of capitalism and refusal of market solutions" (2015b: 392).

Such internal split of JT models can be further unpacked: drawing on Nancy Fraser's influential distinction between *affirmative* and *transformative* remedies for injustice (1995), Jamie Gough (2010) argued that, in the context of JT, affirmation concerns views that call for more equity within the parameters of existing political economy, whereas transformation regards views that push for a radical reshaping of political economy as it is currently designed. Elaborating on this fundamental divide, Dimitris Stevis and Romain Felli (2015) propose three different frameworks to understand JT:

a   The *shared solution* approach claims that a low-carbon economy can be built by involving all stakeholders on fair terms in the transition process. Dialogue is key in this context, and the borders of the capitalist system are elastic enough to affirmatively implement JT: trade unions simply provide workers' interests with institutional voice.

b   The *differentiated responsibility* approach focuses on defending the potential 'losers' of JT, namely those workers employed in the so-called 'brown economy' (e.g. sectors like mining, chemicals and manufacturing), which is supposed to shrink or even disappear if sustainability takes over. It is assumed that capital and labor have unequal responsibility concerning the emergence of the ecological crisis, therefore, calls are made for states' direct intervention by means of 'green industrial policies' to transform the economic status quo and create sustainable jobs.

c   The *socio-ecological* approach sees JT as a process of radically transforming the qualitative composition of production that "requires the democratization of social and economic relations in order to subordinate production to human (and planetary) needs rather than to profit: market forces should not be the ones to decide *what* ought be produced, and *how*" (Stevis and Felli 2015: 39).

At the crossroad between the second and the third options, a good case in point is represented by the South Africa campaign *One Million Climate Jobs* (*OMCJ*): I contend it clearly highlights how CJ can enact an alternative vision of the relationship between labor and climate change. To contextualize the campaign, it is important to recall that South Africa is being severely hit by two global crises: rising inequality and climate change (Cock 2014). Global capital penetrates the country through the uncontested primacy of the so-called minerals–energy complex (MEC), which makes the country's economy the second most energy-intensive in the world. The MEC is structured around large-scale, energy-intensive industry and mining, and consumes over 60% of the country's total electricity output (Hallowes 2011). Moreover, it is underpinned by coal as the fundamental source of energy. The extraction rate of South Africa's rich reserves is ever-increasing particularly to supply coal-fired electricity for transnational corporations such as Anglo American, BHP Billiton and ArcelorMittal. As Patrick Bond (2011) has unmasked, this kind of electricity is among the cheapest in the world since it is provided under apartheid-era pricing agreements. As a consequence, multinational conglomerates are supplied with electricity for less-than-cost (about 1/8 of what domestic consumers pay). Nevertheless, at present over 30% of the South African population have no or minimal access to electricity.

Beyond its unfair production and unjust distribution, from the perspective of climate change the economic dominance of MEC in South Africa presents the further problem of being extremely carbon intensive. In fact, as Patrick Bond, Rehana Dada and Graham Erion have recently documented, "[South African] CO_2 emissions rate in the all-important energy sector – measured per person per unit of output (i.e., the economy's per capita energy intensity) is *twenty times worse than that of even the United States*" (2009: 7). And yet, as the same scholars report, a survey conducted by GlobalScan in 2006 revealed that less than half of South Africans consider climate change a "serious problem". Consequently, they conclude, "more than in nearly any other society, ordinary South Africans have been kept in the dark by government, media and business – with civil society making uneven efforts to address the deficit" (*Ibid.*). Actually, during my research period in Durban, it was common to be exposed to arguments such as: "Never seen such a rainy summer [...] No wonder we are hosting the climate change conference!", in casual conversations with taxi drivers or other Durbanites.

In this context the crucial re-articulation operated by *OMCJ* advocates, lies in the tight integration of climate change, unemployment and inequality. Moreover, it significantly contributes to the process of raising awareness about the damages of global warming. Two further reasons make this specific struggle extremely interesting: on the one hand, this campaign possesses the clear – and somehow rare – advantage of being, at the same time, technically feasible and politically realistic. On the other hand, it assumes the carbon trading dogma of the green economy – capital is able to internalize global warming in such a way that ecological protection and economic growth ideologically appear as reinforcing each other – but immediately disarticulates and inverts it. By means of a strategic move, instead of coupling low impacts and dividends' increase, the *OMCJ* campaign links the transition to a low-carbon economy to the erasure of unemployment, a historical and particularly dramatic plague of the South African workforce.[5] By doing so, it also tackles inequality and puts forward "demands for deep, transformative change meaning dramatically different forms of production and consumption" (Cock 2014: 24).

The basic claim of *OMCJ* is almost self-evident: by shifting crucial productive activities from a fossil fuel-based model to a low-carbon scheme it is possible to create at least one million new jobs. Such jobs must be, and this is a fundamental element, both *decent* and *people-driven*. 'Decency' is defined in terms of social as well as psycho-physical safety and of healthy working conditions, whereas 'people's centrality' is defined along the line of population's primacy over profit.[6] Keeping in mind the three pillars of this transitional strategy – ecological sustainability, social justice and state intervention – the activists list their set of priorities.

As they write:

> We can and must:
>
> - produce our electricity from wind and sun in a way that is driven by the energy needs of all people, and that protects nature;
> - grow enough food for all people through techniques such as agroecology that are labour intensive, low in carbon emissions, protect soil and water, and provide healthy food;
> - protect our natural resources, especially water, soil and biodiversity, to make sure that we can continue to meet the basic needs of all people;
> - provide basic services such as water, electricity and sanitation so that we address the legacies of *apartheid* and build the resilience of our people to withstand the effects of climate change.
>
> (OMJC 2011: 21)

In the materials distributed by South African *OMCJ* campaigners, the specific contents of every listed demand are well articulated, clearly expressed and, crucially, sustained by solid scientific research. This is a key aspect as the collective production of knowledge, which made possible the construction of the campaign, shows the potential of a labor movement–CJ alliance. First, as sketched above, activists assume the starting point of the carbon trading dogma (creating value by means of tackling catastrophic global warming), but immediately disarticulate it by questioning the very notion of value. Just like the green economists, *OMCJ* activists recognize the climate crisis as a terrain for development – as a job creator rather than as a job killer – but do so by privileging the working classes' interests instead of the financial sector's needs. In this sense, Jacqueline Cock argues that a "JT to a low-carbon economy could contain the embryo of an alternative eco-socialist social order" (2014: 33). The proposed transformations do not mainly concern traditionally male jobs in heavy industrial sectors; rather, agriculture and community work stand prominently at the very core of the campaigners' effort. It is this recognition of the internal differentiation of labors, and the centrality attributed to the sphere of reproduction, which allow the campaign to dismiss the rhetoric of Progress and thus to overcome the insidious issue of the – often conflicting – relationships between environmentalists and trade unionists.

Such inclusivity resonates with Andrew Ross' (2011) reflection on the possibility to effectively resist the austerity measures that are sweeping the Eurozone:

> It's very likely that the impact of the new austerity politics will set back the green-labour cause (and it is intended to do so) but there can also be no doubt now about the political potential of synchronizing the movements for social, economic, and environmental justice – a potential that has got a big boost from the climate crisis. Indeed, if the climate crisis did not exist, it may have been necessary to invent it so that this synchrony could finally occur.

Ross' point is definitely applicable to the *OMCJ* campaign: actually, it is refreshing and encouraging to see, as organizations involved in the project, actors as diverse, and once very disconnected, as the COSATU (a federation of over twenty trade unions), the World Wildlife Fund, the Rural People's Movement, the New Women's Movement, the Institute for Zero Waste, and many others. Even more importantly, such process of organizing convergences seems to be immune from the risk of leveling the radicalness of demands since it originates at the intersection between scientific knowledge production/diffusion and local activism; hence, it configures itself as more difficult to be co-opted and/or recuperated. Workers, unemployed, community caregivers and environmentalists are connected not through specific, single-issue political practices, but rather by a new, general understanding of the climate crisis as a political means of social liberation and job creation.[7]

All these features make the *OMCJ* campaign a 'successful' attempt to bridge CJ and labor politics. It must be noted, however, that it failed to reach its immediate goal – to become official state policy. Why did this happen? Possible – and reasonable – explanations may be political instability, economic uncertainty and of course an adverse balance of forces. However, I would like to add a further element. A key point in the *OMCJ* campaign is that the animal spirits of capital must be tamed in order to ensure a people-driven transition to a low-carbon economy. There is no space whatsoever for the technocratic rhetoric so recurrent in carbon trading circles. Exactly this explicit and welcome politicization, however, might represent a limit to the entire radical architecture of the campaign. In fact, who is in charge of this 'taming'? *OMCJ* advocates seem to have no doubts about this: it can only be the nation state. Although, at times, such a state-centrism appears to be counterbalanced by a significant emphasis on community self-governance,[8] it is fair to say that the institutional pivot of the transition is individuated in the (positive) power of the state as opposed to the (negative) influence of the market. Consider, for instance, the following passage:

> A just transition to a low-carbon economy requires state intervention. The imperatives of climate change and job creation on the one hand potentially conflict with trade rules rigged to meet the needs of transnational corporations on the other […] The struggle against climate change requires a struggle against the trade rules 'rigged in favor of the rich'.
>
> (OMCJ 2011: 33)

It seems to me that the problem with this framework does not concern the necessity to limit the market's all-pervasiveness but, rather, the very possibility that such a crucial task might be performed by the contemporary, heavily neoliberalized state (Dardot and Laval 2013), deeply entangled in the cogency of the carbon trading dogma. Similarly, Stefania Barca has aptly argued that such understanding of JT

> does not take into account the fact that the Washington Consensus has forced virtually all governments to terminate social policies wherever possible and ignore (when not destroying) local economies, while adopting a competitiveness model based on ever lower labour costs and the hobbling of union power at the behest of global capital.
>
> (Barca 2015b: 394)

Most states involved in UN-framed climate governance are now accepting their subordination to what James Ferguson defines as "free-market fetishism" (2010: 170). Such subalternity has been detected by Sarah Bracking (2014) in the design-making process of the Green Climate Fund (conceived at COP 15 in Copenhagen, formally adopted at COP 17 in Durban and then further developed). Within a latent conflict between advocates of command-and-control public authorities and supporters of an incrementalist/financial private sector approach, "politicians and country representatives were discouraged from intervening, characterised as they are by the neoliberal self-denying ordinance that capital cannot be interfered with" (2014: 13). Furthermore,

> When benefits to corporate firms and banks are expected to be high, governments and 'green funds' make intonations about money being promised. Conversely, when returns to corporate firms and banks are predicted to be low, and developmental and environmental co-benefits high, these financial promises retreat. The *game itself is financialised*, and as such the poor and vulnerable can expect little from it.
>
> (*Ivi*: 16)

This financialized background is connected to a key feature of the carbon trading dogma, namely the manifest disconnect between its (putative) environmental goal and its (actual) economic means. In fact, although no ecological improvement has been made, a huge amount of value has been created and then transferred to fossil fuel-intensive companies through the production of what can be called *financial climate rent*. In other words, there is no doubt that carbon trading is environmentally irrelevant but economically significant. This friction between environmental irrelevance and financial productivity has led to the entrenchment of the carbon trading dogma. Hence, although the ecological inconsistency of carbon markets has been empirically demonstrated on innumerable occasions, the assumption of a harmonic compatibility between climate stability and sustainable growth keeps orienting policymakers as well as market actors. After all, as Chris Methmann has unveiled, "apparent failure in terms of carbon emission reductions is in fact a success of depoliticizing climate politics" (2013: 69).

The consequence of this line of argument is a strong juxtaposition between market-conceived and state-executed schemes for financialization, and politicized governance innovation imposed by CJ and labor struggles from below. As far as the game itself is financialized, meaningful transformation can hardly be won by respecting its grounding rules. It is more likely that longer-term sources for supporting JT and tackling global warming can be found through bottom-up cooperation, whereby a reduction in the magnitude of investments may be (over)compensated by an increase in the trustworthiness of the political process.

Conclusion

The chapter's main argument is that tightening the bond between CJ and labor movements is an important step for political struggles against catastrophic climate change to gain effectiveness. I have proposed to frame such encounters against the background of recent developments of the capitalist mode of production – cognitization of labor and financialization of the economy – as embodied by a revised version of Ulrich Beck's concept of *definition power*. I have subsequently discussed notions such as carbon trading dogma and JT in order to set the stage for a critical analysis of the highly significant South African *One Million Climate Jobs* campaign. Beside its many merits, I have highlighted what I consider to be an excessive state-centrism. In this Conclusion, I would like to suggest that the prefigurative dimension of the *OMCJ* campaign would benefit from a non-state-based perspective such as that provided by the notion of common/s. The contamination I propose may prove strategic in terms of gaining institutional consistency and resisting capital's and state's co-optation. The main point concerns the configuration of the climate (and, hence, of its crisis) as a common/s to be managed beyond – although not necessarily, and in any case not always, against – the double trap of private and public property.

The definition of the common/s I find most adequate is provided by Sandro Mezzadra and Brett Neilson: they conceive the common/s as the outcome of a process of production, and as such they highlight the unprecedented character of the current phase of capitalist development. Although capital has attempted to pillage the commons ever since its inception – i.e. primitive accumulation – its contemporary configuration diverges from the preceding ones in that the common/s plays the role of a crucial element of production, whose exploitation often assumes a financial form. Thus, a class-related dimension directly affects the common/s. Moreover, the authors contend that its usefulness goes beyond its diagnostic dimension; it can also shape a revolutionary prognosis:

> The concept of the common/s [...] enables the development of a radical perspective on social, juridical, and political matters pertaining to the commons, common goods, the public, and the private. The turn between the singular and the plural that marks the conceptual difference between the common

and the commons is important here. The former signals a process of production, entirely immanent and material, by which instances of the latter acquire
extension in time and space. At the same time, it gives to the plural instances
an intensive quality that brings them into relation in contingent and also
constitutive ways [...] [There is] a moment of excess that characterizes the
common with regard to the commons. Such a moment is without doubt constitutive of rights and institutions, but can never be exhausted by this juridi-
cal dimension.

(Mezzadra and Neilson 2013: 378–379)

Thus, the common/s cuts diagonally through the market-state dichotomy and presents itself as a revolutionary strategy that is based on the translation of singular
struggles into autonomous institutions that constitutively transcend both the state-
form and the enterprise-model. Its strategic core lies in its constructive character:
the common/s cannot be found in a distant past, nor in a putative pristine nature;
rather, it needs to be created as that political goal whose function is precisely to
link singular conflicts in a viable social alternative at a transnational scale. What
is important to underline is that the common/s grows through the simultaneous
production of a unitary political horizon *and* of singular localized conflicts. This
processual character of the common/s is best described by Massimo De Angelis:
"Commoning is the life activity through which commonwealth is reproduced,
extended and comes to serve as the basis for a new cycle of commons (re)produc-
tion, and through which social relations among commoners – including the rules
of a governance system – are constituted and reproduced [...] The first very general key characteristic of commoning is that it is social labour bounded in space/
time, by a given amount of accessible resources and within a commons circuit"
(2017: 201).

To be clear: my point is not that the *OMCJ* campaign should not have engaged
its battle at the state level. More simply, I believe that states are today very much
embedded in the attempt to enhance capital accumulation at the expense of the
climate (and of most people's living conditions). The Paris Agreement is instructive in this regard. Whether CJ activists and labor organizers should reclaim the
state by using the common/s as a pressure tool (Mansbridge 2014) or create new
institutions directly based on the common/s (Hardt and Negri 2017) is an open
question. What is certain, in my opinion, is that for the climate–labor front to be
effective, the common/s must be put at the center stage.

Notes

1 The original *One Million Climate Jobs* campaign was launched in the UK in 2009 (Neale
2009; 2014). Obviously, however, its translation – starting from 2011 – into a specifically South African context has significantly modified both core arguments and practical implications. According to Stefania Barca (2015b), whereas the British campaign
adopted a Keynesian/green growth framework, the South African was more radical and
transformative. It is worth noting that a similar campaign for climate jobs is currently
under way in Portugal (Climáximo 2016).

2 The argument I develop here, largely relys on empirical materials gathered and processed in the course of a three-month long social ethnography I conducted in Durban, South Africa in 2011 (before and during the UNFCCC COP 17). Amongst other things, I collaborated with the organization of the 'People's Space' organized by the Civil Society Committee on the COP 17 (commonly referred to as C 17), a two-week long counter-conference that took place on Howard Campus, at the University of KwaZulu-Natal (Leonardi 2012).

3 The Stern Review has estimated the present value of the future social costs of climate change to be equivalent to 5–20% of global GDP (Stern 2007).

4 Weather-derivatives are designed to price and trade in both the uncertainties of the weather and social uncertainties about the future of climate change. CAT bonds are insurance-like mechanisms that are putatively intended to disperse catastrophic weather risk and, in so doing, protect vulnerable sectors such as agriculture and coastal property. For a compelling analysis of such financial tools, see Cooper (2010).

5 It is important to stress that, although unemployment is a general feature of capitalism, its specifically South African form is irreducible to a universal characterization of the problem. As Franco Barchiesi notes: "The rate of unemployment, presently standing at around 25% of the economically active population, does not in itself explain the full extent of the crisis, or its nature. Nor does the fact that two-thirds of the working-age, able-bodied population aged 18 to 34 have never worked in their lives, or the fact that only one third of the African economically active population is in full-time, formal jobs. More generally, South African society is facing – and this is a reality remarkably impervious to shifts in the economic cycle and in the economic policy discourse – a widespread decline of waged employment as a condition of stable social insertion, citizenship, and the enjoyment of social rights. The most visible impacts of wage labour's decline are deepening labour market inequalities and the expansion of working class poverty, which, encompassing a growing number of workers with formal occupations as well as casual ones, is engulfing urban as well as rural areas" (Barchiesi 2008: 52–53).

6 "Decent jobs are jobs that are safe, provide healthy working conditions, and offer social protection, security and fair wages. They are jobs that, at the very least, meet the International Labour Organisation standards of 'decent work' and are in alignment with goals such as meeting the social needs of the majority of the population. In this sense they should be useful jobs [...] Economic development must be driven primarily by people, not profits. The necessary funding for climate jobs must be allocated by the state, but the implementation and monitoring of the programme must involve local communities" (OMJC 2011: 9).

7 The role of trade unions-inspired JT in facilitating the process of *organizing convergences* became even clearer in the mobilizations around COP 19 in Warsaw in 2013. In that context, ITUC (through its image of respectability [Thörn 2006]) acted as a mediator between affirmative negotiations within the COP-system and transformative CJ demands. ITUC was eventually able to "mobilize mainstream NGOs for more confrontational action such as the Warsaw walkout and the civil disobedience action inside the COP premises in Paris in 2015" (Cassegård, Soneryd, Thörn 2017: 40). This does not mean, however, that all problematic issues are solved: for a start, "the action [Warsaw walkout] was largely a Northern-dominated top-down affair" (*Ivi*: 42).

8 For example, the expression "publicly owned and community-controlled" recurs quite often in *OMCJ* materials.

Bibliography

Barca S. (2012) "On Working-class Environmentalism: A Historical and Transnational Overview" *Interface*, 4(2) 61–80.

Barca S. (2014) "Laboring the Earth: Transnational Reflections on the Environmental History of Work" *Environmental History*, 19(1) 3–27.

Barca S. (2015a) "Labor and climate change: Towards an emancipatory ecological class-consciousness" in EJOLT Report, Refocusing Resistance for Climate Justice (http://www.ejolt.org/wordpress/wp-content/uploads/2015/09/climate-justice-report.pdf) accessed 25 November 2017.

Barca S. (2015b) "Greening the job: Trade unions, climate change and the political ecology of labour" in Bryant R.L. ed *The International Handbook of Political Ecology*. Edward Elgar Publishing, Cheltenham/Northampton.

Barca S. (2016) Labor in the Age of Climate Change (www.jacobinmag.com/2016/03/climate-labor-just-transition-green-jobs/) accessed 25 November 2017.

Barca S. (2017a) "The Labor(s) of Degrowth" *Capitalism Nature Socialism*, 1–10. (https://doi.org/10.1080/10455752.2017.1373300.).

Barca S. (2017b) "Labour and the ecological crisis: the eco-modernist dilemma in western Marxism(s) (1980s–2010s)" *Geoforum* (www.academia.edu/34806191/Labour_and_the_ecological_crisis_the_eco-modernist_dilemma_in_western_Marxism_s_1970s-2000s).

Barchiesi F. (2008) "Hybrid Social Citizenship and the Normative Centrality of Wage Labour in Post-Apartheid South Africa" *Mediations*, 24(1) 52–67.

Barrett P. (2012) It's Global Warming, Stupid, *Bloomsberg Businessweek* (www.bloomberg.com/news/articles/2012-11-01/its-global-warming-stupid).

Beck U. (1992) *Risk Society*. SAGE, London.

Beck U. (2009) *World at Risk*. Polity Press, London.

Bond P. ed (2011) *Durban's Climate Gamble: Trading Carbon, Betting the Earth*. University of South Africa Press, Braamfontein.

Bond P. (2015) "Challenges for the climate justice movement: connecting dots, linking Blockadia and jumping scale" in EJOLT Report, Refocusing Resistance for Climate Justice (www.ejolt.org/wordpress/wp-content/uploads/2015/09/climate-justice-report.pdf) accessed 25 November 2017.

Bond P., Dada R. and Erion G. eds (2009) *Climate Change, Carbon Trading and Civil Society: Negative Returns on South African Investments*. Rozenberg Publishers, Amsterdam.

Bracking S. (2014) "The Anti-Politics of Climate Finance: The Creation and Performativity of the Green Climate Fund" *Antipode,* 47(2) 281–302.

Bracking S. (2015) "Performativity in the Green Economy: How Far Does Climate Finance Create a Fictive Economy?" *Third World Quarterly*, 36(12) 2337–2357.

Butler J. (1993) *Bodies That Matter* Routledge, New York.

Cassegård C., Soneryd L., Thörn H. and Wettergren Å. (2017) *Climate Action in a Globalizing World*. Routledge, London.

Climáximo (2016) Empregos para o clima, Lisbon. Self-published, (www.empregos-clima.pt/wp-content/uploads/2016/08/Livrete-Empregos-para-o-Clima.pdf).

Cock J. (2014) "The 'Green Economy': A Just and Sustainable Development Path or a 'Wolf in Sheep's Clothing'?" *Global Labour Journal*, 5(1) 23–44.

Cooper M. (2010) "Turbulent Worlds. Financial Markets and Environmental Crisis" *Theory Culture and Society*, 27(3) 167–190.

Dardot P. and Laval C. (2013) *The New Way of the World*. Verso, London.

De Angelis M. (2017) *Omnia Sunt Communia*. Zed Books, London.

Edwards P. (2010) *A Vast Machine*. MIT Press, Cambridge.

Ferguson J. (2010) "The Uses of Neoliberalism" *Antipode*, 41(s1) 166–184.

Foucault M. (2007) *Security, Territory, Population*. Basingstoke, New York.

Foucault M. (2008) *Birth of Biopolitics*. Basingstoke, New York.

Fraser N. (1995) "From Redistribution to Recognition? Dilemmas of Justice in a 'Post-Socialist' Age" *New Left Review*, I (212) 68–93.

Gough J. (2010) "Workers' Strategies to Secure Jobs, Their Uses of Scale, and Competing Economic Moralities: Rethinking the 'Geography of Justice'" *Political Geography*, 29(3) 130–139.

Gupta J. (2014) *The History of Global Climate Governance*. Cambridge University Press, Cambridge.

Hallowes D. (2011) *Toxic Futures*. University of KwaZulu-Natal Press, Durban.

Hardt M. and Negri A. (2017) *Assembly*. Oxford University Press, Oxford.

Holmes B. (2010) "Is It Written in the Stars? Global Finance, Precarious Destinies" *Ephemera*, 10(3–4) 222–233.

Layfield D. (2013) "Turning Carbon into Gold: The Financialisation of International Climate Policy" *Environmental Politics*, 22(6) 901–917.

Leonardi E. (2012) Biopolitics of Climate Change. Unpublished PhD Thesis, Centre for the Study of Theory and Criticism, University of Western Ontario.

Leonardi E. (2017a) "For a Critique of Neoliberal Green Economy" *Soft Power*, 5(1) 169–185.

Leonardi E. (2017b) "Carbon Trading Dogma" *Ephemera*, 17(1) 61–87.

Lohmann L. (2011) "Financialization, commodification and carbon" in Panitch L., Albo G. and Vivek C. eds *Socialist Register 2012: The Crisis and the Left*. Monthly Review Press, New York.

Lucarelli S. and Leonardi E. (2015) "Financial governmentality" in M. Pieters, J. Paraskeva and T. Besley eds *The Global Financial Crisis and Educational Restructuring*. Peter Lang, New York.

Lucarelli S. and Vercellone C. (2013) "The Thesis of Cognitive Capitalism: New Research Perspectives" *Knowledge Cultures*, 1(4) 1–14.

MacKenzie D, Muniesa F. and Siu L. eds (2007) *Do Economists Make Markets?*. Princeton University Press, Princeton.

Mansbridge J. (2014) "The Role of the State in Governing the Commons" *Environmental Science & Politics*, 36 8–10.

Marazzi C. (2011) *The Violence of Financial Capital*. Semiotext(e), New York.

Marx K. (1993) *Grundrisse*. Penguin, London.

Methmann C. (2013) "The Sky is the Limit: Global Warming as Global Governmentality" *European Journal of International Relations*, 19(1) 69–91.

Mezzadra S. and Neilson B. (2013) *Border as Method*. Duke University Press, Durham.

Moreno C., Fuchs L. and Speich Chassé D. (2016) Beyond Paris: Avoiding the Trap of Carbon Metrics, (www.opendemocracy.net/transformation/camila-moreno-lili-fuhr-daniel-speich-chass/beyond-paris-avoiding-trap-of-carbon-metr) accessed 25 November 2017.

Neal J. ed (2009) One Million Climate Jobs Now! (http://ccs.ukzn.ac.za/files/Britain%20green%20jobs%20pamphlet.pdf) accessed 25 November 2017.

Neal J. ed (2014) One Million Climate Jobs (www.campaigncc.org/sites/data/files/Docs/one_million_climate_jobs_2014.pdf) accessed 25 November 2017.

One Million Climate Jobs (2011) One Million Climate Jobs (https://womin.org.za/images/the-alternatives/fighting-destructive-extractivism/One%20Million%20Climate%20Jobs.pdf) accessed 25 November 2017.

Räthzel N. and Uzzell D. (2013) "Mending the breach between labour and nature: A case for environmental labour studies" in Uzzell D. and Räthzel N. eds *Trade Unions in the Green Economy: Working for the Environment*. Earthscan, London.

Rosenberg A. (2010) "Building a Just Transition. The Linkages Between Climate Change and Employment" *International Journal of Labour Research*, 2(2) 125–62.

Ross A. (2011) Life and Labor in the Era of Climate Justice (www.uninomade.org/life-and-labor-in-the-era-of-climate-justice/) accessed 25 October 2017.

Stern N. (2007) *The Economics of Climate Change*. HM Treasury, London.

Stevis D. and Felli R. (2015) "Global labour unions and just transition to a green economy" *International Environmental Agreements: Politics, Law and Economics* 15(1) 29–43.

The Economist (2017) Data Is Giving Rise to a New Economy (www.economist.com/news/briefing/21721634-how-it-shaping-up-data-giving-rise-new-economy) accessed 25 October 2017.

Thörn H. (2006) "Solidarity Across Borders" *Voluntas*, 17(4) 285–301.

Part III
New paradigms from below

7 Community economies and climate justice

Gerda Roelvink

Introduction

While there is a long history of social movement struggle centred on the economy, from around the 1990s new forms of collective action emerged that challenge how we *think* about "the economy" *and* are experimenting with new ways of living well with others (see Roelvink 2016). These new forms of collective action depart from social movements centred on a common identity and from traditional Marxist politics centred on a working-class revolution. Instead these movements gather a diverse range of people around common concerns (Latour 2005). They are also much more inclusive than past movements and operate without the singular political identity that many social movements have centred on. In addition to humans, this new form of collective action can include other species and things, such as animals, soil species, new technologies and rivers in the case of concern groups transforming farming (see Gibson-Graham and Roelvink 2010).

Within this new form of collective action are groups that frame their struggle in terms of environmental, and now increasingly climate justice. What is particularly noticeable about environmental justice centred collective action, is the way in which the economy and the environment are linked together; whether it concerns economic initiatives and their social and environmental goals or development work directed at poverty alleviation through climate change mitigation or other issues. The link between environmental and socio-economic injustice is what sets the environmental justice movement apart from other social movements concerned with the environment, particularly environmentalism that is centred on a wildness ethic (Dawson 2010). Rather than separate from human life, and therefore to be protected from humans, the environment is seen as intertwined with social life and, in particular, the different ways certain groups of people are marginalised. This might include, for example, environmental injustices involving racial and class social divisions, with people of colour and or those experiencing poverty bearing the brunt of environmental problems. As Dawson (2010) shows, this makes the struggle against environmental injustice complex; isolating a particular environmental concern, such as campaigning for factory closures or an end to logging, does not necessarily address the intertwined social concerns (i.e. when a particular class or ethnicity is employed in the industry to be closed).

The struggle for environmental justice must therefore address the political–economic arrangements through which the environmental concern has arisen and become intertwined with social concerns.

Climate justice is perhaps the central concern around which different species and things are gathering today. In fact, climate change appears to act as a metanarrative of concern linking different areas of political–economic activism with environmental justice movements. As with struggles for environmental justice, when it comes to the climate justice movement Naomi Klein (2014, 18), a prominent voice in the climate justice movement, suggests that economy and "nature" must to be taken together: "we have not done the things that are necessary to lower emissions because those things fundamentally conflict with deregulated capitalism, the reigning ideology for the entire period we have been struggling to find a way out of this crisis". For Klein, the climate justice movement must "challenge not only capitalism, but also the building blocks to materialism that preceded modern capitalism, a mentality some call 'extractivism' (2014, 25). Klein's work suggests that how we think about economic life more generally, not just in relation to capitalism, needs to be examined in the struggles for climate justice.

The excerpt from Klein above is clearly part of a politics of resistance. Indeed, the environmental justice movement, out of which the climate justice movement has emerged, originates from an oppositional stance towards and fight against the interlinked attacks on the environment and particular social groups (Dawson 2010, Martinez-Alier, Temper, Del Bene and Scheidel 2016). This chapter hopes to contribute to affirmative experimentation with political–economic arrangements in which the environment is central to economic decision making. An important feature I focus on regarding the collectives concerned about climate change (see Roelvink 2016) is the shift they have made from a politics of resistance (such as that associated with the more traditional left, including in academic critique) to one of affirmation (Roelvink 2016). Thus, the kind of social movements concerned with climate change that this chapter explores are not focused on resistance but rather are actively experimenting with new ways of living with others, other species and nature. One of the aims of this chapter, then, is to provide some strategies for affirmative, collective, economic action that other movements centred on climate justice might explore. Rather than focusing on injustice, I examine some of the ways in which just economies are created in response to climate concern.

Many of the affirmative economic initiatives that collectives concerned with climate have worked towards – such as farmers markets, cooperative green enterprises and community supported agriculture – might be taken for granted as part of the economy today; yet a lot of work, both within and outside the academy, has taken place to ensure their recognition. Activist scholars have played an important role in this shift in economic thinking and it is from within this context that the diverse economies' tradition of scholarship has emerged, spearheaded by the work of J.K. Gibson-Graham (see 2006a, 2006b, Gibson-Graham, Cameron and Healy 2013, Roelvink, St. Martin and Gibson-Graham 2015). Central to this scholarship, and a more widely accepted understanding of the economy today (demonstrated, for example, by the inclusion of volunteering work in census data collection), is the view that our economies are full of diverse practices, transactions, institutional forms and property arrangements, some of which are shaped by capitalist class relations but many of which are not (see Gibson-Graham 2006a, 2006b, Gibson-Graham, Healy and Cameron 2013). This diverse economy can be imagined as an iceberg with wage labour, capitalist enterprises and market transactions typically visible at the tip and most of which supports our lives lying hidden underneath the waterline (such as gifts, self-provisioning, cooperatives, fair trade, community gardens and so on) (see Gibson-Graham, Healy and Cameron (2013) for a recent iteration of the diverse economy). This diverse economies' research has provided tools for reading and reframing the economic landscape to enable this fuller version of the economy to emerge (see Gibson-Graham 2006a). This has worked to displace capitalism as 'the economy' or a singular global economic system and thereby displace the thinking that J.K. Gibson-Graham (2006a) characterises as capitalocentricism.

Deconstructing capitalocentricism, or diverse economies' scholarship, has led to the political project of community economies research. This community economies research might be described as the more intentional economic building side of the diverse economies tradition (see Gibson-Graham 2006b and www.communityeconomies.org/Home). Rather than community as such, the community economy is a space of ethical decision making centred on the diverse economies of which we are a part and in particular the way that economic decisions impact upon and shape economic interdependence. Gibson-Graham and their community economies' collective colleagues have developed a number of different tools and coordinates to prompt and direct this decision making, from questions about "what is necessary to personal and social survival" in Gibson-Graham's 2006b book *A Postcapitalist Politics*, to the development of tools to complete a well-being score card in Gibson-Graham, Cameron and Healy's 2013 book *Take Back the Economy*.

Community economies' scholars have begun turning their attention to the challenge of climate change and to thinking about the relationship between the choices we make in our economic lives and the diverse ecologies in which we live. This work speaks to the issue of climate justice. This work has led to a wider examination of our "mode of humanity" (Plumwood 2007), including the extractive mode that Klein mentions above, but also modes through which we might live well with others (Roelvink and Gibson-Graham 2009, Gibson-Graham and Roelvink 2010). The engagement of this work with climate justice has prompted new directions for scholarship, with community economies' scholars beginning to explore, for example, the themes of economic and ecological resilience (Roelvink and Gibson-Graham 2009), belonging (Gibson-Graham 2011), hybrid collective economic initiatives that foreground relationships between different species (Cameron, Manhood and Pomfrett 2011, Hill 2014, Roelvink 2016) and posthumanist economies (Roelvink 2015). This chapter explores and brings together this emerging community economies' approach to climate politics and also considers what our economies might look like when climate justice is foregrounded in economic decision making within a number of different collectives. To do so, the chapter is divided into three central themes, which are at the core of community economies' work. In order to provide some tools for movements concerned with climate justice, I have inserted within these themes strategies and framings that can be used as a guide to economic intervention orientated towards climate justice.

Acting now: thinking outside the spatialities and temporalities of capitalism and climate change

While the climate justice movement may see the "the economy" and climate as intertwined, these two seemingly different yet intersecting spheres are often pitted against each other. As Klein (2014, 21) sees it,

> our economic system and our planetary system are now at war. Or, more accurately, our economy is at war with many forms of life on earth, including human life. What the climate needs to avoid collapse is a contraction in humanity's use of resources; what our economic model demands to avoid collapse is unfettered expansion. Only one of these sets of rules can be changed, and it's not the laws of nature.

She goes on to suggest that "we are left with a stark choice: allow climate disruption to change everything about our world, or change pretty much everything about our economy to avoid that fate" (2014, 22). The economic system we are at war with is widely understood through the lens of capitalism. Here, as seen in the quote from Klein above, climate change is linked to the emergence of capitalism as a global economic system and in order to prevent the worst effects of climate change we need to completely overthrow that system. When our economies are framed as a single capitalist *system*, the struggle for justice is also placed on a global revolutionary scale, tied to the spatial and temporal imaginary of capitalism. From this perspective, local everyday change seems at best insignificant but more often futile. For those less convinced about the possibility of a global revolution, faith is placed in, and then continually dashed by, our politicians (dictated by democratic political cycles) and international governmental bodies to make our economies more sustainable. Taken together, the two options, revolution or global change lead by governments and international bodies, leave little room for hope. Perhaps due to their oppositional stance, many struggles for climate justice have been tied to these spatialities and temporalities of capitalism and contemporary democratic politics.

Moving from the revolution of a system to connection through signification and a politics of assemblage

Community economies' scholars would certainly agree with Klein's call for action and appreciate the devastating impact of human life on our planet, yet they significantly depart from the politics that comes with capitalocentric thinking on climate change. Community economies' work offers several different starting points for thinking about change that is centred on the diverse needs of our societies and how these are intertwined with the environment and climate. The first thing to note is that the discursive shift from a capitalist global economic system to a diverse economy makes an enormous difference to the possibilities of economic action and mobilisation for climate justice. Outside of the capitalocentric framing of our economy as a singular capitalist economic system, we can start the process of transformation from exactly where we are without the formation of some kind of global organisation that will bring about a revolution (Gibson-Graham 2006b). Moving on from this starting point, Gibson-Graham (2006b, xxiv) take inspiration from second-wave feminism to understand how change can be initiated in multiple "disarticulated 'places' – households, communities, ecosystems, workplaces, civic organizations, bodies, public arenas, urban spaces, diasporas, regions, government agencies, occupations – related analogically rather than organisationally and connected through webs of signification". Transformation from this perspective starts with people in place. Key to this placed-based transformation is the articulation of a language that connects the different actions and initiatives. For Gibson-Graham this has initially been the language of economic difference (2006b, xxiv). The environmental injustice movement has come to a similar position. Arguing that the environmental justice movement is global in scope, Joan Martinez-Alier, Leah Temper, Daniela Del Bene and Arnim Scheidel (2016, 747) note that much of the resistance to environmental injustice that has been documented is local and place-based with a globally shared agenda without a central organising body, much like global feminism.

More recently, community economies researchers have understood interventions at a local scale through the lens of an assemblage, which importantly includes more-than-human participants such as the socio-technical aspects and other species (St. Martin, Roelvink and Gibson-Graham 2015). From this perspective, building ethical and just economies involves making connections between different people, species, things in place but also extends to all the other work, practices and entities that stretch beyond place, yet have had a role in making intervention possible. A focus on assemblage greatly expands the scope of justice in terms of who gets included into economic decision making. Reflecting on a community enterprise established through a community economies' research project, for example, St. Martin, Roelvink and Gibson-Graham (2015, 14) note that from an: "assemblage approach, then, we might think of the ginger community enterprise as a sociotechnical assemblage whose constitutive parts exceed any one account of its becoming, as well as any attempt to bound it as essentially local". They further describe this as a:

> politics of horizontal extent, reach, and association rather than a 'politics of scale' where our 'local' interventions and outcomes risk being understood only as subordinate to the 'global' …. Indeed, from the perspective of assemblage, the local and global are outcomes of particular networks and associations rather than inherent qualities or capacities.
>
> (2015, 16)

This approach adds further weight to situated place-based interventions to create justice economies in response to climate change, where economic decisions must concern connections that are unbounded by place. Indeed, this is the kind of unbounded politics that the globe scope of climate change calls for.

Reframing the temporality of change using a generational yardstick

Climate change has provided a new temporal framing for community economies' research, which aims to participate in change here and now. Community economies' scholars ask us to move beyond the capitalocentric Western democratic temporal framing to consider a deeper and longer or altogether different sense of history, such as our existence as a species connected to other species (Roelvink 2016), or our lives within different generations, which span 150 years or more (Gibson-Graham, Cameron and Healy 2013, 2016). Gibson-Graham, Cameron and Healy's (2013, 2016) generational yardstick is one tool that can be used for this kind of work. The generational yardstick enables us to look backwards and forwards 150 years. As Gibson-Graham, Cameron and Healy explain, the yardstick, "places our present in the kind of temporal context that climate change requires us to consider" many generations back and into the future (Gibson-Graham, Cameron and Healy 2013, 138). The generational yardstick looks like a ruler with markings representing years instead of centimetres. A line representing the present is drawn on the yardstick and on either side of the present line, 25-year gaps are marked to represent each generation in the past and in the future. To use the yardstick a particular issue is chosen, such as the ozone commons or climate change discussed by Gibson-Graham, Cameron and Healy (and mentioned further below). With this visual representation of time, researchers can identify and record the different action and events in the past, present and future relating to a particular concern. And with this tool economic questions about climate justice are propelled both backwards and forwards and a greater number of people, species and environments can be taken into account.

The generational yardstick also shows that what we might be doing now, could in fact be laying the ground work for what will one day be seen as rapid change. This is important given the urgency of climate change discourse. Gibson-Graham, Cameron and Healy's (2016) story of the switch to solar power in Australia, for example, looks back to include all the research work in University labs in the 1950s and 1970s, the huge uptake of solar panels by households in the 2000s, government subsidy schemes alongside inaction in international climate change forums and the social movement Solar Citizens:

> Some things seems to happen very quickly such as the rapid take up of solar energy in Australia in the last few years or the two years that it took to get the Montreal Protocol signed. *But if we focus only on these moments we miss the work that can go on for generations to help create the conditions for what seems like rapid transformation.* This is not to say that change happens in a linear or predictable way. The process of change emerges out of any number

of things coming together and entangling to create the conditions for shifts to occur. Only with an inter-generational perspective can we begin to see the multiple temporalities at work and by which change takes place.

(Gibson-Graham 2016, Cameron and Healy 208, emphasis added)

The generational yardstick, then, offers an alternative view to "big" governmental change and also gets us away from the paralysis that comes from focusing on the need to change a "capitalist" system. It enables us to include a wider range of species and environments into economic decision making centred on our interdependence, where questions about justice need to consider a "multi-species planetary community" across time (Gibson-Graham, Healy and Cameron 2016). It also enables us to see rapid change as a cumulative, yet not necessarily linear, effect.

Questioning the liberal human subject who can divert future climate change

There is another temporal element of climate change discourse that is problematic for community economies' approach to climate justice. Alongside, and often in conjunction with capitalocentric temporalities, the temporality of climate change discourse presents something of a barrier to action as this discourse typically displaces climate change into a disconnected future, in the sense that it can still in some ways be diverted. At the same time the liberal human subject (who is separate from the environment) is positioned at the centre of the action that is needed today to divert this future catastrophe (Roelvink and Zolkos 2011). As Magdalena Zolkos and I have argued:

> This understanding of the present as a defining temporality of human activity, possibility and ability masks an investment into a liberal humanist idea of the subject who appears autonomous, rational and self-contained in her/his capacity to exert power in the world. While this subject might be positively aligned with progressive environmental causes, and committed to act on behalf of the non-human environment as its protector, safeguard or custodian, *in some crucial aspects she/he remains disconnected from that environment* – unaffected and unchanged by its "otherness" – and has no part in its vulnerability, pain, or precariousness.
>
> (Roelvink and Zolkos 2011, 47, emphasis added)

With climate change a future to head-off, faith is placed in the liberal subject as saviour. This is a subject who is viewed as separate from the environment. And when it comes to climate politics, the environment must be protected from our economic life rather than seen as intertwined with the economy. This greatly narrows the scope of justice as it ultimately separates human existence from that of others.

Along with the liberal subject, progress and technological advancement are often privileged in climate change discourse. More specifically, the sense of impending future catastrophe that only the action of a liberal rational subject can stop is tied to the technoscientific futurity that María Puig de la Bellacasa (2015) writes about. Here the urgent action that must be undertaken to divert the future ecological crisis is marked by a belief that progress and advancement will save the day, while the preciousness of the present suggests that this action must be undertaken now at all costs (Puig de la Bellacasa 2015, 693–694). Puig de la Bellacasa's work goes further showing how this modernist temporality shapes capitalist discourse and in particular the discourse of productionalism. Ecological destruction brought about through intensified farming, for example, is thus met with technological innovations aimed at maintaining and even increasing production, albeit "sustainably":

> These instances in the history of human-soil relations can also be read in terms of how they expose a combination of anxious restlessness about the future – in the face of disasters such as the dust bowl or fears of mass famine – with ambitious responses based on innovations that confirm the technoscientific productionist drive.
>
> (Puig de la Bellacasa 2015, 696–697)

This scholarship on the temporality of climate change discourse thus suggests the interweaving of capitalocentric and modernist thinking, resulting in more of the same economic practices at an intensified rate and scale. To sum up, climate change discourse is often tied to a capitalocentric vision of the economy and an anthropocentric modernist subject, both of which are problematic for supporting ethical economic action in response to current ecological devastation.

The embodied subject as a site of change

Community economies' scholars question this anthropocentric modernist subject and place affective interdependent relationships with others at the centre of ethical economic action here and now. Social change is understood to be grounded in people whose very subjection to something, whether it is capitalism or something else (perhaps the disabling discourse of climate change), is never complete and thus always contains the potential for change. Inspired by Jane Bennett's work, for Gibson-Graham (2006b, 14) our bodies are dynamic, always engaging with others and the world they are a part of, and with this bodies can change or swerve in new directions and take up "alternative ways of being" in interaction with others. This work presents an embodied economic subject interdependent with others and the world. It suggests that subjective change can arise from even seemingly entrenched subject positions, such as those who feel helpless and paralysed by climate change discourse. This provides an alternative starting point to the rational predetermined action associated with the liberal economic subject. In contrast, an economic response to climate change might be cultivated through the generation of particular subjective experiences that create opportunities for subjects to "swerve". Bearing witness to landscape degradation is one example from my research with Zolkos (2011) that demonstrates that the experience of communal vulnerability when one comes to see their life as intertwined with the environment might prompt an affective swerve, opening the subject to economic experimentation (see also Roelvink 2016). This could also be described as an act of "environmental justice witnessing" (see Grieve 2015). In this and other cases affective change does not just happen. Rather central to the affective changes that Gibson-Graham and Zolkos and I talk about is the subject's involvement in collective life. This has led to a rethinking of the collective, which I turn to in the next section of this chapter.

Exploring more-than-human temporalities

Though not working within a community economies' framing, Puig de la Bellacasa suggests a different temporality to technoscientific futurity, with which one might view and work with soil health where "focusing on experiences of soil care as an involvement with the temporal rhythms of more than human worlds troubles the anthropocentric traction of predominant timescales" (2015, 695). In the case of the food web concept, for example, humans are just one element in a wider interdependent "food web community" and the rhythms of this food web suggest a mode of soil care very different from one centred on production for human needs (Puig de la Bellacasa 2015). This pushes existing community economies' work with temporalities outside of a capitalocentric framing (such as the yardstick mentioned above) to explore temporalities beyond the human, such as the temporalities of inter-species interdependent life. I take up this point in the third section of this chapter. Before getting to more-than-human temporalities and modes of life, however, it is necessary to examine the community economies reframing of the collective and how a rethought collective offers a response to climate change.

Acting together

While one might be ready to start working towards climate justice here and now, knowing where to start can be a daunting task. Community economies' scholars do not presume they know what action to take. Instead, as Gibson-Graham (2010, 332) and I have noted, in the face of climate change community economies' scholars start from a place of silence:

> But how do we put ourselves (and the earth) in the way of such transformations? How do we get from an abstract ontological revisioning to a glimmer or a whiff of what to do on the ground? No answer arrives when we ponder this question—just a spacious silence and a slowing down.
>
> Silence and slowness are openings, of course, opportunities for the body to shift its stance, to meld a little more with its surroundings; chances for the mind to mull over what floats by on the affective tide, or to swerve from its course as momentum decreases. Undoubtedly these are openings for learning.

Not learning in the sense of increasing a store of knowledge but in the sense of becoming other, creating connections and encountering possibilities that render us newly constituted beings in a newly constituted world.

Learning to be affected as a method of economic experimentation in response to climate change

Community economies' scholars approach the tricky questions thrown up by climate change from a position of not knowing and, importantly, from a position of openness to new forms of learning. One way to take action from such a position of openness is to begin experimenting. For Jenny Cameron (2015), experimentation offers a playful, open and hopeful way to begin collective action that responds to climate change. While the word experiment brings much epistemological baggage, the kind of experimentation Cameron has in mind is very different from forms of scientific experimentation associated with technoscienific futurity that take a narrow understanding of objectivity and are centred on control (a form of experimentation that has, in fact, been part of the problem of climate change as discussed above). Instead, Cameron (2015, 100) suggests experimentation as a way for researchers to make "a stand for certain worlds and for certain ways of living on the planet, and taking responsibility for helping to make these worlds more likely and these ways of living more widespread". Researchers (whether they are in academic institutions or in the "wild", to use Callon and Rabeharisoa's (2003) term) wanting to take up a position of experimentation, in response to questions of climate justice, need to be open and playful, and ready to work with others who are engaged in creating new economic practices in a broader collective of concern (Cameron 2015, 100).

Part of this experimental stance, then, is learning from others, not just other humans but also other species and things involved in collectives concerned with climate justice. Central to a community economies' understanding of such collective learning from human and more-than-human others, is Bruno Latour's (2004) idea of learning to be affected. Latour theorises the process of learning to be affected through the case of a person becoming a "nose" in the perfume industry. With a perfume kit consisting of different smells and a teacher, a pupil is taught to differentiate between a range of smells, thus becoming more sensitive and highly attuned to a world of smell. Bodies and worlds change together; the world of smell is co-created with the body becoming a "nose". This could not have happened without the pupil but neither could it have happened without the perfume kit and all the other things needed to for the learning/differentiation to occur. In other words, this could not have happened without the "hybrid collective" through which learning takes place (see Callon and Rabeharisoa 2003, Roelvink 2016 on hybrid collectives). Importantly, then, collectively learning to be affected opens up a more diverse world with new possibilities for action (see Roelvink 2016).

Community economies researchers have taken up and extended this understanding of collective learning to be affected, as a method of economic experimentation in response to climate change (see for example Dombroski 2013, Cameron, Manhood and Pomfrett 2011, Hill 2014). Jenny Cameron, Craig Manhood and

Jamie Pomfrett (2011), for example, see community gardeners as researchers in the wild who are learning to be affected by not only gardens and the differences in plant and insect life as the environment changes but also through interactions with other gardeners. They are part of a community garden collective learning to be affected by a changing climate. Through their research Cameron, Manhood and Pomfrett (2011) seek to extend this learning further by creating opportunities for different community gardens to interact with each other and in doing so to broaden the opportunities for learning to be affected. Importantly, one result of this research is a more highly differentiated vision of community gardening and with this vision, new possibilities for gardeners to experiment with as the climate changes. Another important result of this research is a broader and stronger collective of concern, with the connections between different community gardens strengthened through the research. Creating opportunities for collective learning, and thereby strengthening collectives through community economies research projects, is one way in which community economies scholars are working collectively with others in response to climate change.

Commoning for climate justice

Another entry point to collective change making in response to climate change, has been developed through recent work on the commons. The commons is a central theme within the climate justice movement with several different meanings (Chatterton, Featherstone and Routledge 2013). Approaching the commons as a means of acting together, Gibson-Graham, Cameron and Healy (2016, 195) employ the term common or commoning as a verb, specifically as "a relational process – or more often a struggle – of negotiating access, use, benefit, care and responsibility" of property of any type (private, state-owned, collectively owed and so on) or more generally of communal wealth (such as land but also air, water, the gene pool, the atmosphere and more) (Gibson-Graham 2006b, 96) . In this commoning process, a collective or community is formed and maintained. This is a collective centred on concern rather than identity and also is one that is hybrid and complex. As form of community economy, the collective of commoning shares "being *in* common" (Nancy 1991, cited by Gibson-Graham, Cameron and Healy 2013). Negotiations concerning justice in relation to the commons thus must take into account the interdependence that comes with co-existence. Learning to be affected can be part of the commoning process, as those involved in commoning learn from and are affected by other participants and as a result view the commons in much more diverse ways, in turn opening up new possibilities for caring for the commons.

As an example, Gibson-Graham, Cameron and Healy use the generational yardstick mentioned above to track the commoning of the Australian city of Newcastle's air. This commoning process occurred overtime and involved affected residents, an amalgamated larger city council with greater power, dust deposit gauges, the formation of a state government Smoke Abatement Committee and the resulting Clean Air Act, local media and more:

The commoning action involved residents, across class lines, learning to be affected and acknowledging the impact of the embodied experience of living in a highly polluted environment. It also involved shifts in institutional arrangements and the mobilisation of technological advances. It drew on developments locally and those further afield. As a result, a loose community emerged who were able to take responsibility and care for Newcastle's atmosphere, to manage how the atmosphere was being used, and to ensure that there was access to clean air and that this benefit was shared across the city.

(Gibson-Graham, Cameron and Healy 2016, 201)

This form of commoning could be applied to the climate commons and the creation of affiliated communities, or a global community, and Gibson-Graham, Cameron and Healy (2013) suggest seeking just outcomes in the different ways we relate to and involve the climate in economic life. The Newcastle case is one example of an emerging community of care for the atmospheric commons. Another that Gibson-Graham, Cameron and Healy draw attention to is the action against CFCS (cholorflourocarbons). Gibson-Graham, Cameron and Healy use the generational yardstick to look at the emergence of concern about climate change and the actions alongside this over time. They ask, "what of the future? Might we be able to act now as a global community to care for our atmospheric commons?" and note, "a number of pathways are available" for care centred on the acknowledgement and respect for the interdependence of different life systems (Gibson-Graham, Cameron and Healy 2013, 146).

While some research on the climate justice movement suggests that the theme of the commons complicates and perhaps challenges approaches to climate change that seek to privatise parts of the atmosphere through, for example, carbon trading mechanisms (see Chatterton, Featherstone and Routledge 2013), Gibson-Graham, Cameron and Healy's (2013, 154) work detaches the commons from legal definitions of property, looking instead to how the commons, in a variety of forms, are cared for. Thus, private property can be commoned such as when "non-owners ... have access to and use of privately owned property, thus ensuring that the benefits are more widely distributed". A good example is groups of private landholders establishing conservation covenants in order to protect and restore large areas of land (see Gibson-Graham, Cameron and Healy 2013, 154). Another important part of commoning in this sense is that it involves relations and actions that extend beyond the human frame:

What we have learnt is that the commoning-community is more-than-human. The agent of change, the commoner, is no longer (and perhaps never was) a person or a category such as the working class but an assemblage. Certainly these assemblages include humans, but they also include non-humans; they may include class but also non-class alignments; they may include social movements and grass-roots organisations but also governments, institutions, and firms; they may include non-market mechanisms but also markets; they

may include animate beings who have nothing in common except breathing and living, but also inanimate entities that share an existence on this planet.
(Gibson-Graham, Cameron and Healy, 2016, 207)

Acting outside of capitalocentric and modernist temporalities, as I discussed in the first section, and acting with others through learning to be affected and commoning calls for deeper engagement with the more-than-human world – toward posthumanist community economies to which I now turn.

Posthumanist community economies

In their work to build and support ethical economic life in an era marked by climate change, community economies scholars have begun to engage with the more-than-human world in a new, more conscious and deliberate way. In addition to the work discussed above, this trend towards posthumanist economies (which I explain below) has been developed through conversations with the ecological humanities. Gibson-Graham and I (2009) have explored, for example, the connections between ecological and environmental resilience and highlight the importance of existing community-based economic practices that support not only material well-being but social and environmental well-being as well. What becomes clear in this work is the role that the more-than-human world plays in economic life, whether it is in the "shadow places" (Plumwood 2008), in which our consumables are produced that we do not know about (such as the plants that produce materials for clothing), or right in front of us as we turn on the water (such as rivers) or shop for and eat a meal (such as plants and animals). Gibson-Graham and I go on to ask how we might include the more-than-human world into the ethical economic decision making about what is necessary to our survival, the allocation of surplus, how wealth is to be consumed and in the process of commons making (as discussed above). It is this ethical economic deliberation that performs a community economy and thus by including the more-than-human world into this decision making we also more directly see the more-than-human world as part of a community economy (see also Gibson-Graham and Roelvink 2010).

Caring – with connected earth others

How to include the more-than-human into economic decision making, however, is an ongoing challenge. One way that this challenge has been approached is through thinking on connection. Gibson-Graham (2011) continue to draw on the ecological humanities (such as Weir 2009), in their work on connection and belonging. It should be noted here that this scholarship draws strongly on Indigenous Australian's experience with the environment and their "embodied experience" of "connectivity" (Weir 2009, 51). As Jessica Weir (2009, 51) explains, "This is a perspective that moves beyond an understanding of the world as separated into spheres of human and natural, to an understandings of a world in which our being and the environment are bound together". In addition to the ecological humanities,

Gibson-Graham draw on Jane Bennett's (2010) scholarship on vibrant matter and other authors from both science and philosophy to propose two different yet potentially complementary ways of thinking about connection. The first, coming out of marine science and romantic philosophy, explores the "reciprocity between the species" in encounters between humans and other species (Gibson- Graham 2011, 3). These encounters suggest to Gibson-Graham a connection with others as if part of a large family, where care and love is extended to the more-than-human world when existence is recognised as co-implicated and reciprocal. Gibson-Graham draw on Bennet's work to tease out a second way to think about connection, which displaces the human from the centre of action by focusing on the assemblages that enable action. Here clear distinctions between humans and the more-than-human world are blurred as different entities come together to enable action. For Gibson-Graham (2011, 3):

> Each of these projects of connection constructs a form of belonging – the first is like belonging to the world as one does to a family, suggesting an affect of love and an ethic of care (one that seems to go both ways); the second involves belonging within a 'heterogeneous monism of vibrant bodies' (Bennett 2010, 119), a vital pluriverse, suggesting an affect of uncertain excitement and an ethic of attuning ourselves more closely to the powers, capacities and dynamism of the more than human.
>
> We see these two projects as potentially in productive conversation with each other. While we might feel love for other earth creatures and want to accept a responsibility to care for them, might we also extend our love to parasites, or inorganic matter, or to the unpredictability of technical innovation? And might not an ethics of attunement to vibrant matter produce a more sensitive, experimental mode of assembling within the 'jizz' of our living environments?
>
> (Gibson-Graham 2011, 4)

This work suggests that we might extend our love and care to the more-than-human assemblages through which ethical economic action is performed. This is care, however, that is not care for the other, as in a paternal relationship, but rather a "caring-with" (Tronto 2017) in which all entities are viewed to play an important co-constituting role in supporting interdependent life. Importantly, then, ethical economic deliberation needs to consider interdependence more fully, where our actions affect another's, but also to recognise these others as active participants in our own lives.

An economic ethics that responds to connected others

Another community economies entry point to thinking about economic life in a time of climate change, and in particular exchanges with the more-than-human world, is perhaps surprisingly though research on the species-being of humans

(Roelvink 2013, 2016). Rather than seeing the human species as separate from other species, my work in this area re-examines Marx's theory of the species-being to think about the co-constituting role of other species in the species life of humans. Through this work I suggest that different modes of humanity are performed, in part, as a result of the ways in which other species affect us. I highlight ethical economic decision making that takes into account, and in some way includes, other species involved in economies life, as central to the creation of more liveable worlds in a time of climate change. One example is farmers who, becoming affected by the land and other species and seeing these others as part of themselves, are responding to landscape degradation by distributing part of their surplus to the more-than-human entities on their farms (such as rivers, grasses, cows) (see Roelvink 2016, Roelvink and Zolkos 2011).

Bio-synergy – a strategy to connect the nitty gritty of economic deliberation to broader interdependencies between life systems

By including the more-than-human world into economic decision making we might start to build economies that are not only more just for humans but also for earth others. As the strategies and framings above suggest, a community economies response to climate change focuses our attention and ethical consideration on the "nitty gritty" (Gibson-Graham and Roelvink 2011); on the entities that enable our everyday lives. Yet the global scope of climate change seems to suggest that we also need to think more generally about a range of different economies and how they connect to each other. Work in the environmental humanities suggests that continued attention to the nitty gritty of economic ethics still remains vital to building just economies alongside broader considerations. In fact, Freya Mathews (2011) shows that the two are inseparable. More specifically, while debate over climate change may place the fate of all species together, Mathews (2011) notes that our economic response to climate change may not necessarily take into account other species on their own terms to secure the survival of the planet. In other words, when our primary focus is on the planet as a whole our response to climate change may not take into consideration the lives of other species but could instead be centred on ensuring the planetary conditions for human survival. For example, if we focus the technoscientific solutions to climate change, then it is conceivable that while ensuring the survival of humans these "solutions" may further endanger other species (Mathews 2011). There is a need for, Mathews argues, a "bio-centric" approach to climate change in which justice is conceived not only in terms of the earth's biosphere but also in terms of all the different species and environments.

I would suggest that the way forward is to maintain our traditional environmental commitment to local ecosystems as moral ends-in-themselves, and not allow this commitment to be subsumed under the new global perspective emanating from climate change. In other words, concern for the biosphere as a whole needs to be balanced with concern for its component parts if we wish to retain a biocentric orientation. As long as earth is valued exclusively as a global system its parts may be sacrificed for the sake of the whole.

(Mathews 2011, 52)

Community economies' scholars have drawn on Mathews work to connect economic ethics to considerations of how different economic assemblages interact and to work towards global interdependence. In my work (2015), for example, I pick up on Mathews (2011, 53) thinking on conatus and synergy, and her description of "bio-synergy" that characterises an economy based on these principles:

> By the term, conativity, I mean the innate impulse of living things to maintain and increase their own existence, each in their own particular mode or style. By synergy, I understand a form of relationship between two or more conative parties who engage with each other in such a way that something new and larger than either of them, but true to the conative tendency of each, is born. Synergy is a modality which brings novelty and change into the world but in a way that is consistent with the conative grain of things at any given moment in the self-unfolding of nature.

A community economies approach centred on bio-synergy takes into account the needs of others to maintain their own existence in ethical economic deliberation, as in the work by Gibson-Graham and myself discussed above, with the added dimension of exploring the partnerships between different entities and assemblages. Community economies' scholars are concerned with whether these partnerships are respectful of and in tune with the modes of living of each of the entities and assemblages involved. One example that I have explored is from agriculture, where rivers have been harnessed for agricultural production without consideration of the water necessary for the rivers to maintain and increase their existing systems. In response to this some farmers have conducted historical research on the river systems from which they draw and as a result they have transformed their farming practices to incorporate the river's own mode or characteristic of existence into their farming, such as by respecting wet lands, swamps and floodplains. These "radical" forms of farming are shown to support and enable rivers to restore their health as well as being of benefit to the farmer who has improved soil and reduced costs from chemicals, erosion and irrigation (see Roelvink 2015).

Mathews suggests how diverse actions centred on synergy, might be connected and come to characterise economies that stretch far and wide. She describes these economies in terms of bio-synergy. An economy centred on bio-synergy, Mathews suggests by way of example, could connect economic practices characterised by foraging (harnessing that which is already available), such as solar power and Indigenous forms of foraging and bush foods modelled on the role of a predator in maintaining ecological balance. This economy may also include practices that will ultimately change biological systems if these changes are in line with their modes of existence:

We might, for example, increase the number of water holes in an arid region, thereby increasing the density of wildlife there. Such an action would need to be offset by other actions, since increasing the density of wildlife in a fragile arid ecosystem might well incur degradation of the vegetation. But a judicious selection of actions might result in the "evolution" of the original ecosystem into one with higher biomass and higher biodiversity than the original system. If we judge the conative tendency of living things to include the impulse not only towards self-maintenance but also towards self-increase, it is arguable that such a change in an ecosystem – in the direction of greater vitality and diversity – would qualify as consistent with the system's own conativity. In this sense it may be possible for us to intervene in biological systems to increase their "productivity" without violating their integrity.

(Mathews 2011, 60)

Community economies have provided a starting point to create just economies not only for humans but also for other species. This is largely focused on particular actions, practices and entities but also extends further when we consider these as part of an assemblage spanning different generations. While wary of thinking about the economy as a system (see Gibson-Graham 2006a), we can look at community economy interventions in light of the conative tendencies of other species, places and ecologies and try to work with these earth others following the idea of bio-synergy.

In light of this work, community economies might be now described as post-humanist. This is not to entirely displace the human from economic consideration, rather it "draws attention to the embodied life of the human in relation to others, and how it is precisely through our engagement with others that we become human. So while posthumanist scholarship *decentres* the human by highlighting the connections that enable life it also attends to the *specificity* of the human being" in relation to those other interdependent entities with their own specificities (Roelvink 2015, 227).

Conclusion

There are no straightforward rights and wrongs here. As in all ethical negotiations, there's a weighing of the practical opportunities and possibilities available in the situation with our longings as to how the world might be.
(Gibson-Graham, Cameron and Healy 2013, 129)

For community economies researchers it is through ethical deliberation about economic interdependence that just economies are achieved. The foundation of questions of justice then lie in the conceptualisation of a community based on interdependence and solidarity in co-existence, and the ethical deliberation about which economic practices and forms support this. The environment has always been a core part of this decision making with, for example, questions around consumption including the consumption of earth's resources and the commons taken as vital to well-being (see Gibson-Graham 2006b). With growing awareness and concern about climate change, and with these new questions of climate justice, community economies researchers have not only broadened the scope of the coordinates of economic ethics, such as by using ecological footprint calculations to explore diverse labour practices (see Gibson-Graham, Cameron and Healy 2013), but have also radically rethought the parameters of ethical economic action. This chapter has outlined these parameters of change.

There will always be trade-offs in ethical deliberation; when it comes to climate justice these are no longer trade-offs between humans alone but now also between a range of different entities concerned with economic experimentation and different forms of life. As Mathews (2011, 59) notes, "It must be remembered, in other words, that bio-synergy is a two-way street – it allows us to act on nature, but it also permits nature to act on us, trimming our ends, and with them our self-expressiveness, to the conative contours of ecosystems". Perhaps when we learn to be affected by earth others, these modifications will be seen less as trade-offs and concessions to others and more as the recognition and response to those who support and make us.

References

Bennett, J. (2010) *Vibrant Matter: A Political Ecology of Thing* Duke University Press, Durham.

Callon, M. and Rabeharisoa, V. (2003) "Research 'in the Wild' and the Shaping of New Social Identities" *Technology in Society*, 25(2): 193–204.

Cameron, J. (2015) "On Experimentation" in Gibson, K. Rose, D. and Fincher, R. eds, *Manifesto for Living in the Anthropocene* Punctum Books, Brooklyn, 99–102.

Cameron, J., Manhood, C. and Pomfrett, J. (2011) "Bodily Learning for a Climate (Changing) World: Registering Difference through Performative and Collective Research" *Local Environment*, 16(6): 116–129.

Chatterton, P., Featherstone, D. and Routledge, P. (2013) "Articulating Climate Justice in Copenhagen: Antagonism, the Commons, and Solidarity" *Antipode*, 45(3): 602–620.

Dawson, A. (2010) "Climate Justice: The Emerging Movement against Green Capitalism" *South Atlantic Quarterly*, 109(2): 313–338.

Dombroski, K. (2013) Babies' Bottoms for a Better World: Modernities, Hygiene and Social Change in Northwest China and Australasia Unpublished PhD Thesis, University of Western Sydney.

Gibson-Graham, J.K. (2006a) *The End of Capitalism (As We Knew It): A Feminist Critique of Political Economy with a New Introduction* University of Minnesota Press, Minneapolis.

Gibson-Graham, J.K. (2006b) *A Postcapitalist Politics* University of Minnesota Press, Minneapolis.

Gibson-Graham, J.K. and Roelvink, G. (2010) "An Economic Ethics for the Anthropocene" *Antipode*, 41(1): 320–346.

Gibson-Graham, J.K. (2011) "A Feminist Project of Belonging for the Anthropocene" *Gender, Place and Culture*, 18(1): 1–21.

Gibson-Graham, J.K., Cameron, J. and Healy, S. (2013) *Take Back the Economy. An Ethical Guide for Transforming Our Communities* University of Minnesota Press, Minneapolis.

Gibson-Graham, J.K., Cameron, J. and Healy, S. (2016) "Commoning as a Postcapitalist Politics" in Amin, A. and Howell, P. eds, *Releasing the Commons: Rethinking the Futures of the Commons* Routledge, London and New York 192–212.

Grieve, S. (2015) *Environmental Justice Witnessing in the Modernist Poetry of Lola Ridge, Muriel Rukeyser, Gwendolyn Brooks, and Elizabeth Bishop* Unpublished PhD Thesis, Arizona State University.

Hill, A. (2014) *Growing Community Food Economies in the Philippines* Unpublished PhD Thesis, Australian National University.

Klein, N. (2014) *This Changes Everything: Capitalist Vs. The Climate* Simon and Schuster, New York.

Latour, B. (2004) "How to Talk about the Body? The Normative Dimension of Science Studies" *Body and Society*, 10(2–3): 205–229.

Latour, B. (2005) "From Realpolitik to Dingpolitik: or How to Make Things Public" in Latour, B. and Weibel, P. eds, *Making Things Public: Atmospheres of Democracy* MIT Press, Cambridge, Massachusetts: 14–41.

Martinez-Alier, J. Temper, L. Del Bene, D. and Scheidel, A. (2016) "Is there a Global Environmental Justice Movement?" *The Journal of Peasant Studies*, 43(3): 731–755.

Nancy, J. (1991) *The Inoperative Community* University of Minnesota Press, Minneapolis.

Plumwood, V. (2007) "A review of Deborah Bird Rose's Reports from a Wild Country: Ethics of Decolonisation" *Australian Humanities Review*, 42(August): 1–4.

Plumwood, V. (2008) "Shadow Places and the Politics of Dwelling" *Australian Humanities Review*, 44 (March): 1–9.

Puig de la Bellacasa, M. (2015) "Making Time for Soil: Technoscientific Futurity and the Pace of Care" *Social Studies of Science*, 45(5): 691–716.

Mathews, F. (2011) "Moral Ambiguities in the Politics of Climate Change" in V. Nanda eds, *Climate Change and Environmental Ethics* Transaction Publishers, New Brunswick, New Jersey: 43–64.

Roelvink, G. (2013) "Rethinking Marx's Species Being in the Anthropocene" *Rethinking Marxism*, 25(1): 52–69.

Roelvink, G. (2015) "Performing Posthumanist Economies" in Roelvink, G., St. Martin, K. and Gibson-Graham, J.K. eds, *Making Other Worlds Possible: Performing Diverse Economies*, University of Minnesota Press, Minneapolis: 225–243.

Roelvink, G. (2016) *Building Dignified Worlds: Geographies of Collective Action* University of Minnesota Press, Minneapolis.

Roelvink, G. and Gibson-Graham, J.K. (2009) "A Postcapitalist Politics of Dwelling" *Australian Humanities Review*, 46(May): 145–158.

Roelvink, G. and Zolkos, M. (2011) "Climate Change as Experience of Affect" *Angelaki*, 16(4): 43–57.

Roelvink, G., St. Martin, K. and Gibson-Graham, J.K. (2015) *Making Other Worlds Possible: Performing Diverse Economies* University of Minnesota Press, Minneapolis.

St. Martin, K., Roelvink, G. and Gibson-Graham, J.K. (2015) "Introduction: An Economic Politics for Our Times" in Roelvink, G., St. Martin, K. and Gibson-Graham, J.K. eds, *Making Other Worlds Possible: Performing Diverse Economies* University of Minnesota Press, Minneapolis: 1–25.

Tronto, J. (2017) "There is an Alternative: Homines Curans and the Limits of Neoliberalism" *International Journal of Care and Caring*, 1(1): 27–43.

Weir, J. (2009) *Murray River Country: An Ecological Dialogue with Traditional Owners* Aboriginal Studies Press, Canberra ACT.

8   Growth, power and domination

Degrowth and perspectives for climate justice

Ulrich Brand

Introduction

Currently, the relationship between economic growth and prosperity is being debated intensively (D'Alisa et al. 2014, Kallis 2017, Konzeptwerk Neue Ökonomie 2017, Eversberg and Schmelzer 2018, Muraca 2013, Demaria et al. 2013). This is due largely to the current economic crisis and decreasing rates of economic growth in the Organisation for Economic Co-operation and Development (OECD) countries as well as a re-politicisation of the ecological crisis, particularly climate change. The latter has mainly to do with the obvious fact that international environmental politics has largely failed (Conca et al. 2008) and that environmental destruction is in many areas accelerating (UNEP 2012). The widely recognised study published by Rockström et al. (2009) shows that in many respects the "planetary boundaries" have already or almost been reached; in addition to biodiversity loss and nitrogen flow, climate change is the most severe problem. Additionally, estimates about peak oil and peak everything stirs the debate about whether and how to rethink economic growth (IEA 2011, Murray and King 2012). The common denominator is that the classical orientation towards the annual growth of production and consumption of market-mediated goods and services is no longer considered adequate. In fact, many reflections and strategies towards climate justice are, at least implicitly, close to a de-growth perspective (Jacobsen 2018). Both aim at a radically different cultural political economy (from a climate justice perspective, cf. Bullard and Müller 2012, Newell and Paterson 2010, Chatterton et al. 2013, Campaign against Climate Change 2014).

In the following, I will briefly condense the motives behind the increasing criticism of the *intense* quest for economic growth and discuss substantial proposals that argue for different approaches to growth. This overview[1] of the current state of the art creates the foundation for my main argument: the critical debates referring to the paradigm of quantitative growth usually blank out a crucial dimension: economic growth as social relations is linked to societal domination and, hence, to reproducing social structures. Contributions developed from perspectives of critical theory – especially feminist and Marxist ones – insist on the domination-formed character of economic growth as an integral part of capitalist societalisation (*Vergesellschaftung*). Societal domination, I argue, in the tradition of the "older" Frankfurt School, is also the basis for domination-formed societal nature relations (Görg 2011, Brand et al. 2008) and should be considered as a main driver of current socio-ecological problems and a major obstacle for alternative approaches.

Domination is hereby understood as a complex political, economic and cultural mode of reproduction of societal structures along class, gender, ethnic, generational or national intersections. Domination can be exercised by open violence but is more commonly reproduced through the internalisation of the dominator's will by the dominated. Such a relational understanding of domination stands in the tradition of Max Weber (1922/1978).

Thus, I refer to relations ingrained in structures of domination and power, to processes that produce and are reproduced by active or passive consent among the dominated (Gramsci 1991: 101–102; Thomas 2009). The concept of hegemony attempts to show that dominant social forces intend to universalise their interests in society and how they become hegemonic, i.e. to exercise domination via political, moral, and intellectual leadership – especially promising and securing growth and progress by pursuing their accumulation strategies – and consensus through accepted institutions. Civil society is a sphere in which social consensus is decisively worked out through power-shaped discourses and practices. Gramsci intended to elucidate the complex mechanisms of "the agreement of associated societal wills" (Gramsci et seq. 1991: 1536). Against this background, hegemony refers to domination-shaped consent based on a more or less functioning capitalist political economy, and the ability and willingness of the dominating classes to compromise.

Hegemony is not represented by explicit agreements among subjects but by a comprehensive practice that involves "the day-to-day activities of individuals and social groups in which their acceptance of domination is manifested as active self-subjection to the shared customs of a large collective" (Demirovi 1997: 257, translation U.B.). Consent, in a Gramscian sense, is not only conviction or false consciousness, but also lived practice. It has a "material core" (Gramsci 1996: 1567), especially with respect to the material reproduction of the everyday lives of people. It is broadly accepted and deeply inscribed into economic, political and cultural practices and norms. Under the prevailing conditions, this material core is not at all sustainable. Manifold societal institutions, like the capitalist market and the capitalist state, assured certain hegemony of destructive and domination-shaped societal nature relations.

Such a Gramscian perspective has an agential or relational dimension as well: The ruling class(es) that organise other forces in a hegemonic power bloc manage to "assert itself, to extend itself throughout the whole of society. In so doing, it creates uniformity not just of economic and political objectives, it also creates intellectual and ethic unity; all the issues over which struggles rage are elevated by it to the 'universal' level, that is, beyond the merely corporatist level. Thus the hegemony of one of the basic groups of society over a number of subordinate groups is established" (Gramsci 1996: 1561, translation U.B.). Finally, domination has a great deal to do with the dominant and marginal forms of the societal appropriation of nature or, more precisely, *societal nature relations*.

This paper is organised as follows. In section two, I summarise major issues of the debate. In section three, my own argument on economic growth and societal domination is outlined, referring to the feminist and neo-Marxist debate and enhanced from a perspective of political ecology towards domination-formed societal nature relations. The reintroduction of democracy to the debate is established in section four and linked to some aspects of the recent debate around social–ecological transformation.

Recent contributions

The most significant critique of economic growth over the last 40 years and the claim for "qualitative" growth has centred around the argument of the ecological limits to growth (c.f. the comprehensive overview in Pirgmaier and Hinterberger 2012). After the study of the Club of Rome in 1972, an intense scientific and social debate commenced (Meadows et al. 1972). The central assumption is that there were scarce resources, notably fossil fuels, for energy production. This debate was complemented in 1990 by the concept of sustainable development, a discussion of the limits of the capacity of forests and oceans to operate as "sinks", as well as the ability of the atmosphere and the stratosphere to cope with emissions (CO_2, chemicals, waste of any kind). Since the 2000s, the discussion has been more and more related to the destruction of interdependent ecosystems.

In this tradition, the most common claim is to foster technological innovation and societal changes towards qualitative growth. Ecologically oriented alternatives to quantitative economic growth are currently emerging under the banner of Green Growth, Smart Growth or a Green Economy (UNEP 2011, OECD 2011a, overview in Hinterberger et al., 2012, criticism in Lander 2011, Unmüßig 2012, Brand 2012a). Also, most of the contributions under the header "beyond GDP" and about more comprehensive indicators argue for another form of economic growth (prominently Stiglitz et al. 2009, OECD 2011b).[2]

Other contributions are critical of the role of money and interest rates because monetary systems are considered to force economies to grow, and public and private entities to become indebted. These mechanisms have in turn caused the economic and financial crisis (Binswanger 2009, New Economics Foundation (NEF) 2009). However, minimal growth rates are considered necessary because profits compensate capital owners for their risks and assure that they provide capital (Binswanger 2009). The aspect of societal domination is hereby tackled implicitly and affirmatively, insofar as existing social structures are not seen as a problem but are simply assumed as given.

The motives and arguments of a fundamental, i.e. *strong* criticism of economic growth are many and varied, labelled as décroissance, de-growth or Jenseits des Wachstums. They consider that growth, as the crucial economic policy point of reference and as an indicator of prosperity and quality of life, no longer holds (Latouche 2010, Jackson 2009, van den Bergh 2011, Kallis 2011, a brief intellectual history of the de-growth debate and its links to ecological economics in Martínez-Alier et al. 2010).

Besides all analytical and strategic differences (van den Bergh 2011, Kallis 2011), an important theoretical reference is the concept of a steady state economy – in the tradition of John Stuart Mill's stationary state – where the costs and benefits of economic activities are accounted for separately and where material and energy throughput and not just output is considered (Daly 1999, Common and Stagl 2005). The (im-)possibility of markets to deal with ecological and social problems, especially, are a core commonality. Some argue for an internalisation of ecological and social costs, others go further; they add that more structural changes as well as a decolonising of economics and minds from economism towards another collective imaginary are preconditions for eligible change (Latouche 2009, Kallis 2011).

The consequence of many contributions is a call for stronger support of grassroots movements (e.g. Martínez-Alier et al. 2010, Wallis 2010 refers especially to indigenous movements). It is argued that environmental justice organisations (EJO) of the Global South are the counterparts of struggles for de-growth in the Global North (Martínez Alier 2012, Rodríguez Labajos et al. 2017, Klein 2014, cf. for many EJO experiences on: www.ejolt.org).

Other contributions rather focus on an adequate political framework (e.g. van den Bergh 2011), different individual behaviours, the reduction of wage–labour hours or, more generally, "a multi-faceted political project that aspires to mobilise support for a change of direction, at the macro-level of economic and political institutions and at the micro level of personal values and aspirations. Income and material comfort is to be reduced for many along the way, but the goal is that this is not experienced as welfare loss" (Kallis 2011: 878). Normative principles like cooperation and social justice are being reintroduced, while social movements are seen as the major subjects of change. Many contributions aimed at de-growth do not focus so much on crises or secular trends of diminishing growth rates in highly industrialised countries. Rather, on the contrary, they propose a "voluntary, smooth and equitable transition to a regime of lower production and consumption" (Schneider et al. 2010: 511, Kallis 2011: 574). De-growth is thought of as a conscious societal process based on a change of values.

Van den Bergh (2011) argues that an orientation towards *a*-growth might be more instructive since the focus should be put on concrete alternative policies and not so much on de-growth, as this would be politically more feasible, environmentally more effective and economically more efficient.

I share this overall perspective and would also argue for the priority of qualitative changes of societal relations and societal nature relations – though I am possibly not as optimistic towards the state as van den Bergh nor as focused on social movements as Martínez-Alier, Kallis and others. Despite the fact that – in contrast to the debate around qualitative growth – power and competition play a role, the contributions to the de-growth and a-growth debate fail to think through the manifold structures and processes of societal domination more thoroughly.

Power and domination commonly refer to the power of the state or political actors like parties, associations or corporations. Of course, this perspective is relevant, however, I contend that a more sophisticated conception of domination helps us to achieve a more differentiated understanding of reality.

Another school of thought focuses on the social limits to growth. Leopold Kohr argued in the 1950s that industrialised countries had become too big and that economic growth did not contribute to progress but diminished it because the duration of product lifetimes became shorter (Kohr 1957, overview in Steurer 2002). In the 1970s, Fred Hirsch (1977) developed his prominent argument of the social limits to growth.

Recent research on happiness and well-being can be seen in the tradition of this school of thought. It argues that there is a correlation between inequality and unhappiness, i.e. not-well-being: "Economic growth, for so long the great engine of progress, has, in the rich countries, largely finished its work. Not only have measures of well-being and happiness ceased to rise with economic growth but, as affluent societies have grown richer, there have been long-term rises in rates of anxiety, depression and numerous other social problems. The populations of rich countries have got to the end of a long historical journey" (Wilkinson and Pickett 2009: 19, Layard 2005, Frey 2008). Greater equality creates better social relationships, and conversely, health and social problems rise significantly in countries with large income gaps (Wilkinson and Pickett 2009, Helliwell et al. 2012).

Beyond a certain level of growth of income, economic growth actually exacerbates social problems, since, in societies in which subsistence is secure, the pressures of competition and consumerism increase. Correspondingly, people need to take a different perspective on their own societies in order to come to a broader understanding of what constitutes quality of life (also, Frey 2008, Layard 2005).

The boundaries of the different contributions on ecological and social limits to growth are blurred. One of the most prominent critics in the German-speaking debate, Niko Paech, adopts the above-mentioned themes and translates these into a radical social diagnosis. His perspective integrates all the five dimensions van den Bergh (2011) detects in the de-growth debate: GDP, consumption, work-time and material de-growth linked to a radical change by overcoming the capitalist economy and capitalist values (Paech 2012). The diagnosis claims that people in Western societies live beyond their own means and beyond the means of the locally and regionally available resources (also, Binswanger 2009).

This diagnosis reveals an appealing message: the necessary reduction of resource consumption and the use of sinks through less and different industrial output can be associated with a more stable satisfaction of needs and greater happiness in the sense of subjective well-being. This may require cultural changes, especially the change toward "creative subsistence" through one's own production and through communal usage of longer lasting consumer goods (Paech 2012: 120ff.). The growth drive of businesses can be mitigated by a shift towards local and regional production. Shorter, less complex chains of production promote trust, which "encourages investors to be satisfied with lower interest rates and smaller returns on investment" (Ibid.: 108, translation U.B.). In addition, there would be a reduction and redistribution of working hours and a shift in consumer demand towards longer lasting consumer goods. In his widely discussed book, *Prosperity without Growth*, Tim Jackson asks (2009), whether in a world with increasing population growth and limited resources, a prosperity can be "one in which it is possible for human beings to flourish, to achieve greater social cohesion, to find higher levels of well-being and yet still to reduce their material impact on the environment" (Ibid.: 35). He is distrustful of both economic growth and technological solutions, claiming that a sustainable economic system requires a political framework (such as ecological tax reform and limits on emissions and the consumption of resources), cultural changes (such as the delegitimation of consumerism), reduced work hours, reduced inequality, enhancement of skills and social capital among the populace and support to developing countries in restructuring their economies (Ibid.: 171ff., Martínez Alier 2009: 1099–1119). Like Binswanger, Jackson reveals the systemic effects of interest and hence public debt as a core problem and accelerator of the current economic and financial crisis (Jackson 2009). However, his consequences are more radical towards no-growth.

Finally, a conservative critique of growth considers the ecological and social problems as a result of the short-term orientation of people, human greed and, therefore, excessive consumption and the increasing indebtedness of people and institutions (prominent in the German-speaking discussion: Miegel 2010, 2012). Historically, the increasing orientation towards individual material wealth and growth started developing at the beginning of the 18th century. Conservative perspectives point out a destruction of traditional family structures, the menace of existing institutions and public order ever since (Steurer 2010: 426). De-growth is not so much a political project but considered as a fact, i.e. important economic actors pursue different aims to those who contribute to economic growth. Economic growth is simply no longer viable nor desirable in highly industrialised societies. This goes hand in hand with a change of deeply ingrained preconceptions. In these conservative diagnoses and proposals, the consideration of domination and power is completely absent. The points of reference are "people" or "peoples" (*Völker* in German) or different types of countries, but social structures and the implications of social power and domination are largely absent.

To summarise this first section, the different contributions are an attack on mainstream social sciences and especially economics as those implicitly or explicitly assume that societal differentiation and modernisation as well as economic growth are fundamentals of modernity.

Many open questions in this vivid and important debate remain unanswered. For instance, Steurer (2010) argues that the growth debate is full of problematic assumptions because extrapolations of current trends remain uncertain. Discussions in and between the disciplines of environmental economics and ecological economics, environmental governance and social and political ecology centre around qualitative growth or de-growth. Here, questions emerge about implicit assumptions of the role substitution of "natural capital", of technology, prices and the possibilities of the internalisation of externalised costs, the rebound effect and, in sum, the effects of relative decoupling and absolute reduction. The relationship between monetary and physical factors and their growth or use, respectively, is not clear and requires more research. One criticism of the proposals towards a de-growing economy is its weak macroeconomic foundation (Victor 2008, Jackson and Victor 2011). However, some important aspects are formulated, such as the necessity to reduce the working times of wage labour and to redistribute work equally as a foundation to maintain productivity growth without economic growth.

Whereas claims for qualitative growth propose changes largely within the existing institutional settings (of state, market and civil society), the consensus within the de-growth debate – I pragmatically include here the recent plea for a-growth – is that there is a need for in-depth social change or social–ecological transformation in order to address social and ecological problems. The orientation towards economic growth is mainly seen as part of the problem, not as the solution. Prosperity without growth is conceivable, feasible, and moreover, it is essential.

Growth and domination

Meanwhile, the growth critique runs the risk of underestimating or even denying the key moments of capitalist economic growth, namely its broader societal foundations and consequences in terms of societal power relations and domination. Economic growth is not just a (questionable) process of material well-being and (re)distribution. It is based upon and reinforces social relations in which life opportunities and spaces of action, assets and income are distributed unevenly. It guarantees economically, politically and culturally manifold social inclusion and exclusion, class and property relations, the asymmetrical relationship between men and women, between majority and minorities, as well as international inequalities. These issues will be addressed below. What is understood by capitalist growth and thus what it denies also needs to be scrutinised.

I maintain that the growth critical debate could be more fertile if growth is perceived in its connection with the ruling capitalist mode of production and living, including related politics, cultural norms and subjectivities (Brand and Wissen 2017, 2018). This is not just a system of producing and consuming goods and services, but also a system of power and domination – especially over nature. A broader perspective opens the debate concerning an alternative growth or post-growth future to the important question of how society can be made more democratic. Democracy is more than enhanced participation to improve governance and the legitimacy of the political system. Democracy means first and foremost to ask the question: Who and what mainly define which societal development should be considered as problematic (and what are the respective dominant scientific and societal interpretations of the problems themselves)? And it includes a normative standpoint: How can societal relations be shaped in a way that assures sustainability and productivity, justice, freedom and democracy. I conclude that democracy is the precondition for a society which is liberated from the compulsion towards capitalist economic growth. This is often mentioned in the debate – led mainly by economists – but not really explored.

Feminist critiques of growth

The heterogeneous feminist critique of growth – liberal, Marxist or poststructuralist feminism are important political and intellectual currents – adopts many of the above motifs. Nevertheless, feminist insights are again and again overlooked in other growth-critical articles (a view on the debate in the journal "Ecological Economics" is a good example). A major intention of the respective contributions is to make hierarchical societal relations visible, in particular gender relations. Hence, gender relations are represented in a social structure, which produces an order of inequality and it is both the basis and outcome of capitalist growth.

Growth-critical feminist contributions see, first, the capitalist system as excessive in itself, indifferent to the consequences of growth. The reasons they cite are, among other things, the limitlessness of money and the profit-driven compulsion for accumulation (Biesecker et al. 2012). Second, the capitalist economy is an economy of separation. Particularly the way market processes, capital and wage labour enforce underlying conditions by separation – namely unpaid work, particularly care work, and the natural resources that are not saleable goods. The everyday reproduction and well-being of humans and society is not just based on paid income but also on the mostly invisible domestic and care work done primarily by women. Thus, a broader understanding of (re)productivity is required, which is more comprehensive than the sole integration of formal production and labour processes. The fact that well-being depends on the production and consumption of commodities but also on non-market production and consumption in turn, depends on asymmetric gender relations – on societal evaluations of work, which are "valuable" or "not valuable" (Biesecker and Baier 2011: 54–63). Thus, the externalisation of costs is not a market failure, which might be addressed by the State through relevant regulation, as economics claims, but a "principle", which contributes significantly to the functioning of the capitalist economy. Third, economic growth is strongly associated with a male, rationalist and Western understanding of development that is first and foremost part of patriarchal relations oriented towards the mastery of nature.

From a feminist perspective, different understandings of wealth and its production and consumption are necessary – and thus we require a much broader understanding of economics, one that goes beyond the capitalist market and money mediated economy. The focus should be also on the "careholder value" (Kennedy 2011: 39, quoted by Biesecker et al. 2012: 12). This refers to non-capitalist economies, manifested in, among other things, so-called community economies (Gibson and Graham 2006, Salleh 1997/2017). Social structures are not just those constructed along class lines but need to be seen from an intersectional perspective. The scope of understanding becomes considerably broader here: It includes the material production and reproduction of life, especially in the form of a precautionary business practices, and requires a working definition that goes beyond wage labour. Most important is the strengthening of principles of cooperation and responsibility, of a sense of sufficiency and equity (Habermann 2011: v, Winterfeld 2011: 57–65).

The (neo-)Marxist critique of growth

The (neo-)Marxist tradition is also quite heterogeneous (Koch 2018, Dietz and Wissen 2009, Chertkovskaya and Paulsson 2016, Altvater 1993, Forster 2000, Löwy 2006, Wallis 2010) but has a strong common ground. Its critique of growth claims that social dynamics are determined first by the production of exchange values and not by the production of concrete use values. Goods, represented by their exchange value, "have absolutely no connection with their physical properties and with the material relations arising therefrom" (Marx 1968: 86). Marx was sensitive to this, writing that through capitalist accumulation dynamics, the natural "sources of all wealth" would be undermined. In addition, to be economically quantified resources, such as non-paid work force, public services or aspects of nature, tend to be converted into commodities and exchange values. Capitalist competition and the associated drive to accumulate are further reasons why more commodities would be produced more cheaply, along with the natural tendency to use and overuse free resources. Capital, "fanatically bent on making value expand itself, (…) ruthlessly forces the human race to produce for production's sake (…) and competition makes the immanent laws of capitalist production to be felt by each individual capitalist, as external coercive laws" (Ibid.: 618 also, Altvater 2005). This is especially visible in the process of globalisation, which has led to more intense competition and an enormous increase in resource consumption.

The domination-formed societal division of labour is crucial. Historically, there was an emergence of a class of owners of the means of production and other assets, who aimed to multiply their assets. The overwhelming majority of people possess little or no assets, but sustain themselves through wage labour, in terms of which the capitalist surplus value is produced. The more people subsist through wage labour, the more the production of goods and thus capitalist growth is encouraged. We see this in the past two decades in China, where hundreds of millions of people were drawn into wage labour to produce commodities for the world (probably the majority do this willingly, although one must take into account the specific social and environmental conditions). Indeed, class structure has become more diversified in many countries. Nevertheless, if people subsist from wage labour they, and their organisations like trade unions, have an interest in the perpetuation and expansion of capitalist production as their wages depend on it, thus reinforcing capitalist class relations. As wage earners, most people accept not only the machinery of capitalist growth, but also the underlying relations of control and ownership, though this is largely involuntary and impotent (Marx 1969: 34).

Many drivers of growth are mentioned in the debate: technological progress, productivity growth, consumerism and its social-psychological dimensions, the debt and repayment cycle, globalisation and urbanisation. These are all clearly important factors. Yet it should be remembered from a Gramscian perspective that the societal relations of domination in the minds of those who are dominated are usually not perceived as such, but rather as silently enforced anonymous relations; as the uncontrolled processes of technological progress and global markets; of globalisation and productivism. In other words, most people experience their daily life as relatively powerless individuals – notwithstanding all of the new management methods and approaches to the transfer of responsibility and political participation. This is the basis of capitalist culture. Moreover, there exist central social and economic dynamics which, as conditions of capitalist competition, transform more and more aspects of society into marketable goods, i.e. capitalist commodities. This relates not only to nature and to people who sell their labour. In this respect, the capitalist market or economy not only constrains the sphere of social innovation and the production, allocation and consumption of resources, but also the manner in which power relations are constituted and reproduced along dispositives of class, gender and ethnic lines.

Although Martínez-Alier et al. (2010: 1744) argue that the French approach of décroissance refers to Marxist debates and the (neo-)Marxist Régulation school, my impression is that regulationists increasingly refer both to Keynesian economics and sociological institutionalism. Most explicitly, a critique of social forms and domination was formulated in the German-speaking version of the regulation school as well as by Bob Jessop, which linked it to Antonio Gramsci's theory of hegemony and Nicos Poulantzas' state theory (Esser et al. 1994, Jessop 1990, Hirsch 1997). This might be a fruitful way to link insights of the critique of political economy with the structures, processes and imaginaries of capitalist growth – understood as domination-formed social structures.

In my own work and together with Christoph Görg and Markus Wissen, I propose the concept of "post-Fordist societal nature relations". It is a Régulationist and Gramscian perspective on the aftermath of the crisis of Fordism. It points out and defines the connections of both fundamental contradictions within capitalist accumulation and its inherent mechanisms to appropriate nature. One further aspect, crucial to the continuation of unsustainable societal nature relations, is the globalisation of the "imperial mode of living", the propagation of an exploitative Western mode of living on a global scale (Brand and Wissen 2017, 2018).

Here it becomes quite obvious: The de-growth perspective is closely linked to questions of climate justice. Beyond an increasingly dominant understanding that climate justice largely means the even distribution of emission rights among global people or countries (Warlenius 2018, Bond 2018), a de-growth perspective means to take seriously the profound transformation of capitalist and imperial modes of production and living and to orient alternatives at the principles of participation, democracy and justice as well as the serious dealing with unequal historical and current responsibilities for and the exposure to risks of climate change. Here, questions of power and domination come in: Climate justice, and in a broader sense environmental justice, as well as de-growth are sensitive to the power of financial and industrial capital, as well as the governments and international political institutions supporting them that are interested in maintaining the industrialist capitalism that rests on fossil fuels and growth. Domination comes in when we look at the hegemonic, i.e. broadly accepted forms of production and living among in the Global North and increasingly in the Global South. As well as de-growth, the term and slogan climate justice is part of an "activist-led science", it's rather part of radical transformation than technocratic aims set by governments.

Limits of the planet or of the valorisation of nature?

My second aim is to adapt the central ideas of the feminist and Marxist critiques of growth to the relationship between society and nature or, more precisely to *societal nature relations.*[3]

The ecological justifications for a new conception of prosperity are usually cited as the overuse and destruction of nature (beside the above mentioned social limits). Concepts like "environmental space" (Opschor 1994) or "planetary boundaries" (Rockström et al. 2009) are prominent here, as metaphors like the ecological footprint (Wackernagel and Rees 1996) gain importance. The human race, as well as individual societies, ought to consume only as much in a year as the Earth's ecosystem can reproduce over the same period without long-term damage. This would be achieved by greater resource efficiency and technological progress, but also by a social process of ecological modernisation, brought about by a political change to the framework in which we value and evaluate ecological factors. As we saw, critical perspectives argue for more profound changes or transformations. However, at the ontological level, most approaches tend to reproduce a dichotomy between society and nature (e.g. the recent critique of ecological economics of Spash 2012). This weakens an analytical way of thinking and political strategising causing profound transformations.

I suggest that, in the growth-critical debate, a somewhat broader perspective to the crisis-ridden relationship between society and nature should be taken. The famous dictum of the "Dialectic of Enlightenment" by Max Horkheimer and Theodor Adorno was: "Any attempt to break the laws of nature, will be broken by nature (i.e. to move away from dependence on nature, UB), only bringing all the more deeply under nature's control (thus increasing the dependency, U.B.)" (Horkheimer and Adorno 1944/2006: 19, translation U.B.). This is what we are experiencing today: the attempt to replace the energy supplied by oil with "clean" agrofuels, results in countries like Indonesia converting huge tracts of land from smallholder farms into capitalist-managed oil palm plantations (Brad et al. 2015, Backhouse 2016). Strategies to free the global economy from its dependence on fossil fuels – like the project of a Green Economy – create new dependencies. In capitalist societies, the privileged solution to many challenges seems to lie in the expansion of capitalist market and growth mechanisms. If there is money to be made, however, investors will not stand idly by. The states and wage earners also have an interest in the development of green industries. Therefore, a fundamentally different energy base and increased efficiency of production, and thus a green capitalism or a green economy, is quite conceivable. Whether this degradation of natural resources will be effectively halted is not yet clear. So far there is no evidence that it will.

My point here is that commodification – which is frequently referred to in the de-growth debate – is also a social relation that secures hegemony and asymmetric social structures of domination along different lines.

As Horkheimer and Adorno might have argued, a green economy is going to be selective and polarising. The primary profit motives stem from competitiveness and Western technological rationality, they are manifested as a process of an ecological or, more precisely, multiple crisis. However, the domination and thus destruction of nature accelerates because societal nature relations are not fundamentally ingrained (see also, Görg 2003, Brand 2009: 103–117). At the same time, social control increases as a green economy emerges out of the control of capital and the social relationships to nature (Wichterich 2011: 5–7, Brand 2012: 28–32). This double nucleus of economic growth – the domination of man over man and society over nature – is given too little attention in the popular growth-critical debate.

Democratic socio-ecological transformations?

In many pro-growth contributions, the necessity of economic growth is justified with the "need" of the Global South to develop to alleviate hunger and poverty. In particular, "China" serves as a foil when it comes to the unsustainability of catch-up modernisation and industrialisation in the global geopolitical and geo-economic competition.[4] In fact, most governments, as well as the upper and middle classes of the Global South, are set on economic growth, which results in an intensive commodification of work-force and nature. In this case, we can see, too, that capitalist economic growth is based on and reproduces existing societal structures, especially class and gender structures. This is supported by the strategies concerning the supply of raw materials propounded by the governments of the Global North and by international institutions. The local population usually gains little from the exploitation of resources, while they bear many of the negative environmental consequences and upheavals. In the countries of the Global South, therefore, one may ask just how democratic economic and social development has been. Which social groups benefit from the dominant development and growth models and which do not? Are the deaths of miners due to less secure operations stemming from savings measures? Are small-scale farmers the neglected "collateral damage" of growth and development? Do we simply accept the dictum of economics as a truth that during the early stages of development social inequality massively increases? Or should we look more closely at whether there are scientific and political debates, as well as political forces, which might oppose too brutal a capitalist modernisation? Qualitative changes to social relations like work or politics as well as the forms of the social satisfaction of needs need to be taken into account (cf. Kothari 2014, Acosta and Brand 2017, Brand et al. 2017).

The de-growth debate does not have to be restricted to the "rich" countries. If we consider struggles around the "environmentalism of the poor" (Martínez-Alier 2002) against commodification and for the defence of livelihoods, it becomes clear that economic growth is not a "necessity" but an enhancement and deepening of capitalist societal relations and dynamics.

This claim is even more important when the protagonists of the de-growth debate claim that they aim at "an equitable and *democratic* transition to a smaller economy with less production and consumption" (Martínez-Alier et al. 2010: 1741, emphasis added). Democracy as a principle is, on the one hand, in conflict (not necessarily in contradiction) with the principle of capitalist economy and seems to be, on the other hand, stabilised through capitalist economic growth and its potential for (re)distributional politics. A climate justice perspective elucidates that the material conditions of democracy, i.e. the well-being of more or less people within the Global North and also in the Global South, are largely secured through further environmental destruction and accelerating climate change. Timothy Mitchell (2011) proposed the powerful notion of "carbon democracy" to point at the intrinsic links between liberal democracy, the organisation of workers, material well-being under capitalist conditions for some and environmentally destructive dynamics.

Therefore, the conception of democracy takes place on a contested terrain and it is crucial to thinking of a social–ecological transformation as a collective attempt to address socio-economic and ecological crises. Democracy should not be boiled down to political participation, improvement of governance and an increase in life satisfaction. It can mean so much more than the fulfilment of the important principles of economic stability, sustainability and distributional justice (Jackson 2009, as a prominent example). At the same time, within the de-growth debate, democracy is mainly conceptualised in the tradition of Cornelius Castoriadis as a rather abstract principle of the self-institution of society (Asara et al. 2013, Deriu 2012, on important antinomies of democracy under post-political conditions see Blühdorn 2013).

A democratic approach must ask first of all: Who and what determines what is considered to be a problematic development of society? How can all members be taken into consideration? What are the socio-economic aspects of democracy, i.e. the organisation of a "material core" (Gramsci) in non-destructive ways? This necessarily includes forms of economic democracy (Demirovi 2007).

A "growth-free society" (Wolfgang Sachs) would have to tackle different forms of social domination – class-, race-, gender-specific and internationally – as well as the domination of nature. Up until now, the dominant experience of most people is to play no role in shaping society. The levers of political and economic power are wielded by others who make the essential political and economic decisions. And these people make sure – this must be taken into account in the current crisis – that it stays this way. Democratic processes toward a post-growth society, and the democratic transformation of society, include appealing and democratically designed forms of production and the provision of food and clothing, of housing and living together: What will sustainable cities look like? What does the solidarity in mobility mean? What foods are sustainable, fairly produced and internationally distributable in sufficient quality, while tasting good and being healthy? How will conflicts among *global players* in the transnational food industry play out when food is once again produced locally and regionally?

An important role is played by socio-ecological experimentation, and "Pioneers of Change", such as inventors, companies, political activists, consumers and non-governmental organisations in various fields such as urban development, energy and agriculture, will determine "what the options for overcoming our economic dependence on the use of fossil resources are, testing and advancing the development of new models or visions towards which social change can be oriented. The pioneers initially emerge as niche players, but may have an increasingly key impact in promoting the transformation of development"(WBGU 2011: 6 et seq.). So that this pioneering work is followed through, however, questions of policymaking should be linked to questions of economic and political power and domination. Precisely for this reason, it seems essential to insist on the question of democracy in the sense of a conscious design of the economy, of technology and development and of society at large.

At the level of societal projects, the concept of "socio-ecological transformation" seems more adequate to me than fostering a perspective of "sustainable degrowth" (Brand 2012b, Brand 2016, Görg et al. 2017, Brie 2014). At the tactical level, it inscribes itself into the vivid mainstream debate about transformation and attempts to push this to a more structural take, i.e. to clarify that within the existing institutional system aimed at "great transition" – called transformation in German – (WBGU 2011) is impossible.

At the strategic level, the intentions behind the claim for sustainable de-growth as "a new overarching vision" do not only counter the imperative of growth (Kallis 2011: 874). In fact, many respective policies are close to some proposals of a socio-ecological transformation. Still, those claims mostly remain umbrella concepts, thus uncovering a new oxymoron which needs to be filled with differentiable meaning.

The common ground is that the decline of GDP as an effect of transformation should not be crisis driven, leading to recession or depression, but that "this can happen in a socially and environmentally sustainable way" (Kallis 2011: 874).

Politics of time, different modes of reproduction with their own logics and a strengthening of non-commodified social relations like solidarity economy are considered crucial. This critically points at the strong grammar of commodification and the unquestioned privilege of the capitalist market as the best societal institution to secure growth and well-being. The (re)production of wealth and well-being needs to take place under socially just and socio-ecological sustainable conditions.

To realise an attractive mode of production and living requires sustainable and democratic societal nature relations, i.e. very different forms of mobility and communication, food and agriculture, housing, the (re)production of cities and country-sides. It needs another notion of well-being that includes different forms of technological and social innovation, political and societal steering and discourses as well as subjectivities.

Results and conclusion

In this chapter I intended to show that the growth critical debate in principle – in the versions which point at qualitative growth as well as those around the notions of de-growth – overlooks issues of power and domination, which is intrinsically linked to the societal structures and processes of capitalist growth. Feminist and Marxist contributions, which are mainly neglected in the debate, have the most advanced conceptual proposals and they have the potential to push the debate to another level: to acknowledge societal domination like property, class and gender relations and domination-formed societal nature relations as a major basis and driver of economic growth, to conceptualise the market differently, i.e. not just as a mechanism of production and exchange but also as a means to reproduce unequal and alienating societal structures, to understand the state not as a regulator and promoter of growth or alternatives but also as a social relation which reproduces and is reproduced by societal power relations.

Such a different perspective adds important insights to the literature in order to both analyse current dynamics and to follow a new approach towards a society beyond the growth imperative, i.e. by recognising non-market activities as crucial for social and individual well-being as well as by insisting on the democratic and conflict-based character of socio-ecological transformation.[5] Therefore, such an enhanced understanding of de-growth can contribute to better understand the obstacles to and potentials of climate justice.

Notes

1   I hereby refer to the English- and German-speaking debate. It would be interesting to consider motives and arguments of a critique of economic growth in Latin America or China given their different experiences.
2   The debate about indicators is not at all new (see, Steurer 2002, Brangsch 2011).
3   Gesellschaftliche Naturverhältnisse in German, which seems even more precise to overcome the danger of a dichotomy; the exact translation would be "societal relationships with nature".The term "Naturverhältnisse" was used once by Marx in *Capital*.
4   In China, an intense discussion has emerged about the scarcity and the ecological consequences of the model of catch-up capitalist industrialisation. In addition, the government has begun to calculate a "green GDP", in which environmental degradation is accounted for. However, in response to criticism from some provinces, these calculations have not been released. In this discussion, the term "growth critique" has yet to be used. I am indebted to Joseph Baum and Daniel Fuchs for this information.
5   At the level of current strategic debates on Green Economy the crucial question posed by the NGO Erosion, Technology, Concentration (ETC Group) should be considered: Who controls the Green Economy? (www.etcgroup.org).

References

Acosta A. and Brand U. (2017) *Salidas del Laberinto Capitalista. Decrecimiento y Postextractivismo.* Icaria Publisher, Barcelona.
Altvater E. (1993) *The Future of the Market.* Verso/Monthly Review Press, London/New York.
Altvater E. (2005) *Das Ende des Kapitalismus, wie wir ihn kennen.* Westfälisches Dampfboot, Münster.
Asara V., Profumi E. and Kallis G. (2013) "Degrowth, democracy and autonomy". *Environmental Values*, 22(2), 217–239.
Backhouse M. (2016) "The discursive dimension of green grabbing – palm oil plantations as climate protection strategy". *Pléyade*, 18, 131–157.
Biesecker A. and Baier A. (2011) "Gutes Leben braucht andere Arbeit". *Politische Ökologie*, 29 (125), 54–63.

Biesecker A., Wichterich C. and von Winterfeld U. (2012) Feministische Perspektiven zum Themenbereich Wachstum, Wohlstand, Lebensqualität Background Paper for the Enquete Commission "Growth, Well-Being, Quality of Life" of the German Bundestag, March (www.rosalux.de/en/publication/id/6177/f45dd8259a9694857a74e 8ef50a01c06/) accessed 16 January 2018.

Binswanger H. C. (2009) *Vorwärts zur Mäßigung.* Murmann, Hamburg.

Blühdorn I. (2013) "The governance of unsustainability: Ecology and democracy after the post-democratic turn". *Environmental Politics*, 22 (1), 16–36.

Bond P. (2018) "Climate Justice, Big Oil and Natural Capital", in Jacobsen, S. G. ed. *Climate Justice and the Economy: Social Mobilization, Knowledge and the Political.* Routledge, London.

Brad A., Schaffartzik A., Pichler M. and Plank C. (2015) "Contested territorialization and biophysical expansion of oil palm plantations in Indonesia". *Geoforum*, 64, 100–111.

Brand U. (2009) "Environmental crises and the ambiguous postneoliberalising of nature". *Development Dialogue*, 51, 103–117.

Brand U. (2012a) "Green economy – the next oxymoron? No lessons learned from failures of implementing sustainable development". *GAIA*, 21(1), 28–32.

Brand U. (2012b) "Green economy and green capitalism: Some theoretical considerations". *Journal für Entwicklungspolitik*, 28 (3), 118–137.

Brand U. (2016) "How to get out of the multiple crisis? Towards a critical theory of social-ecological transformation". *Environmental Values*, 25 (5), 503–525.

Brand U. and Wissen M. (2017) "The Imperial Mode of Living", in Spash C. ed. *Routledge Handbook of Ecological Economics: Nature and Society.* Routledge, London 152–161.

Brand U. and Wissen M. (2018) *The Limits to Capitalist Nature: Theorizing and Overcoming the Imperial Mode of Living.* Rowman & Littlefield International, London.

Brand U., Görg C., Hirsch J. and Wissen M. (2008) *Conflicts in Global Environmental Regulation and the Internationalization of the State. Contested Terrains.* Routledge, London.

Brand U., Boos T. and Brad A. (2017) "Degrowth and post-extractivism: Two debates with suggestions for the inclusive development framework" .*Current Opinion in Environmental Sustainability*, 24 (February), 36–41.

Brangsch L. (2012) "Economic 'Indicators' are Really About Power. Political Dimensions of Object and Method in Debates on Growth", in Eskelinen T. ed. *The Left between Growth and De-Growth.* Transform, Brussels 44–57.

Brie M. ed. (2014) *Futuring. Perspektiven der Transformation im Kapitalismus über ihn hinaus.* Westfälisches Dampfboot, Münster.

Bullard N. and Müller T. (2012) "Beyond the 'green economy'. System change, not climate change?" *Development*, 55 (1), 54–62.

Campaign against Climate Change (2014) *One Million Climate Jobs. Tackling the Environmental and the Economic Crisis.* Campaign against Climate Change, London.

Chatterton P., Featherstone D. and Routledge P. (2013) "Articulating climate justice in Copenhagen". *Antipode*, 45 (3), 602–620.

Chertkovskaya E. and Paulsson A. (2016) "The growthocene: Thinking through what degrowth is criticising" *Entitle Blog* (https://entitleblog.org/2016/02/19/the-growthocene-thinking-through-what-degrowth-is-criticising/) accessed 27 November 2017.

Common M. and Stagl S. (2005) *Ecological Economics. An Introduction.* Cambridge University Press, Cambridge.

Conca K., Finger M. and Park J. eds. (2008) *The Crisis of Global Environmental Governance.* Routledge, London.

D'Alisa G., Demaria G. and Kallis G. (2014) *Degrowth. A Vocabulary for a New Era* Routledge, London.

Daly H. ed. (1999) *Ecological Economics and the Ecology of Economics*. Edward Elgar, Cheltenham.

Demaria F., Schneider F., Sekulova F. and Martinez-Alier J. (2013) "What is degrowth? From an activist slogan to a social movement". *Environmental Values*, 22 (2), 191–215.

Demirovi A. (2007) *Demokratie in der Wirtschaft*. Westfälisches Dampfboot, Münster.

Deriu M. (2012) "Democracies with a future: Degrowth and the democratic tradition". *Futures*, 44 (6), 553–561.

Dietz K. and Wissen M. (2009) "Kapitalismus und 'natürliche Grenzen'. Eine kritische Diskussion ökomarxistischer Zugänge zur ökologischen Krise". *PROKLA 156. Zeitschrift für kritische Sozialwissenschaft*, 39 (3), 351–369.

Esser J., Görg C. and Hirsch J. eds. (1994) *Politik, Institutionen und Staat. Zur Kritik der Regulationstheorie*. VSA, Hamburg.

EU Commission (2010) *Europe 2020 – A European Strategy for Smart, Sustainable and Inclusive Growth* (http://ec.europa.eu/eu2020/pdf/COMPLET%20EN%20BARROSO%20%20%20007%20-%20Europe%202020%20-%20EN%20version.pdf) accessed 27 November 2017.

Eversberg D. and Schmelzer M. (2018) "The degrowth spectrum: Convergence and divergence within a diverse and conflictual alliance". *Environmental Values*, forthcoming.

Forster J. B. (2000) *Marx's Ecology: Materialism and Nature*. Monthly Review Press, New York.

Frey B. S. (2008) *Happiness: A Revolution in Economics*. MIT Press, Cambridge.

Gibson-Graham J. K. (2006) *The End of Capitalism (As We Knew It). A Feminist Critique of Political Economy*. University of Minnesota Press, Minneapolis.

Görg C. (2003) *Regulation der Naturverhältnisse. Zu einer kritischen Theorie der ökologischen Krise*. Westfälisches Dampfboot, Münster.

Görg C. (2011) "Societal Relationships with Nature: A Dialectical Approach to Environmental Politics", in Biro A. ed. *Critical Ecologies. The Frankfurt School and Contemporary Environmental Crises*. University of Toronto Press, Toronto 43–72.

Görg C., Brand U., Haberl H., Hummel D., Jahn T. and Liehr S. (2017) "Challenges for social-ecological transformations: Contributions from social and political ecology". *Sustainability*, 9 (7), 1045.

Gramsci A. (1991, 1996) *Gefängnishefte* Vol. 1 and Vol. 7. Bochmann K. and Haug W. eds. Argument, Hamburg.

Habermann F. (2011) "Ecommony statt economy. Wir werden nicht als egoist_innen geboren". *Frauenrat. Informationen für die Frau: Green Economy. Gerechtigkeit oder Begrünung des Kapitalismus?* 5 17–19.

Helliwell J., Layard R. and Sachs J. eds. (2012) *World Happiness Report*. The Earth Institute, Columbia University, New York.

Hinterberger F., Freytag E. and Pirgmaier E. eds. (2012) *Growth in Transition*. Earthscan, London/New York.

Hirsch F. (1977) *Social Limits to Growth*. Outledge & Kegan Paul, London/Henley.

Hirsch J. (1997) "Globalization of capital, nation-states and democracy". *Studies in Political Economy*, 54, 39–58.

Horkheimer M. and Adorno T. W. (1944/2006) *Dialektik der Aufklärung*. Fischer, Frankfurt/M.

IEA – International Energy Agency (2010) *World Energy Outlook*. IEA/OECD, Paris.

Jacobsen S. G. (2018) "Climate Justice as Radical Economic Mobilization", in Jacobsen S. G. ed. *Climate Justice and the Economy: Social mobilization, knowledge and the political*. Routledge, London.

Jackson T. (2009) *Prosperity Without Growth. Economics for a Finite Planet*. Earthscan Publications, London.

Jackson T. and Victor P. (2011) "Productivity and work in the 'green economy'. Some theoretical reflections and empirical tests". *Environmental Innovation and Societal Transitions*, 1 (1), 101–108.

Jessop B. (1990) *State Theory. Putting States in der Place*. Polity Press, Cambridge.

Kallis G. (2011) "In defence of degrowth". *Ecological Economics*, 70 (5), 873–880.

Kallis G. (2017) *In Defense of Degrowth. Opinions and Minifestos*. Creative Commons, self-published (https://indefenseofdegrowth. com).

Klein N. (2014) *This Changes Everything. Capitalism vs the Climate*. Allen Lane, London.

Koch M. (2018) "Growth and Degrowth in Marx's Critique of Political Economy", in Chertkovskaya E., Paulsson A. and Barca S. eds. *The End of Growth as we Know it: Contributions to the Political Economy of Degrowth* Rowman & Littlefield International, London (forthcoming).

Kohr L. (1957) *The Breakdown of Nations*. Routledge & Kegan Paul, London.

Konzeptwerk Neue Ökonomie and DFG Research Group Post-Growth Societies (2017) *Degrowth in Bewegung(en): 32 Alternative Wege zur sozial-ökologischen Transformation*. Oekom, München (English: www.degrowth.info/en/dim/degrowth-in-movements/) accessed 27 November 2017.

Kothari A. (2014) Degrowth and Radical Ecological Democracy: A View from the South (www.degrowth.info/en/2014/06/degrowth-and-radical-ecological-democracy-a-view-from-the-south/) accessed 27 November 2017.

Lander E. (2011) The Green Economy. The Wolf in Sheep's Clothing (www.tni.org/en/publication/the-green-economy-the-wolf-in-sheeps-clothing) accessed 27 November 2017.

Latouche S. (2009) *Farewell to Growth*. Polity Press, Cambridge.

Latouche S. (2010) "Degrowth". *Journal of Cleaner Production*, 18 (6), 519–522.

Layard R. (2005) *Happiness. Lessons from a New Science*. Allen Lane, London.

Löwy M. (2006) "Eco-Socialism and Democratic Planning", in Panitch L. and Leys C. eds. *Socialist Register 2007: Coming to Terms with Nature*. Merlin Press, London 294–309.

Martínez-Alier J. (2002) *Environmentalism of the Poor. A Study of Ecological Conflicts and Valuation*. Edward Elgar, Cheltenham.

Martínez-Alier J. (2009) "Socially sustainable economic de-growth". *Development and Change*, 40 (6), 1099–1119.

Martinez-Alier J. (2012) "Environmental justice and economic degrowth: An alliance between two movements". *Capitalism Nature Socialism*, 23 (1), 51–73.

Martínez-Alier J., Pascual U., Vivien F.-D. and Zaccai E. (2010) "Sustainable de-growth. Mapping the context, criticisms and future prospects of an emergent paradigm". *Ecological Economics*, 69 (9), 1741–1747.

Marx K. (1968) *Das Kapital. Erster Band* Vol. 23. Marx-Engels-Werke, Berlin.

Marx K. (1969) *Die Deutsche Ideologie* Vol. 3. Marx-Engels-Werke, Berlin.

Meadows D. H., Meadows D. L., Randers J. and Behrens W. W. (1972) *The Limits to Growth: A Report for the Club of Rome's Project on the Predicament of Mankind*. Universe Pub, New York.

Miegel M. (2010) *Exit. Wohlstand ohne Wachstum*. Ullstein, Berlin.

Miegel M. (2012) "Welches wachstum und welchen wohlstand wollen wir?". *Aus Politik und Zeitgeschichte*, 62 (27–28), 3–8.

Mitchell T. (2011) *Carbon Democracy: Political Power in the Age of Oil.* Verso, London/ New York.

Muraca B. (2013) "Décroissance: A project for a radical transformation of society" *.Environmental Values*, 22 (2), 147–169.

Murray J. and King D. (2012) "Oil's tipping point has passed". *Nature*, 481 (7382), 433–435.

NEF – The New Economics Foundation (2009) *The Great Transition. A Tale of How It Turned Out Right* (www.neweconomics.org/publications/great-transition) accessed 27 November 2017.

Newell P. and Paterson M. (2010) *Climate Capitalism: Global Warming and the Transformation of the Global Economy.* Cambridge University Press, Cambridge.

OECD (2011a) Towards Green Growth (www.keepeek.com/Digital-Asset-Management/ oecd/environment/towards-green-growth_9789264111318-en#.WhwkrHq1P-U) accessed 27 November 2017.

OECD (2011b) *How's Life? Measuring Well-Being.* OECD Publishing, Paris.

Opschor H. (1994) *Sustainable Development and Paradigms in Economics. Research Memorandum 1994–30* Faculteit der Economische Wetenschappeu en Econometrie. Vrije Universiteit, Amsterdam.

Paech N. (2012) *Befreiung vom Überfluss.* Oekom Verlag, München.

Pirgmaier E. and Hinterberger F. (2012) "What Kind of Growth is Sustainable? A Presentation of Arguments", in Hinterberger F., Pirgmaier E., Freytag E. and Schuster M. eds. *Growth in Transition.* Earthscan, London/New York 13–53.

Rodríguez Labajos B., Bond P., Greyl L., Munguti S., Ojo G., Overbeek W. and Yanez, I. (2015) "Environmental Justice in the South and Degrowth. Are there really bases for an alliance?" (under preparation).

Rockström J. et al. (2009) "Planetary boundaries. Exploring the safe operating space for humanity", *Ecology and Society* 14 (2), (www.ecologyandsociety.org/vol14/iss2/ art32/) accessed 27 November 2017.

Salleh, A. (2017/1997) *Ecofeminism as Politics. Nature, Marx and the Postmodern.* Zed Books, London.

Schneider F., Kallis G. and Martinez-Alier J. (2010) "Crisis or opportunity? Economic degrowth for social equity and ecological sustainability". *Journal of Cleaner Production*, 18 (6), 511–518.

Spash C. (2012) "New foundations for ecological economics". *Ecological Economics*, 77, 36–47.

Stiglitz J., Sen A. and Fitoussi J.-P. (2009) *Report by the Commission on the Measurement of Economic Performance and Social Progress* (http://ec.europa.eu/eurostat/documents/ 118025/118123/Fitoussi+Commission+report) accessed 27 November 2017.

Steurer R. (2002) *Der Wachstumsdiskurs in Wissenschaft und Politik: Von der Wachstumseuphorie über "Grenzen des Wachstums" zur Nachhaltigkeit.* Verlag für Wissenschaft und Forschung, Berlin.

Steurer R. (2010) "Die wachstumskontroverse als endlosschleife. Themen und paradigmen im überblick". *Wirtschaftspolitische Blätter*, 4, 423–435.

Thomas P. D. (2009) *The Gramscian Moment. Philosophy, Hegemony and Marxism.* Brill Academic Publications, London.

UNEP (2011) *Towards a Green Economy: Pathways to Sustainable Development and Poverty Eradication* (https://sustainabledevelopment.un.org/content/documents/126 GER_synthesis_en.pdf) accessed 27 November 2017.

UNEP (2012) *Responsible Resource Management for a Sustainable World. Findings from the International Resource Panel.* UNEP, Paris.

Unmüßig B. (2012) The Green Economy – The New Magic Bullet? Expectations from the Rio+20 Conference (https://lb.boell.org/sites/default/files/unmuessig_green_economy_magic_bullet.pdf) accessed 27 November 2017.

van den Bergh J. (2011) "Environment versus growth – a criticism of 'degrowth' and a plea for 'a-growth'". *Ecological Economics*, 70 (5), 881–890.

Victor P. (2008) *Managing Without Growth – Slower by Design Not Disaster.* Edward Elgar, Cheltenham.

von Winterfeld U. (2011) "Vom Recht auf Suffizienz" in Rätz W., Egan-Krieger T., Muraca B., Passadakis A., Schmelzer M. and Vetter A. eds. *Ausgewachsen!* VSA, Hamburg 57–65.

Wackernagel M. and Rees W. (1996) *Our Ecological Footprint: Reducing Human Impact on the Earth.* New Society Publishers, Gabriola Island, British Columbia.

Wallis V. (2010) "Beyond 'green capitalism'". *Monthly Review*, 61 (9), (https://monthly review.org/2010/02/01/beyond-green-capitalism/) accessed 27 November 2017.

Warlenius R. (2018) "Climate Debt: The Origins of a Subversive Misnomer". in Jacobsen, S. G. ed. *Climate Justice and the Economy: Social Mobilization, Knowledge and the Political.* Routledge, London.

Weber M. (1922/1978) *Economy and Society.* University of California Press, Berkley.

Wichterich C. (2011) The Future WE Want. Occupy Development (http://wideplusnet work.wordpress.com/news/the-future-we-want-occupy-development/) accessed 27 November 2017.

Wilkinson R. and Pickett K. (2009) *The Spirit Level: Why More Equal Societies Almost Always Do Better.* Allen Lane, London.

WBGU – German Advisory Council on Global Change (2011) *World in Transition. A Social Contract for Sustainability.* WBGU, Berlin.

9   On social ecology and the movement for climate justice

Brian Tokar

As the immediate consequences of global climate disruptions become increasingly difficult to ignore, a host of long-range, systemic questions are capturing the attention of activists and scholars. Can economic and political structures be sufficiently transformed to accommodate a rapid transition to a fossil-free economy? Will economies continue to grow as fossil fuel infrastructure is replaced by renewable energy sources, or can a functioning growth-free economy be sustained? Could capitalist institutions collapse under the weight of massive stranded investments in fossil fuels, perhaps overturning their insidious and widespread political influence? What manner of transitions are feasible in the Global South, where the daily effects of climate disruptions are the most extreme and the imperatives of poverty reduction are perennially co-opted by elites still focused on economic growth (Bidwai 2012)? What new political strategies can emerge to aid community resilience and help facilitate a more thoroughgoing transformation? And how can we transcend the limits of today's often defensive environmental struggles to nurture a movement better able to confront the problems ahead?

All these questions share the assumption that a rational and organized transition to a more sustainable future remains possible in this historical period. This is far from certain in an era of profound social upheaval, with progressive political tendencies frequently on the defensive and well-funded neo-fascist movements vying for political power. With the world rapidly approaching climate tipping points, we no longer have the luxury of several decades to plan for a just transition, as was once the case. With the magnitude of extreme weather events growing every year, and at least 240 million people already affected by climate related events annually (Oxfam International 2009), the scientific consensus now suggests that there is virtually no time left for the measured and gradual transition that policymakers and economic elites clearly prefer.

From the earliest popular writings about global warming, authors have suggested that a failure of preventive action would raise the likelihood of an authoritarian response to climate instability. For example, in his 1992 book, *Earth in the Balance*, then U.S. Senator Al Gore remarked that societal responses to past weather catastrophes paralleled the rise of "the bureaucratic, administrative tendencies of the modern state." If societies are unable to anticipate and prevent climate-related disasters it could necessitate "a new worldwide bureaucracy to manage the unimaginable problems caused by massive social and political upheavals" (Gore 1992, 73, 79). Other prominent voices suggest that human civilizations are not only doomed to collapse, but that the collapse of civilization may be an inevitable or even necessary precondition for the preservation of biodiversity (Jensen 2006, Kingsnorth and Hine n.d.). Such doomsday scenarios are rarely consistent, however, with a justice-centered perspective that aims to sustain human development and advance social equality. Furthermore, the doomsayers often ignore the central lesson of climate justice: that those who contribute the least to climate disrupting forms of pollution have long experienced the severest consequences (Samson et al. 2011). Thus, it is more urgent than ever before to seek out a political outlook that is both critical and forward-looking, which offers a systemic critique of status-quo politics and a coherent vision of an ecologically transformed society. Social ecology, which emerged in the 1960s and has influenced a wide array of social movements, represents such a view, and one that has already contributed to the unfolding global movement for climate justice.

To better contextualize social ecology's contributions, it is useful to first review the various social movement influences that have converged to shape the climate justice perspective. In earlier work I have identified 3 principle currents that have become most visible and influential in various international forums over the past decade (Tokar 2013, 2014). Foremost are the diverse array of indigenous and other land-based people's movements from around the world that have effectively highlighted their extreme vulnerability to climate disruptions along with their continued resilience in the face of colonizing influences. These include rainforest dwellers opposing new mega-dams and palm oil plantations, African and Latin American communities resisting land appropriations for industrial agriculture and agrofuel production, Pacific Islanders facing the loss of their homes due to rising seas, and peasant farmers fighting for food sovereignty and basic land rights, among many others. A second key influence has come from representatives of environmental justice communities, primarily from North America. These mainly African American, Latino and Native American activists represent communities that have resisted daily exposure to chemical toxins and other environmental hazards for decades, highlighted the links between environmental and racial justice, and contributed an essential perspective of frontline leadership around a wide array of climate-related concerns. Organizations such as the Indigenous Environmental Network (ienearth.org) that help bridge these two complementary worlds of struggle have been in the forefront of articulating and advancing a compelling climate justice framework ever since the mid-1990s.

A third central influence upon the evolution of climate justice has evolved from the global justice or "alterglobalization" movements that arose in opposition to the World Trade Organization (WTO) and other international financial institutions, including the annual G7/G8/G20 economic summits, during the 1990s and early 2000s. A discussion paper by European activists hoping to sustain the momentum from mass protests around the 2009 UN climate conference in Copenhagen, suggested that "Climate Justice means linking all struggles together that reject neoliberal markets and working towards a world that puts autonomous decision making power in the hands of communities" (Anon. 2010). This tendency is generally anti-capitalist in its outlook and has advanced systemic critiques of carbon markets and other policies widely viewed as false solutions to the unfolding climate crisis. The international Rising Tide network (risingtide.org.uk, risingtidenorthamerica.org), is one continuing organizational expression of this approach that has helped sustain opposition to controversial fossil fuel projects in North America, the UK, Australia, and beyond.

The theory and praxis of social ecology have helped guide numerous efforts to articulate a radical, counter-systemic ecological outlook since the 1960s, with its goal of transforming society's relationship to non-human nature and reharmonizing human communities' ties to the natural world. For many decades, social ecologists have articulated a fundamental ecological critique of the institutions of capitalism and the nation state and proposed an alternative vision of empowered communities organized confederally in pursuit of a more harmonious relationship to the natural world. Social ecology has helped shape the 1960s to 1970s New Left and antinuclear movements, the emergence of Green politics in many countries, the alterglobalization movement and the present struggle for democratic autonomy by Kurdish communities in Turkey and Syria, among many others. This chapter will review the distinct perspective of social ecology and then aim to address a variety of challenging political questions for climate justice that this approach may help clarify. These include the assessment of transition strategies for a fossil-free future, the potentialities and limitations of a localist, community-centered response to climate disruptions, the problems underlying market-driven models of renewable energy development, and the potential contribution of reconstructive, neo-utopian outlooks to contemporary climate politics.

Locating social ecology

The philosophy and praxis of social ecology were initially developed by the social theorist Murray Bookchin during the early 1960s to early 2000s and have been further elaborated by his colleagues and many others throughout the world, including writers and activists working presently in the Scandinavian countries, the U.K., Turkey, and throughout southern and eastern Europe (Eiglad 2015). It is a unique synthesis of utopian social criticism, historical and anthropological investigation, dialectical philosophy, and political strategy. Social ecology can be viewed as an unfolding of several distinct layers of understanding and insight, spanning all of these dimensions, and more. It begins with an understanding that environmental problems are fundamentally social and political in nature, and are rooted in the historical legacies of domination and social hierarchy. Bookchin was among the first thinkers in the West to identify the growth imperative of capitalism as a fundamental threat to the integrity of living ecosystems, and he consistently argued that social and ecological concerns are fundamentally inseparable, questioning the narrowly instrumental approaches advanced by many environmentalists to address particular issues.

This critical outlook on the nascent environmental movement, spurred many years of research into the evolution of the relationship between human societies and non-human nature. Bookchin challenged the common Western notion that humans inherently seek to dominate the natural world, concluding instead that the domination of nature is a myth rooted in relationships of domination among people that emerged from the breakdown of ancient tribal societies in Europe and the Middle East (Bookchin 1982). He sought to highlight various egalitarian social principles that many indigenous cultures – both past and present – have held in common and elevated these as guideposts for a renewed social order. Such principles have been described by progressive anthropologists and indigenous thinkers alike, and include concepts of interdependence, reciprocity, unity-in-diversity, and an ethics of complementarity, *i.e.* the balancing of roles among various social sectors, especially by actively compensating for differences among individuals. The inherent conflict between these guiding principles and those of increasingly stratified hierarchical societies has shaped the contending legacies of domination and freedom through much of human history.

Next, social ecology's philosophical inquiry examines the emergence of human consciousness from within the processes of natural evolution. Reaching back to the roots of dialectical thought, from Aristotle to Hegel, Bookchin (1990) advanced a unique approach to ecophilosophy, emphasizing the potentialities that lie latent within the evolution of both natural and social phenomena and celebrating the uniqueness of human creativity and self-reflection. Social ecology eschews the common view of nature as a realm of necessity, instead viewing natural evolution as striving, in a sense, to actualize an underlying potentiality for consciousness, creativity and freedom. For Bookchin, a dialectical outlook on human history compels us to reject what merely is and follow the potentialities inherent in natural history that suggest an expanded view of what could be, and ultimately what ought to be. While the realization of a free, ecological society is far from inevitable, it may perhaps be the most rational outcome of 4 billion years of natural evolution.

These historical and philosophical explorations provide an underpinning for social ecology's political strategy, which is described as libertarian (or confederal) municipalism or, more simply, as *communalism*, stemming from the roots of key ideas in the legacy of the Paris Commune of 1871. Social ecology reclaims the ancient Greek roots of the word "politics" as the democratic self-management of the *polis*, or municipality. Bookchin argued for liberated cities, towns, and neighborhoods, governed by open popular assemblies, which confederate to challenge parochialism, encourage independence, and build a genuine counter-power to currently dominant institutions. He celebrated the lasting Town Meeting traditions in Vermont and throughout the New England region of the U.S., describing how the region's Town Meetings and colonial legislatures assumed an increasingly radical and egalitarian character in the years prior to the American Revolution (Bookchin 1996, 154–55, 196–97). Bookchin believed that the limits of local action can be overcome by confederations of cities, towns and neighborhoods, joining together to sustain counterinstitutions aimed at challenging centralized power, overcoming parochialism, promoting interdependence, and advancing a broad liberatory agenda (Bookchin 2015, 67–82). Furthermore, the stifling anonymity of the capitalist market can be replaced by a moral economy in which economic, as well as political relationships, are guided by an ethics of mutualism and reciprocity (Bookchin 1986).

Social ecologists believe that whereas institutions of capitalism and the state heighten social stratification and exploit divisions among people, alternative structures rooted in direct democracy can foster the expression of a general social interest toward social and ecological renewal. "[I]t is from the municipality," Bookchin wrote (1992, 283), "that people can reconstitute themselves from isolated monads into a creative body politic and create and existentially vital … civic life that has institutional form as well as civic content: the block committees, assemblies, neighborhood organizations, cooperatives, citizens' action groups, and public arenas for discourse that go beyond such episodic acts as demonstrations and retain a lived as well as organized community." People inspired by this view have brought structures of direct democracy through popular assemblies into numerous social movements in the U.S., Europe and beyond, from popular direct-action campaigns against nuclear power in the late 1970s to the more recent alterglobalization and Occupy Wall Street movements. The prefigurative dimension of these movements – anticipating and enacting the various elements of a liberated society – has encouraged participants to challenge the status quo and advance transformative future visions.

Social ecologists have also sought to renew the utopian tradition in Western thought. Institute for Social Ecology co-founder Dan Chodorkoff argues for a practical utopianism, combining social ecology's theoretical insights and political praxis with advanced principles from green urban design and building, together with ecotechnologies to produce food, energy and other necessities (Chodorkoff 2014). Ecological design concepts like permaculture that encourage a more profound understanding of the patterns of the natural world resonate with social ecology's view that human beings can participate in nature in creative, mutually beneficial ways, while seeking to overturn historical legacies of abuse and destruction.

The influence of these ideas upon popular movements began with the largely underground distribution of Bookchin's essays during the 1960s. Ideas he first advanced, such as the need for a fundamentally radical ecology in contrast to technocratic environmentalism, were embraced by growing numbers of ecologically informed radicals. Bookchin and his colleagues at the Institute for Social Ecology participated in some of the earliest efforts to "green" cities and bring alternative, solar-based technologies into economically marginalized urban neighborhoods.

By the late 1970s, social ecology was playing quite a visible role in the rapidly growing movement against nuclear power in the U.S. Following the mass arrest of over 1,400 people who sought to nonviolently occupy a nuclear construction site on the coast of New Hampshire in 1977 – an event inspired by long-term nuclear site occupations in Germany and elsewhere – decentralized anti-nuclear alliances that began to appear across the U.S. These groups were committed to direct action, nonviolence, and grassroots organization, and many were captivated by the utopian dimension of the emerging "appropriate technology" movement for which Bookchin and other social ecologists provided an essential theoretical and historical grounding. New England's anti-nuclear Clamshell Alliance was the first to adopt the model of the "affinity group" as the basis of a long-range regional organizing effort – a concept that Bookchin (1971, 1977) first brought to the attention of U.S. activists through his research on the Spanish revolutionary tradition, and which continued to shape the structures of decentralized direct action movements in North America and beyond for decades to come (Kauffman 2017).

Also beginning in the 1970s, feminist thinkers informed by social ecology began to articulate a distinctive approach to "ecofeminism" that sought to re-evaluate the legacy of the historical association between women and non-human nature in Western culture, rejecting the essentialist and biological determinist notions that are typically linked to this association. A dialectical outlook informed by social ecology enabled writers like Ynestra King and Chaia Heller to eschew roman-ticized views of a women–nature connection, while consciously embracing the knowledge that women have acquired from an oppressive past to advance the goal of a free society that liberates women and men alike (King 1989, Heller 1999).

By the mid-1980s emerging Green political movements in many countries were torn between conventional party politics and strategies rooted in radically democratic, ecologically centered grassroots movements. Social ecologists on both sides of the Atlantic argued for a strategy rooted in issue-oriented local campaigns, ultimately seeking structural changes that would devolve decision making to directly democratic cities, towns, and neighborhoods. While Greens in most countries ultimately favored more traditional electoral routes, those who remained committed to their social movement base significantly influenced key policy positions (Tokar 2006) and set the stage for the renewal of ideas about radi-cal democracy in various kindred movements.

In the global justice movements of the 1990s and early 2000s, social ecologists raised support for a politics of direct democracy to challenge centralized economic and political institutions, advanced longer-range reconstructive visions within the movement, and established grassroots democratic organizing and decision-making structures that helped shape the aspirations of social movement actors for a genera-tion to come (Staudenmaier, et al. 2000). In the New England region of the U.S., where traditions of local Town Meeting governance evolved prior to the American Revolution and continue to this day, social ecologists have initiated local resolution campaigns around several issues where political progress appeared deadlocked at a national level. One such effort, challenging the proliferation of genetically modi-fied foods in the early 2000s, led to the passage of local Town Meeting resolu-tions in 120 towns in Vermont and other New England states (ISE Biotechnology Project 2005). While efforts in many towns served a primarily educational role, furthering public discussions of a relatively new area of concern for most people, the campaign also raised pressure on state legislatures to address the issue and a few towns were able to use local zoning rules and other measures to prevent the growing of GMOs (genetically modified organisms).

More recently, social ecology has become a central theoretical and strategic influence for militants in the Kurdish regions of the Middle East, where ethnically diverse populations, long marginalized by colonial powers and modern states alike, have created institutions of confederal direct democracy in one of the world's most war-torn regions. Despite persistent sectarian warfare and religious violence, Kurdish towns near the Turkish–Syrian border are working toward gender equity and ecological reconstruction, significantly informed by social ecology and other critical social outlooks. Drawing upon concepts first elaborated by Murray Bookchin, Kurdish communities have established multi-ethnic confederal councils to manage the economy in areas they control, and are developing "a new political architecture, one that is based on a critique of the state and a connection to a praxis based on the self-governing abilities of people" (Jongerden 2017, 254).

Social ecology and current movements

Before approaching some of the particular challenges faced by today's climate justice movement, it may be useful to clarify some general principles that underlie social ecology's contributions to social movements.

First, social ecology offers an uncompromising ecological outlook that challenges the entrenched power structures that underlie the systems of capitalism and the nation-state. A movement that fails to confront the underlying causes of environmental destruction and climate disruption can, at best, only superficially address those problems. Climate justice activists generally understand, for example, that false climate solutions such as carbon markets, geoengineering, and the promotion of natural gas obtained from fracking as a "bridge fuel" on the path to renewable energy, mainly serve the current economic system's imperative to keep growing. To fully address the causes of climate change and other compelling environmental and social problems requires movement actors to raise long-range, transformative demands that the dominant economic and political systems may prove unable to accommodate. Using tools developed by social ecologists, activist campaigns can help illuminate hidden structures of oppression and hierarchy, and reveal how various oppressions intersect, even while dramatically illustrating the long-range, reconstructive potential of the movement (Heller 1999, 149–171).

Second, social ecology offers us a lens to better comprehend the origins and historical emergence of ecological radicalism, from the nascent movements of the late 1950s and early sixties right up to the present. Over more than 5 decades, the writings of Murray Bookchin and his colleagues have reflected upon important on-the-ground debates within ecological and social movements with passion and polemic, as well as with humor and long-range vision. Social ecology also played a central role in exposing and challenging the inherent anti-ecological biases of much of twentieth-century Marxism, and thus serves as an important complement to current efforts to reclaim Marx's ecological legacy. While the understanding of Marx's long-ignored ecological writings, as advanced by authors such as Foster (2010) and Saito (2016), is essential to the emerging eco-left tradition, so are the political debates and theoretical insights that unfolded over decades when the

Marxist left was disturbingly and often quite vehemently uninterested in environmental matters. Movements that are aware of their history, and comprehend the lessons of their past, are far better equipped to discuss where we may be headed.

Third, social ecology offers the most comprehensive treatment of the origins of human social domination and its historical relationship to abuses of the earth's living ecosystems. Social ecology highlights the origins of ecological destruction in social relations of domination, in contrast to conventional views suggesting that impulses to dominate non-human nature are a product of historical necessity. Social ecologists celebrate the ways that humans can participate meaningfully and supportively in the processes of natural evolution, not solely as a disruptive force.

Fourth, social ecology presents a framework for comprehending the origins of human consciousness and the emergence of human reason from its natural context. Bookchin's philosophy reaches far beyond popular often solipsistic notions of an "ecological self," grounding the embeddedness of consciousness in nature in a coherent theoretical framework with roots in both classical nature philosophies and modern science. It challenges us to overcome popular acceptance of the world as it is and consider how the social and political world perhaps ought to be. Furthermore, social ecology's attempt to forge an ethics grounded in natural evolution has helped generations of activists articulate a coherent challenge to ecophilosophical tendencies that can sometimes veer toward atavism, biological determinism, and "blood and soil" ethnocentrism (Biehl and Staudenmaier 2011).

Fifth, social ecology offers a comprehensive historical and strategic grounding for discussing the promise of direct democracy. Social ecologists have worked to bring the praxis of direct democracy into popular movements since the 1970s, and Bookchin's writings offer an essential historical and theoretical context for this continuing conversation. Social ecology offers a comprehensive strategic outlook that looks beyond the role of popular assemblies as a form of public expression and outrage toward more fully realized self-organization, confederation, and a revolutionary challenge to entrenched nation-state institutions.

Finally, social ecology asserts the inseparability of effective oppositional political activity from a reconstructive vision of an ecological future. Bookchin viewed most popular dissident writing as incomplete, focusing on critique and analysis without also proposing a coherent way forward. At the same time, social ecologists have spoken out against the accommodation of many alternative institutions—including numerous formerly radical cooperatives and collectives—to a stifling capitalist status quo (Bookchin 1986; Tokar 1992, 115–17, 146). The convergence of oppositional and reconstructive strands of activity is a crucial step toward a political movement that can ultimately contest and reclaim political power. This is realized within the international climate movement through the creation of new political spaces that embody the principles of "blockadia" and "alternatiba" (Combes 2014). The former term, popularized by Naomi Klein (2014), was coined by the activists of the Tar Sands Blockade in Texas, who engaged in an extended series of nonviolent actions to block the construction of the Keystone XL oil pipeline. The latter is a French Basque word, adopted as the theme of a bicycle tour that encircled France during the summer of 2015 and highlighted scores of local alternative-building projects (see alternatiba.eu/en/).

What kind of transition?

Having outlined these general principles, how can they help address several of the central dilemmas facing climate justice movements today? Can local action help drive a sufficiently robust and timely transition to a fossil-free economy? Is such a transition compatible with capitalist growth, or is a more thoroughgoing transition in the offing? How can humanity sustain a sense of hope and possibility in the face of potential climate catastrophe? The questions we face today tend to elude straightforward answers, but social ecology's principles and praxis may help illuminate the way forward.

Climate scientists have long been in the forefront of mapping out the magnitude of the challenges we all face. A decade ago, James Hansen and his colleagues demonstrated that carbon dioxide levels need to stabilize around 350 parts per million (ppm) to sustain a hope of "preserving a planet resembling the one on which civilization developed" (Hansen, et al. 2007, 1926). More recently, his group at Columbia University determined that total global emissions will need to peak by around 2030 in order to return to 350 ppm within 2–300 years, and that a slower recovery time could result in a highly unstable climate regime lasting many thousands of years (Hansen, et al. 2013). Several of Europe's leading climate scientists have calculated that to prevent average warming beyond 1.5 degrees Celsius – as demanded by Global South delegates over years of climate negotiations and affirmed in the 2015 Paris agreement – will require an emissions peak no later than 2020 and the halving of anthropogenic emissions every subsequent decade (Rogelj, et al. 2015, Rockström, et al. 2017). Less ambitious scenarios that would further delay the emissions peak bring potentially devastating human and ecological consequences.

Kevin Anderson, one of Britain's most prominent and politically engaged climate scientists, has calculated that even a 50 percent chance to avoid more than 2 degrees of average warming would require a 10 percent annual decline in emissions between 2020 and 2040 (2012, 24). While recent decades have seen a decoupling of emissions growth from economic growth in many countries (Smith 2017), it appears unlikely that such a magnitude of reduction can be achieved without significant economic contraction. In capitalist economies, that almost invariably results in widespread loss of employment and livelihoods (Magdoff and Foster 2011, 55–59), along with a potential political backlash. Others argue, in contrast, that a period of significant economic expansion may be necessary to support a sufficiently rapid transition to a renewable energy economy that also fosters job creation and global poverty relief (Pollin 2015, Schwartzman and Schwartzman 2013). A series of widely cited studies by Mark Jacobson and his colleagues at Stanford University aim to demonstrate the feasibility of such a conversion, mandating the construction of over 1.7 billion new renewable energy installations in the coming decades and utilizing just under 2 percent of the potentially accessible global land mass available for such projects (Jacobson and Delucchi 2011).

While critics have challenged several of the specific assumptions behind these projections (Clack, et al. 2017), such "green growth" proposals raise a variety of more fundamental questions. For example, Jacobson and Delucchi argue in some detail (2011, 1161–64) that a combination of metals recycling and substitution of alternatives for rare minerals may be sufficient to address the material needs of such a large-scale deployment of new technology, but this is far from certain. Furthermore, economists have suggested since the 19th century coal boom, that technological changes, even if they improve the efficiency of resource consumption, tend to *increase* the demand for energy and materials as capitalists learn how to do more with less while continuing to grow the economy. This is known as the Jevons Paradox, after research by the British economist William Stanley Jevons on patterns of coal use during the Industrial Revolution (Foster 2009). To cite one current example, jet fuel consumption per passenger-mile has fallen 82 percent since the late 1950s, however the rapid expansion of air travel has led to a seven-fold increase in total fuel use (Lohmann and Hildyard 2013, 36). Richard York from the University of Oregon has calculated (2012) that as little as a quarter of non-fossil energy currently replaces fossil fuels, and only a tenth of non-fossil electricity; the rest is simply adding new capacity to the system. While some studies suggest that global carbon emissions may be reaching a plateau (Jackson, et al. 2016), global emissions spiked significantly in 2016, even before a new U.S. administration began to dismantle environmental regulations and aggressively promote new fossil fuel extraction (Friedman 2017).

Investment in renewable energy grew rapidly through the first decade of this century but leveled off in 2012 and has substantially declined in some recent years (Frankfurt School of Finance & Management 2015, 12). Andreas Malm (2016, 370–71) further documents the cancellation of renewable investments by several major corporations, explaining how in capitalist terms, the industry has become a victim of its own success. As technology costs continue to fall – making renewable energy more affordable throughout much of the world – investors may face a trend of steadily declining asset value. Malm laments how renewable energy has "lost so much of its exchange-value at the very same time that its social use-value – slowing down climate change – rose toward priceless heights" (2016, 371).

The U.K.-based Corner House research group, managed by former editors of *The Ecologist* magazine, argues that future technology projections such as the Jacobson group's may indeed be asking the wrong questions. First, they posit future scenarios as if a "class of hypothetical independent, impartial, supremely powerful global or national regulators" were empowered to make decisions about the world's energy resources (Lohmann and Hildyard 2013, 19). At the very least, they imply a far more robust and agile public sector than currently appears within reach; the logic of the market, in contrast, is far more chaotic and less predictable. But, more fundamentally, such projections perpetuate an "abstract concept of 'energy'" that "has largely been a creation of fossil-fuelled industrial capitalism" (Lohmann and Hildyard 2013, 26). With annual coal, oil, and gas consumption now burning the equivalent of 400 years of terrestrial plant growth each year, fossil fuels have encouraged us to ignore "time, place or context," viewing energy as an abstract commodity that is ever-present rather than as a means to perform a diverse range of discrete useful tasks. This ultimately furthers the destructive myth of unlimited production and consumption, even as the world needs to rapidly curtail emissions of greenhouse gases.

Furthermore, the scale and character of current renewable energy installations tends to reflect what Bookchin (1982) described as the "social matrix" of technology. Technological innovations are not simply products of the particular social relations of industrial capitalism but are developed specifically to reinforce and strengthen those relationships. For example, the trend toward ever larger-scaled wind turbines can be justified in terms of their increased power output and efficiency, but it has also served to shift control of wind power production toward larger corporations and undermine the many local, cooperative arrangements that drove earlier waves of wind power development (Maegard 2010, Shaffer 2016). The increasingly massive scale and centralized ownership of renewable energy installations has also increased local opposition to wind and solar energy projects in many rural areas, impeding overall progress toward a renewable future (Phadke 2011, Agnew 2017).While social ecologists are generally optimistic about the potential for an informed human engagement with ecological processes to help enhance the integrity of natural systems, there is also considerable resonance with the critique of gigantism and preference for smaller-scale solutions that have driven the European degrowth movement (Demaria 2013). Bookchin consistently argued, however, that "small" is not enough, and that the ethical and political character of the solutions we propose are ultimately what matters most (1992, 265).

Global inertia, local response

Following the exuberant but ultimately disappointing conclusion of the 2015 UN climate conference in Paris, many climate justice activists have embraced a return to the local. While delegates to the conference tended to echo Ban Ki-moon's appraisal of the Paris agreement as ushering in a "new era of global cooperation" (UNFCCC 2015a), the civil society response was generally skeptical. Friends of the Earth International (2015) denounced the agreement as a "sham of a deal" and Kevin Anderson said it was "weaker than Copenhagen" and "not consistent with the latest science" (Chivers and Worth 2015). Tens of thousands of people who assembled on the streets of Paris on the last day of the conference described the agreement as having crossed dangerous "red lines," and the global 350.org network went on to initiate an international series of actions the following spring urging the world to "Break Free from Fossil Fuels" (breakfree2016.org).

While the Paris agreement's Preamble embraced many of the concerns that various countries and their civil society representatives brought to the table – even citing "the importance for some of the concept of 'climate justice'" (UNFCCC 2015b, 21) – activists condemned the agreement's fundamentally voluntary nature and the absence of enforcement measures (Tokar 2015). Article 15 of the agreement proposed a "mechanism to facilitate implementation and promote compliance," but only in the form of an international "expert-based" committee that is to be "transparent, non-adversarial and non-punitive" (UNFCCC 2015b, 29). The document offered a nod to Global South concerns to address current climate-related losses and damage, but the text explicitly denied, at the insistence of the U.S. and other wealthy countries, "a basis for any liability or compensation" (UNFCCC 2015b, 8). The U.S. administration added insult to injury in June of 2017 by announcing its withdrawal from the agreement, threatening to undermine even the voluntary process that had drawn most of the world's nations to bring their emissions reduction plans to the table.

In response to the announced U.S. withdrawal, an alliance of over 200 cities and counties, along with some 1600 businesses and investors, announced their intention to uphold the commitments the previous administration had brought to Paris (Tabuchi and Friedman 2017). But this represents only a modest step forward, for 3 main reasons. First, the sum of all the "national contributions" that countries brought to Paris is only a partial step toward keeping average warming below 1.5 or 2 degrees (www.climateactiontracker.org, www.climateinteractive. org). Second, the Obama administration's Climate Action Plan offered little to advance the actual historic pace of U.S. emissions reductions (Komanoff 2015). And third, financial analysts from institutions such as Bloomberg and Morgan Stanley now suggest that rapidly falling prices for renewable energy could accelerate the deployment of alternatives considerably faster than any current policy initiatives (Schlanger 2017, Shankleman and Warren 2017). Beyond the electrical sector, at least 3 European countries – Norway, Germany, and France – have announced plans to ban the sale of petroleum powered vehicles in the next decade or two, with some auto companies promising a much faster transition (Chow 2017). However, the continuing relevance of the Jevons Paradox suggests that even these measures will not necessarily translate into economy-wide emissions reductions. A far more ambitious, people-driven effort is necessary to address the fundamental inadequacy of international climate agreements, market-oriented approaches, and symbolic local measures.

The history of local measures to reduce energy use and greenhouse gas emissions is reasonably encouraging. In the U.S., cities and states have mandated important measures to save energy and further incentivize alternatives. These include "renewable portfolio standards" that require utilities to obtain a rising share of their power supplies from renewable sources, net metering and feed-in tariffs to stabilize costs for subsidized home- and farm-scale producers of solar and wind energy, and measures to attach loans for fuel-saving equipment to home mortgages to facilitate easier financing. Over several decades, U.S. cities have advanced local zoning changes to encourage higher downtown population densities and thereby limit urban sprawl, strengthened building codes to mandate energy savings, built infrastructure to charge electric vehicles, and supported urban farms and relocalized food systems (Linstroth and Bell 2007). A few U.S. cities are even expanding public transportation systems, despite continuing pressures toward fiscal austerity. Numerous European cities have taken steps to significantly redesign their central cores to reduce traffic, air pollution, and fossil fuel use (Schneibel 2016). Internationally, more than 2,500 cities from Oslo to Sydney have submitted plans to the UN to reduce their greenhouse gas emissions, sometimes in defiance of their national governments' more cautious commitments (Doyle 2017).

Popular grassroots pressure can also help reshape national policies. In Germany, for example, decades of local efforts – from successful anti-nuclear campaigns and citizen initiatives in the 1970s to the more recent emergence of hundreds of energy cooperatives and Bioenergy Villages – led to the passage of a pioneering renewable energy law in 2000 that helped increase renewable electricity use to a third of the nation's total production (Mueller 2017). Even the landmark U.S. environmental laws of the 1970s resulted in part from successful local efforts to regulate pollution; a wave of environmental regulations and lawsuits in numerous cities and states helped convince influential business interests that a uniform set of national standards and funding mechanisms to implement pollution controls was a far better option (Tokar 1997, 58). A parallel scenario for overcoming political deadlocks around climate policy is not difficult to envision.

Locally focused campaigns have also had a large impact in many areas of the Global South, from Gandhi's historic drive to reinvigorate rural economies to land defense movements in present-day India and the movement of landless people in Brazil, among many others. Each of these movements in turn has significantly impacted domestic politics and also provided a living example for social movement actors throughout the world. One recent report described two local popular *consultas* in Columbia that moved to reject mineral and oil exploitation within their territories, citing the affiliation of one of the towns with the Italian-based "Slow Cities" movement (Weinberg 2017). The latter is an outgrowth of the famous Slow Food movement that has helped raise the social and cultural standing of local food producers in Italy and many other countries. A Slow Cities statement of principles suggests that by "[w]orking towards sustainability, defending the environment and reducing our excessive ecological footprint" communities are "committing … to rediscover traditional know-how and to make the most of our resources through recycling and reuse, applying the new technologies" (Cittaslow International n.d.). In contrast to the somewhat similar Transition Town movement, whose reach has only minimally extended beyond the English-speaking world, the Slow Cities website lists scores of affiliated cities and towns in countries including Germany, Poland, Turkey, South Korea, and China.

The ability of localist movements to build support and pressure for broader institutional changes is central to their political importance in a period when social and environmental progress is stalled in many countries. Actions initiated locally may also have more staying power than those mandated by higher authorites. They are far more likely to be democratically structured and accountable to people who are most affected by the outcomes. They help build relationships among neighbors and strengthen the capacity for self-reliance. They enable us to see that the institutions that now dominate our lives are far less essential for our daily sustenance than we are often led to believe. And, perhaps most important, local initiatives can challenge regressive national policies that favor fossil fuel corporations and allied financial interests.

Of course, not all social movements at local level seek forward-looking, progressive changes. In both Europe and North America, forces of the far right have adopted the rhetoric of local control toward regressive, ultra-nationalist, and often racist ends. For example, when the U.K. Independence Party, which helped lead the drive for British withdrawal from the European Union, proclaimed that "real decision-making should be given to local communities," it only thinly veiled their intent to marginalize immigrant populations, oppose renewable energy projects, and even ban discussions of climate change in some local schools (Hopkins 2014). Racist organizations in the American South have long hidden behind localist rhetoric, as does the militia movement and other far right pseudo-populist formations that support the Trump presidency in the U.S. At least one prominent voice of "anti-civilization" environmentalism has written in support of a nationalist response to globalism (Kingsnorth 2017). Bookchin was well aware of such tendencies, and of the potential for atavistic forms of ecological thought to turn in a reactionary direction but remained hopeful that a more consistently liberatory localism would emerge from the practice of direct democracy, with communities acting as "a school for creating a new kind of citizenship," rooted in participatory self-governance and an expansive ecological ethics (1986, 95). Whether this can ultimately serve to counter the current neo-populist wave still remains to be seen.

For the most part, recent local initiatives in the U.S. and beyond have mainly evolved in a progressive, socially liberatory direction. The Center for Immigration Studies, which seeks to reduce immigration rates into the U.S., lists over 160 cities and counties that have declared themselves as "sanctuaries" in defiance of the Trump administration's elevated enforcement of U.S. immigration laws (Griffith and Vaughan 2017). Thirteen U.S. and Canadian cities are implementing steps toward participatory budgeting at neighborhood level, a practice that originated in the 1980s in Porto Alegre, Brazil (Hagelskamp et al. 2016). Several U.S. cities have raised their local minimum wage well above state and national levels, along with other measures to help mend a threatened social safety net. Indeed, several Republican-dominated state legislatures have responded to the threat of progressive local measures by passing controversial new "pre-emption" laws designed to overturn local initiatives to protect refugees, guarantee the rights of gay, lesbian, and transgender people, and encourage local hiring on public works projects (Badger 2017). The Texas legislature passed a law prohibiting cities and towns from banning fracking for oil and gas. This replicates an earlier wave of state pre-emption measures over a decade ago that prohibited local jurisdictions from banning smoking, restricting pesticide use, and regulating the use of genetically modified seeds, among other measures (Newman 2006). Ongoing political and legal battles over the rights of municipalities vs. states speak to the continuing political potency of socially and environmentally progressive measures emerging from the local level.

Social and environmental justice activists in the U.S. are also challenging the trend of right wing electoral victories at the national and many state levels by running and winning bold campaigns for a variety of local positions, from city councils, to top law enforcement posts and mayors' offices. Perhaps most noteworthy is the successful 2017 campaign of Chokwe Antar Lumumba, who was elected mayor of Jackson, Mississippi, in the heart of the Deep South, with a program focused on human rights, local democracy, and neighborhood-based economic and ecological renewal. Lumumba ran as the voice of a movement known as "Cooperation Jackson", which has put forward numerous ideas resonant with social ecology, including empowered neighborhood assemblies, cooperative economics, and a dual-power political strategy (Akuno 2014). Cooperation Jackson takes its inspirations mainly from traditionally Black American and Global South sources, including the resistance struggles of enslaved Africans before and after the U.S. Civil War, the Zapatista movement in southern Mexico, and recent international popular uprisings. Another central source of inspiration for the climate justice movement is the legacy of active collaborations between environmental justice and labor activists, a 30-year effort that has advanced demands for energy democracy and a just transition for workers in the fossil fuel sector and other polluting industries (Sweeney 2014, jtalliance.org, labor4sustainability.org).

Utopian visions

The projections of climate science highlight the difficulty of transforming our societies and economies quickly enough to prevent a descent into a planet-wide climate catastrophe. Science also affirms that the actions we undertake today can mean the difference between a future climate regime that is disruptive and difficult and one that rapidly descends toward apocalyptic extremes. While some authors focus on the most dire future scenarios, hoping that people can be shocked into realizing the magnitude of changes that are necessary, this approach appears more likely to inspire despair and withdrawal than meaningful action. Author Eddie Yuen describes the problem of "catastrophe fatigue," which typically pacifies rather than energizes people, and argues that real solutions to the climate crisis "must be prefigurative and practical as well as visionary and participatory," appealing to "community and solidarity" rather than "austerity and discipline" (2012, 16, 42).

This resonates strongly with the utopian dimensions of social ecology, and with the continually renewed history of utopian thought over many centuries. While we need to be completely realistic about the potentially devastating consequences of continuing climate disruptions, a genuinely transformative movement needs to be rooted in a forward-looking view of an improved quality of life for most people in the world in a future freed from fossil fuel dependence. As Naomi Klein has written (2014), the climate crisis demands not only an end to the unlimited exploitation of people and the earth, but also a restructuring of society around the egalitarian, community-centered values that progressive movements have championed for generations.

While centrist thinkers, especially since the fall of the Soviet Union, have often condemned the pursuit of utopian solutions as a harbinger of totalitarianism, the utopian impulse has historically been a popular expression of human strivings for a better world. It has deep roots in ancient thought and came fully into its own with the emergence of secular culture in the West, as the desire for a better world was freed from narrowly religious forms of expression (Chodorkoff 2014, 121–143; Touraine 2000). The pioneering German sociologist Karl Mannheim believed that "The utopian mentality is at the base of all serious social change" and invoked "the reality-transcending power of utopia" (quoted in Sargent 2000, 14; Kumar 2000, 265). World systems theorist Immanuel Wallerstein (1998) has proposed a renewed study of "utopistics" that broadly examines future possibilities and reveals "the substantive rationality of alternative possible historical systems."

In a world confronting the possibility of a rapidly deteriorating natural order, with unprecedented weather-related catastrophes and an epochal wave of mass extinctions of living species, humanity's future may depend on our ability to envision and create a better world. Partial measures are far from sufficient, but the cumulative impact of local efforts to challenge entrenched interests and actualize living alternatives – combined with coherent revolutionary visions and strategies toward a radically transformed society – may perhaps be enough to fend off a dystopian future of deprivation and authoritarianism. Whether local democratic initiatives are aimed at pressuring and transforming established institutions or at fully superseding and abolishing them, they remain our best hope to meaningfully reshape the future. Perhaps the threat of climate chaos, combined with our deep knowledge of the potential for a more humane and ecologically harmonious future, can indeed help inspire the profound transformations that are necessary for humanity and the earth to continue to thrive.

References

Agnew O. (2017) "Vermont and the Meaning of Green" Nexus Media. Accessed 14 July 2017 from: https://nexusmedianews.com/vermont-and-the-meaning-of-green-aa5c0b5f7003

Akuno K. (2014) "People's Assembly's Overview: The Jackson People's Assembly Model" Accessed 10 May 2017 from: https://mxgm.org/peoples-assemblys-overview-the-jackson-peoples-assembly-model/

Anderson K. (2012) "Climate Change Going Beyond Dangerous – Brutal Numbers and Tenuous Hope" in Hällstrom N. ed, *What Next Volume III: Climate, Development and Equity* Dag Hammarskjöld Foundation, Uppsala 16–40.

Anonymous. (2010) "What does Climate Justice mean in Europe? A Discussion Paper" *Climate Justice Action*. 26 March, via email.

Badger E. (2017) "Blue Cities Want to Make Their Own Rules. Red States Won't Let Them" *New York Times*, 6 July.

Bidwai P. (2012) "Climate Change, Equity and Development: India's Dilemmas" in Hällstrom N. ed, *What Next Volume III: Climate, Development and Equity* Dag Hammarskjöld Foundation, Uppsala 147–59.

Biehl J. and Staudenmaier P. (2011) *Ecofascism Revisited: Lessons from the German Experience* New Compass Press, Porsgrunn, Norway.

Bookchin M. (1971) "A Note on Affinity Groups" in *Post-Scarcity Anarchism* Ramparts Press, Berkeley, 221–22.

Bookchin M. (1977) *The Spanish Anarchists: The Heroic Years, 1868–1936* Harper Collophon, New York.

Bookchin M. (1982) *The Ecology of Freedom* Cheshire Books, Palo Alto, California.

Bookchin M. (1986) "Market Economy or Moral Economy" in *The Modern Crisis* New Society Publishers, Philadelphia 77–97.

Bookchin M. (1990) *The Philosophy of Social Ecology: Essays on Dialectical Naturalism* Black Rose, Montreal.

Bookchin M. (1992) *Urbanization Without Cities: The Rise and Decline of Citizenship* Black Rose, Montreal.

Bookchin M. (1996) *The Third Revolution: Popular Movements in the Revolutionary Era*, Volume 1 Cassell, London.

Bookchin M. (2015) *The Next Revolution: Popular Assemblies and the Promise of Direct Democracy* Verso, London.

Chivers D. and Worth J. (2015) "Paris Deal: Epic Fail on a Planetary Scale" *New Internationalist*. 12 December, via email.

Chodorkoff D. (2014) *The Anthropology of Utopia* New Compass, Porsgrunn, Norway.

Chow L. (2017) "France to Ban Sale of Cars Powered by Gasoline and Diesel" *Ecowatch. com*, 6 July.

Cittaslow International (n.d.) "Our Principles" Accessed 17 July 2017 from: http://cittaslow.org/content/our principles

Clack C.T.M., Qvist S.A., Apt J., Bazilian M., Brandt A.R., Caldeira K., Davis S.J., Diakov V., Handschy M.A., Hines P.D., and Jaramillo P. (2017) "Evaluation of a proposal for reliable low-cost grid power with 100% wind, water, and solar" *Proceedings of the National Academy of Sciences USA*. Accessed 26 June 2017 from: www.pnas.org/cgi/doi/10.1073/pnas.1610381114

Combes M. (2014) "Towards Paris 2015: Challenges and Perspectives" Attac France, Paris. 18 November, via email.

Demaria F. (2013) "What is degrowth? From an activist slogan to a social movement" *Environmental Values* 22:2 191–215.

Doyle A. (2017) "In Race to Curb Climate Change, Cities Outpace Governments" *Reuters*, 13 March. Accessed 14 March 2017 from: www.reuters.com/article/us-climatechange-cities-insight/in-race-to-curb-climate-change-cities-outpace-governments-idUSKBN16K0JI

Eiglad E., ed. (2015) *Social Ecology and Social Change* New Compass Press, Porsgrunn, Norway.

Foster J.B. (2009) "The Jevons Paradox: Environment and Technology Under Capitalism" in *The Ecological Revolution: Making Peace with the Planet* Monthly Review Press, New York 121–28.

Foster J.B. (2010) *The Ecological Rift: Capitalism's War on the Earth* Monthly Review Press, New York.

Frankfurt School of Finance & Management. (2015) "Global Trends in Renewable Energy Investment" 2015. Accessed 2 April 2015 from http://fs-unep-centre.org/publications/global-trends-renewable-energy-investment-2015

Friedman L. (2017) "Climate-Altering Gases Spiked in 2016, Federal Scientists Report" *New York Times*, 13 July.

Friends of the Earth International. (2015) "Paris climate deal is a sham" 12 December. Accessed 13 December 2015 from www.foei.org

Gore A., (1992) *Earth in the Balance: Ecology and the Human Spirit* Houghton Mifflin, Boston.

Griffith B. and Vaughan J. (2017) "Map: Sanctuary Cities, Counties, and States" Center for Immigration Studies, Washington. Accessed 17 July 2017 from: http://cis.org/Map-Sanctuary-Cities-Counties-and-States

Hagelskamp C., et al. (2016) "Public Spending, by the People: Participatory Budgeting in the United States and Canada in 2014–15" Public Agenda, San Francisco. Accessed 17 July 2017 from: www.publicagenda.org/pages/public-spending-by-the-people

Hansen J., Sato M., Kharecha P., Russell G., Lea D.W., and Siddall M. (2007) "Climate change and trace gases" *Philosophical Transactions of the Royal Society A* 365:1856 1925–54.

Hansen J., Kharecha P., Sato M., Masson-Delmotte V., Ackerman F., Beerling D.J., Hearty P.J., Hoegh-Guldberg O., Hsu S.L., Parmesan C., and Rockstrom J. (2013) "Assessing 'Dangerous Climate Change'" *PLOS One* 8:12.

Heller C. (1999) *Ecology of Everyday Life* Black Rose Books, Montreal.

Hopkins R. (2014) "Four Reasons Why too much Local Democracy can be a Bad Thing." Accessed 3 June 2014 from: https://transitionnetwork.org/

ISE Biotechnology Project (2005) *Vermont Towns vs. Genetic Engineering: A Guide to Reclaiming Our Democracy* Institute for Social Ecology, Plainfield, Vermont.

Jackson R.B., Canadell J.G., Le Quéré C., Andrew R.M., Korsbakken J.I., Peters G.P., and Nakicenovic, N. (2016) "Reaching Peak Emissions" *Nature Climate Change* 6:1 7–10.

Jacobson M.Z. and Delucchi M.A. (2011) "Providing all global energy with wind, water, and solar power, Part I" *Energy Policy* 39:3 1154–1169.

Jensen D. (2006) *Endgame* (2 volumes) Seven Stories, New York.

Jongerden J. (2017) "The Kurdistan Workers' Party: Radical Democracy and the Right to Self-Determination Beyond the Nation-State" in Stansfield G. and Shareef M. eds, *The Kurdish Question Revisited* Hurst Publishers, London 245–58.

Kauffman L.A. (2017) *Direct Action* Verso, London.

King Y. (1989) "The Ecology of Feminism and the Feminism of Ecology" in Plant J. ed, *Healing the Wounds: The Promise of Ecofeminism* New Society Publishers, Philadelphia 18–28.

Kingsnorth P. (2017) "The Lie of the Land: Does Environmentalism Have a Future in the Age of Trump?" *The Guardian*, 18 March.

Kingsnorth P. and Hine D. (n.d.) "Uncivilisation: The Dark Mountain Manifesto". Accessed 12 May 2010 from: www.dark-mountain.net/about-2/the-manifesto

Klein N. (2014) *This Changes Everything: Capitalism vs. the Climate* Simon & Schuster, New York.

Komanoff C. (2015) "Transformational It's Not: Running the Numbers on Obama's Latest Climate Regs" 3 August. Accessed 28 August 2015 from http://carbontax.org

Kumar K. (2000) "Utopia and Anti-Utopia in the Twentieth Century" in Schaer R., Claeys G., and Tower Sargent L. eds, *Utopia: The Search for the Ideal Society in the Western World* Oxford University Press, New York 251–67.

Linstroth T. and Bell R. (2007) *Local Action: The New Paradigm in Climate Change Policy* University of Vermont Press, Burlington.

Lohmann L. and Hildyard N. (2013) *Energy Alternatives: Surveying the Territory* The Corner House, Dorset, U.K.

Maegard P. (2010) "Denmark: Politically-Induced Paralysis in Wind Power's Homeland and Industrial Hub" in Abramsky K. ed, *Sparking A Worldwide Energy Revolution* AK Press, San Francisco 489–94.

Magdoff F. and Foster J.B. (2011) *What Every Environmentalist Needs to Know About Capitalism* Monthly Review Press, New York.

Malm A. (2016) *Fossil Capital: The Rise of Steam Power and the Roots of Global Warming* Verso, London.

Mueller T. (2017) *Diversity is Strength: The German Energiewende as a Resilient Alternative* New Economics Foundation, London.

Newman N. (2006) "Governing the Nation from the Statehouses: The Rightwing Agenda in the States and How Progressives Can Fight Back" Progressive Legislative Action Network, New York. Accessed 24 February 2006 from http://progressivestates.org

Oxfam International (2009) *The Right to Survive: The Humanitarian Challenge for the Twenty-First Century* Oxfam, London.

Phadke R. (2011) "Resisting and reconciling big wind: middle landscape politics in the new American West" *Antipode* 43:3 754–76.

Pollin R. (2015) "The new green economy" *The Nation* 16 November 13–18.

Rockström J., Gaffney O., Rogelj J., Meinshausen M., Nakicenovic N., and Schellnhuber H.J. (2017) "A roadmap for rapid decarbonization" *Science* 355:6331 1269–71.

Rogelj J., Luderer G., Pietzcker R.C., Kriegler E., Schaeffer M., Krey V., and Riahi K. (2015) "Energy system transformations for limiting end-of-century warming to below 1.5°C" *Nature Climate Change* 5:6 519–27.

Saito K. (2016) "Marx's ecological notebooks" *Monthly Review* 67:9 25–42.

Samson J., Berteaux D., McGill B.J., and Humphrie M.M. (2011) "Geographic disparities and moral hazards in the predicted impacts of climate change on human populations" *Global Ecology and Biogeography* 20:4 532–44.

Sargent L.T. (2000) "Utopian Traditions: Themes and Variations" in Schaer R et al. eds *Utopia: The Search for the Ideal Society in the Western World.* Oxford University Press, New York 8–17.

Schlanger Z. (2017. "Renewable Energy is Becoming so Cheap the US will meet Paris Commitments even if Trump Withdraws" *Qz.com*, 9 July.

Schnibel K. (2016) Personal communication, on behalf of Alleanza per il Clima (climatealliance.it)

Schwartzman D. and Schwartzman P. (2013) "A rapid solar transition is not only possible, it is imperative" *African Journal of Science, Technology, Innovation and Development* 5:4 297–302.

Shaffer D. (2016) "Wind Power Industry Surges, and Expects Steady Growth" *Minneapolis Star Tribune*, 28 January.

Shankleman J. and Warren H. (2017) "Solar Power Will Kill Coal Faster Than You Think" *Bloomberg News*, 15 June. Accessed 16 June 2017 from www.bloomberg.com/news/articles/2017-06-15/solar-power-will-kill-coal-sooner-than-you-think

Smith N. (2017) "Capitalism Can Thrive Without Cooking the Planet" *Bloomberg News*, 22 June.

Staudenmaier P., Driskell J., Milstein C., Heller C., Foelsche A., del Moral A., and Toft A. (2000) *Bringing Democracy Home* Institute for Social Ecology, Plainfield, Vermont.

Sweeney S. (2014) "Working Toward Energy Democracy" in Worldwatch Institute ed, *State of the World 2014: Governing for Sustainability* Island Press, Washington 215–27.

Tabuchi H. and Friedman L. (2017) "U.S. Cities, States and Businesses Pledge to Measure Emissions" *New York Times*, 11 July.

Tokar B. (1992) *The Green Alternative: Creating an Ecological Future* R & E Miles, San Pedro, California.

Tokar B. (1997) *Earth for Sale: Reclaiming Ecology in the Age of Corporate Greenwash* South End Press, Boston.

Tokar B. (2006) "The Greens as a Social Movement: Values and Conflicts" in Zelko F. and Brinkmann C. eds, *Green Parties: Reflections on the First Three Decades* Heinrich Böll Foundation North America, Washington 97–107.

Tokar B. (2013) "Movements for Climate Justice in the US and Worldwide" in Dietz M. and Garrelts H. eds, *Routledge Handbook of the Climate Change Movement* Routledge International Handbooks Series, Oxford 131–46.

Tokar B. (2014) *Toward Climate Justice: Perspectives on the Climate Crisis and Social Change* New Compass, Porsgrunn, Norway.

Tokar B. (2015) "The Paris Climate Agreement: Hope or Hype?" 30 December. Accessed from:www.commondreams.org/views/2015/12/31/paris-climate-agreement-hope-or-hype

Touraine A. (2000) "Society as Utopia" in Schaer R., Claeys G., and Sargent L.T. eds. *Utopia: The Search for the Ideal Society in the Western World.* Oxford University Press, New York 18–31.

UNFCCC. (2015a) "Historic Paris Agreement on Climate Change" (Press Release) UN Framework Convention on Climate Change, Paris. 12 December. Accessed 13 December 2015 from: http://newsroom.unfccc.int

UNFCCC. (2015b) "Adoption of the Paris Agreement" United Nations Framework Convention on Climate Change, Paris. 12 December. Accessed 13 December 2015 from: http://unfccc.int

Wallerstein I. (1998) *Utopistics: Or Historical Choices of the Twenty-first Century* The New Press, New York.

Weinberg B. (2017) "Colombia: still more 'consultas' reject extractivism" Countervortex. org, 14 July.

York R. (2012) "Do Alternative Energy Sources Displace Fossil Fuels?" *Nature Climate Change* 2:6 441–443.

Yuen E. (2012) "The Politics of Failure Have Failed: The Environmental Movement and Catastrophism" in Lilley S., McNally D., Yuen E., and Davis J., *Catastrophism: The Apocalyptic Politics of Collapse and Rebirth* PM Press, Oakland 15–43.

Index

Note: page numbers in **bold** indicate a table; *n* denotes a note

For Product Safety Concerns and Information please contact our EU
representative GPSR@taylorandfrancis.com
Taylor & Francis Verlag GmbH, Kaufingerstraße 24, 80331 München, Germany

www.ingramcontent.com/pod-product-compliance
Ingram Content Group UK Ltd.
Pitfield, Milton Keynes, MK11 3LW, UK
UKHW020954180425
457613UK00019B/685